NOT-FOR-PARENTS

THE TRAVEL BOOK

MICHAEL DUBOIS   KATRI HILDEN   JANE PRICE

the story of
THE NOT-FOR-PARENTS TRAVEL BOOK

Everyone knows which is the world's highest mountain, but do you know which country banned chewing gum? Or what's the world's **stinkiest fruit**? Or who invented **roller skates**? Or which building leans more than the Leaning Tower of Pisa? Or where can you eat fried spiders as a snack?

Here at Lonely Planet we decided to make a *book* about the world's countries for children, not parents. The world is **a very big place**, and in The Not-for-Parents Travel Book we've concentrated on the really interesting bits to create **a snapshot** of what each country is like. (Warning to parents: these might not be the same "really interesting bits" that you like...where to buy coffee, how many stars the hotel has, what's the phone number for the airport, blah, blah, blah.)

In this *book* are the epic events, amazing animals, **hideous histories**, funky foods, and **crazy facts** that make the world's 200 countries so fascinating. Each country has a page to itself—so tiny Tuvalu gets as much space as superpower USA.

If you want to know **all the cool stuff** about every country in the world, turn the page...

Contents

CANADA
★Ottawa

★ Official languages: English, French
★ Population: 33,487,208
★ Currency: Canadian dollars
★ Area: 3,855,103 sq miles (9,984,670 sq km)

There are fewer than 25,000 polar bears in the world. They are the top predators in the Arctic.

Daredevil!
A 63-year-old teacher named Annie was the first person to go over Niagara Falls in a barrel, in 1901.

HI (hi)

This country is the second largest in the world after Russia. Canada is 3,855,103 sq miles (9,984,670 sq km) and the USA is 3,794,100 sq miles (9,826,675 sq km), so they're roughly the same size...but more than 300 million people live in the USA while just 33 million enjoy big, empty Canada. Niagara Falls is on the border between the two countries. When you head north, you'll find totem poles, ice hockey rinks, and maybe even a polar bear.

CANADA'S TOP 5 Weird Place Names

1. Moose Jaw
2. Bacon Cove
3. Scugog
4. Precious Corners
5. Happy Adventure

What's your totem? Native Americans of British Columbia carved totem poles from giant cedar trees. The poles told stories or showed family totems, objects believed to have spiritual significance. Many were placed in doorways to guard homes from evil.

Inside an Igloo
The Inuit people have lived in the Arctic region in far north Canada for thousands of years. They used to travel on sleds pulled by dogs and build igloos – domed shelters made with snow blocks. Now many Inuit drive snowmobiles to get around and live in wooden houses.

Catching your man
Canada's famous mounted police force was founded in 1873. It's so successful at catching criminals that people say: "The Mountie always gets his man."

Hockey at Home
Canadians are so crazy about their national game of ice hockey that some families flood the backyard in the winter. When the water freezes they have their own personal skating rink.

UNITED STATES OF AMERICA
★Washington, DC

Twister! Around 1,000 tornadoes hit the USA each year, many of them in Tornado Alley in the Central Plains.

Snurf's up! Snowboarding was invented here in 1965. It was originally called "snurfing."

★ Official language: English
★ Population: 307,212,123
★ Currency: US dollars
★ Area: 3,794,100 sq miles (9,826,675 sq km)

HI (hi)

Howdy and welcome to the USA, home of Wild West cowboys, baseball, beauty pageants, the Empire State Building, the Hollywood film industry, and fast food (although several countries claim the hamburger as their own). This is a land of extremes—the Grand Canyon is 6,000ft (1,829m) deep and California's General Sherman tree is about as tall as a 23-story building. The USA won the Space Race to land on the moon. Only 12 men have ever walked on the moon and all are American.

Invented Here

Who put the hole in the middle of the doughnut? The invention of the ring-shaped doughnut is credited to a 16-year-old sailor on a US ship in 1847. He didn't like the greasy center of his bun so punched a hole through it with a tin box.

Baseball crazy Baseball is America's national sport and players in this country can become as famous as movie stars.

One giant leap for mankind On July 20, 1969, Neil Armstrong and "Buzz" Aldrin were the first men to walk on the moon.

FIRST MAN ON THE MOON UNITED STATES

Crazy Fact

Mt. Rushmore

Sculptor Gutzon Borglum spent 14 years carving the faces of four great presidents into the granite of Mt. Rushmore, South Dakota. Dynamite shaped 90% of the heads. The presidents are Washington, Jefferson, Theodore Roosevelt, and Lincoln. Each face is more than 60ft (18m) high.

Vroom! Go-karts were invented in California in the 1950s. Some early engines were modified chainsaw motors.

A gift from France The Statue of Liberty is the most famous symbol of American freedom but she isn't even American! She was built in France, then broken into pieces and shipped to New York City in crates in 1885 as a gift.

Lose the "Land"

The famous Hollywood sign was put up in 1923 by a real estate agent to advertise a new Los Angeles housing development, but the original sign said "Hollywoodland."

HOLLYWOOD

MEXICO
★Mexico City

★ Official language:
  Mexican Spanish
★ Population: 111,211,789
★ Currency: Mexican pesos
★ Area: 733,594 sq miles
  (1,900,000 sq km)

Have a bash A *piñata* is a big, bright clay or papier-mâché figure, filled with toys and treats and hung from a big string. Kids take turns whacking it with a stick so all the treats fall out.

Crazy Facts

- Mexico City is sinking by 4in (10cm) a year.
- The ancient Toltec tribe went to war armed with wooden swords—so they wouldn't kill their enemies.
- Mexico has more Spanish–talking people than Spain.
- The chihuahua (chi wa wa) is the world's smallest dog, growing only to about 6in (15cm) high—half a ruler.
- Mexico has the world's three longest underwater caves.

HOLA (oll ah)

The sun in Mexico is very hot, so don't forget to wear a *sombrero* and do a Mexican hat dance. The people love eating chocolate chicken (called chicken *mole*), tacos and hot chillies—but also you can gobble fly eggs that you mix with chopped cactus to make a fly-egg omelette! Before Hernán Cortes landed in 1519 and claimed the land for Spain, the Maya and Aztecs sacrificed people to the gods. Sadly, diseases brought by the Spanish wiped out 20 million more.

They grow on you
Imagine growing a new leg! Axolotls can. These "walking fish" are really salamanders and can regrow hurt body bits.

Taco

Hideous History

Heads Up

At Chichén Itzá there is a huge ball court where players would try to hit a 11lb (5kg) rubber ball—or perhaps a human head—through high stone hoops. Losers were put to death!

Happy hat *Sombreros* are big straw hats you can wear, or put on the ground and dance around.

Counting the days

Chichén Itzá is an old pyramid with 365 steps—one for each day of the year. In spring and autumn, a shadow shaped like a snake slides down the steps to join a stone snake head at the bottom. (For another New Wonder of the World, see the Taj Mahal on page 166.)

Scary Stuff

Day of the Dead

Every November 2 the dead come back to say hello. Not a horror movie, but a happy day as people put out food, flowers, and treats in their homes for their dead pals to enjoy. Some light candles in graveyards and sing and dance together.

Heads through here, please.

7 ONE OF THE NEW WONDERS OF THE WORLD

BELIZE
★ Belmopan

WORLD'S TOP 5 Loudest Animals

1. **Tiger pistol shrimp:** Atlantic Ocean
2. **Blue whale:** world's oceans
3. **Howler monkey:** South America
4. **Gray wolf:** North America
5. **Elephant:** Africa, India

Now hear this Howler monkeys are one of the loudest animals in the world. Their growls can be heard 3 miles (5km) away.

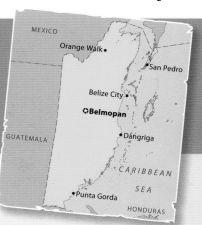

★ Official language: English
★ Population: 307,899
★ Currency: Belizean dollars
★ Area: 8,867 sq miles (22,966 sq km)

Map labels: MEXICO, Orange Walk, San Pedro, Belize City, ◇Belmopan, GUATEMALA, Dangriga, CARIBBEAN SEA, Punta Gorda, HONDURAS

ARRIGHT? (arr rite?)

Tiny Belize has one of the world's least populated capital cities, Belmopan, with only 20,000 people. Maybe there are so few people because Belize is the home of El Sisimito, a mythical creature with backward feet and no knees that eats human flesh! Jaguars and pumas lurk in the country's jungles, which hide hundreds of Mayan ruins, some of them 4,000 years old. The sea is also full of life—the Belize Barrier Reef is the world's second largest, after Australia's Great Barrier Reef.

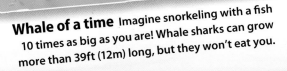

Whale of a time Imagine snorkeling with a fish 10 times as big as you are! Whale sharks can grow more than 39ft (12m) long, but they won't eat you.

Scary Stuff

Queen Eats Rat!

When Queen Elizabeth II visited Belize in 1985, she was served a local rodent called a gibnut, which some people say looks a bit like a giant rat without a tail. It tastes like rabbit.

Hole Lot of Water

The Great Blue Hole on Lighthouse Reef is 984ft (300m) wide and 427ft (130m) deep. It's so big you can see it from outer space! It's full of bright corals, colorful fish—and sharks.

Lizard lunch In Belize, they call iguana meat "bamboo chicken." They grow big green iguanas on farms to eat them.

Hideous History

Sparkling Bones

Ancient Maya sacrificed humans to the gods in the Actun Tunichil Muknal caves more than 1,000 years ago, and the bones are still there. The Crystal Maiden is the skeleton of a teenage girl, probably a sacrifice victim, whose bones sparkle.

GUATEMALA
★Guatemala City

★ Official language: Spanish
★ Population: 13,276,517
★ Currency: Quetzales
★ Area: 42,042 sq miles (108,889 sq km)

HOLA (oll ah)

Earth's center is trying to escape in Guatemala. It is home to 37 volcanoes—four of them still active. People have been living among the eruptions for at least 12,000 years and the old Mayan civilisation is still very much alive here: more than half the population are modern Maya, and at least 20 Mayan languages are spoken now. An old Mayan custom that people still follow is to sweep out their house every December and burn the rubbish to chase off the devil.

Flying feast During the Feast of St. Thomas, people leap off 98ft (30m) poles, tied to a rope attached to the top. It's a bit like bungee jumping (see page 194) or land diving (see page 195). Crazy!

Cacao pod

Invented Here

The ancient Maya used chocolate as a medicine to help sick people feel stronger and put on weight. Sometimes they used it to sweeten bitter powders and potions made from plants, crocodiles, insects, fish, and birds.

Epic Event

Can't Touch the Bottom

Surrounded by three volcanoes and Mayan villages, Lake Atitlan is the deepest lake in Central America. It is about 1,115ft (340m) deep, and at its widest is 10 miles (16km) across. It was formed 85,000 years ago by a volcanic explosion 30 times larger than what buried Pompeii in Italy.

No Worries

If young children have fears, their parents give them "worry dolls" made from wood and pieces of colored cloth. The children tell their worry to the doll, then place it under their pillow when they go to sleep. The next morning the doll is gone, along with the worry.

Guatemalan currency

Welcome party When you visit the ancient Mayan city of Tikal, deep in the jungle, you have to first get past the tarantulas, jaguars, howler monkeys, and toucans.

Feathery funds
The resplendent quetzal (ket sal) is the national bird of Guatemala. The currency of Guatemala is also called the quetzal, because ancient Maya used quetzal tail feathers as money.

Lizard soup

A *garrobo* is like an iguana, about 20in (50cm) long. It is still made into a special dinner called *garrobo* soup, which is meant to have magical powers. In Spanish, the soup is called *levanta muertos*, or "raise the dead!"

EL SALVADOR
★San Salvador

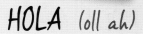

- ★ Official language: Spanish
- ★ Population: 7,185,218
- ★ Currency: US dollars
- ★ Area: 8,124 sq miles (21,041 sq km)

Sad story This mural, in typical folk art style, shows an old couple who were killed in a nasty war. The gunman is a guerilla (go ril ah) fighter.

HOLA (oll ah)

El Salvador is bursting at the seams in more ways than one. The "Tom Thumb of the Americas" is both Central America's smallest and most densely populated country. It also has many volcanoes and experiences plenty of earthquakes. That is because it sits on the Pacific Ring of Fire. Six of its 22 volcanoes may erupt at any time. One eruption buried an old village under a thick layer of volcanic ash, just like Pompeii in Italy. El Salvador has also had many years of bloody civil wars.

The Soccer War

During the 1969 World Cup soccer match between El Salvador and Honduras, the government of El Salvador invaded Honduras and bombed its airports. Luckily the "war" lasted fewer than 100 hours.

Tamales Corn dumplings wrapped in banana leaves are a popular snack.

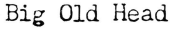

Big Old Head

The Olmec people made stone sculptures of giant heads, such as this one, in El Salvador and Mexico. Some are up to 4,000 years old.

Eggsellent idea If you catch the bus in El Salvador, you might have to share your seat with a chicken or a pig. That's because locals use the brightly painted country buses to transport livestock. Tourists call them "chicken buses."

About 70,000 people died during the civil war in El Salvador, back in the 1980s.

HONDURAS
★ Tegucigalpa

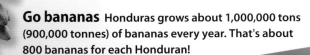

★ Official language: Spanish
★ Population: 7,792,854
★ Currency: Lempiras
★ Area: 43,278 sq miles (112,090 sq km)

Go bananas Honduras grows about 1,000,000 tons (900,000 tonnes) of bananas every year. That's about 800 bananas for each Honduran!

Dazzling Macaws are parrots with amazingly bright feathers and powerful beaks.

HOLA (oll ah)

Explorer Christopher Columbus first landed on the American mainland in 1502 in a spot that is now part of Honduras. He named it Honduras because of the deep water off its coast: *honduras* means "depths." The country has lots of dense rain forests where brightly colored birds such as macaws and crazy-looking toucans live. In the Bay Islands off the coast you can swim with bottlenose dolphins, manta rays, parrot fish, tiny seahorses, and huge whale sharks.

The white-tailed deer is the national animal of Honduras.

Forests in the Sky

Up in the highest mountains of Honduras you'll find "cloud forests." These forests sit in a blanket of thick, moist fog.

Off to bed The tiny Honduran white bats like to go camping every night. Before they go to sleep they fold leaves around themselves to form a tent, then huddle together for protection.

Home grown The ceiba or kapok tree can grow 230ft (70m) high and live for 200 years. Each tree provides a safe home for hundreds of birds, mammals, amphibians, insects, and other plants.

What's in a Name?

Garifuna People

Also known as the Black Caribs, the Garifuna people are descendants of Caribs, Indians, and African slaves who were shipwrecked on the island of St. Vincent. Today, many live in villages in Honduras, in houses made of wild cane or palm leaves. They are good at fishing.

Scary Stuff

Ancient Kingdom

The city of Copán, with many stone carvings and sculptures, was part of an ancient Mayan kingdom called Xukpi. The city was at its most powerful between AD 400 and AD 800. It had step pyramids, plazas, and palaces; like Greece (see page 67), it also had an acropolis. It had a large court for playing a deadly ball game; a nicer version of the game, *ulama*, is still played.

Hippity hop About 90 frog species live in Honduras—some in the cloud forests.

NICARAGUA
★ Managua

Freaky beaks
Five of the world's 40 species of toucans live in Nicaragua's forests: the collared aracari, yellow-eared toucanet, keel-billed toucan (below), black-mandibled toucan, and the emerald toucanet.

See a Lake
Lake Nicaragua is so big that you can't see from one shore to the other. It is more like the sea than a lake. It has waves, islands, and sharks: its bull sharks are able to live in the lake's freshwater, so look out if you go swimming!

★ Official language: Spanish
★ Population: 5,891,199
★ Currency: Cordobas
★ Area: 50,336 sq miles (130,370 sq km)

Big bullies Bull sharks can get quite aggressive and sometimes attack people.

HELP, HELP!
Every year thousands of sea turtles dig a nest on Nicaragua's beaches and lay their eggs. They can live for up to 80 years, but they are now endangered because people eat them as meat and also steal their eggs. Thousands of turtles are killed each year.

HOLA (oll ah)

Nicaragua is named after Nicarao, the chief of a tribe who lived near Lake Nicaragua hundreds of years ago. Even though it is prone to natural disasters—hurricanes, volcanic explosions, landslides, and earthquakes—Nicaragua calls itself the "Land of Poets," because poets are national heroes here. Nicaragua has the second-largest rain forest in the Americas, after the Amazon Rainforest. In it hide armadillos, green chocoyo parrots, toucans, macaws, jaguars, and shy ocelots.

Tamandua anteater This furry critter shuffles around the forests of Nicaragua. It has massive claws for ripping into ant nests.

Great Granada!
The best way to explore the beautiful buildings of Granada is on foot.

So Slooow...
Three-toed sloths live in forests and can travel only 6.5ft (2m) per minute. They are so slow that algae grows on them.

COSTA RICA
★San José

★ Official language: Spanish
★ Population: 4,253,877
★ Currency: Costa Rican colones
★ Area: 19,730 sq miles (51,100 sq km)

Scientists think about 500,000 different species of animals live in Costa Rica, including 300,000 different types of insects, and about 2,000 different kinds of spiders!

HOLA (oll ah)

Christopher Columbus and Spanish explorers thought they had struck it rich when they landed here and spied the gold jewelry the native Indians wore. They called the place Costa Rica, which means "rich coast" in Spanish. Today this small country is rich with wildlife, its thick jungles teeming with animals of all kinds—no other country on the planet has such an astounding variety. Volcanoes spew ash and lava almost every day. Many huge fish live off its coast.

Mystery balls

No one knows where Costa Rica's hundreds of smooth stone balls (las bolas) came from. Some are as small as marbles; others are up to 6ft 6in (2m) across and weigh up to 16.8 tons (15 tonnes). Were they thrown up by fiery volcanoes, or carved by ancient people?

Epic Event

Peace, Man

Costa Rica is a peaceful place. It is one of the few countries in the world without an army. It got rid of its army in 1949.

Amazing Animals

- About 90% of Central America's butterfly species live in Costa Rica. The blue morpho butterfly is one of them.

- The Costa Rican zebra tarantula has black and white stripes. It can grow to more than 4in (10cm).

- The giant anteater eats up to 30,000 insects every day.

Humming Along

A tiny hummingbird can beat its wings 80 times a second. It is the only bird that can fly backward. Costa Rica has more than 50 varieties.

Mighty Hercules We would have to be able to carry an army tank, a semitrailer, or a giant dinosaur to be as strong as the Hercules beetle. It grows to about 6in (16cm) long and can lift 850 times its own bodyweight.

Funky Food

- Costa Ricans love to eat "spotted rooster," which is actually a dish of fried rice and red beans.

Missing Link

The 30,000 miles (48,000km) Pan American Highway from northern Alaska down to Chile comes to a halt in Panama, at a place called the Darien Gap. The jungle here is too thick and too dangerous to build a road through. The highway starts up again about 62 miles (100km) south.

Pretty deadly The strawberry poison-dart frog is too poisonous to touch. Its skin oozes a deadly toxin, which comes from the insects it eats. The Choco Indians use the poison on their blow darts.

PANAMA
★Panama City

★ Official language: Spanish
★ Population: 3,360,474
★ Currency: Balboas
★ Area: 29,120 sq miles (75,420 sq km)

ATLANTIC OCEAN
CARIBBEAN SEA
COSTA RICA
Colón
Panama Canal ◇ **Panama City**
David
PACIFIC OCEAN
COLOMBIA

HOLA (oll ah)

Panama is covered in dark, mysterious rain forests. Its lush jungles are home to a huge range of tropical plants, animals, and birds—some found nowhere else in the world. It is thought that in a local language, Panama meant "place of fishes"—not surprising, as the country has plenty of coastline. Funnily enough, the famous Panama hat doesn't come from Panama, but from Ecuador. And if somone sells you barbecued "monkey meat," don't worry—it's really beef or pork.

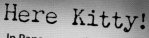

CANAL ZONE POSTAGE
AIR MAIL

Deadly Ditch

Nearly 30,000 people died building the Panama Canal, mainly from diseases such as malaria and yellow fever, and because of landslides. The canal cuts through Panama and joins the Atlantic and Pacific oceans.

Here Kitty!

In Panama you'll find five of Central America's six big cats: the jaguar, puma, ocelot, jaguarundi, and margay. (The one that got away is the bobcat.)

World's strongest
The massive harpy eagle is Panama's national bird. It stands 3 ft 3in (1m) tall, and has a wingspan of up to 8ft (2.5m). Even though it is the world's strongest bird of prey, it is now becoming rare.

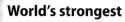

Being shaped like an "S," Panama is the only place where you can see the sun rise in the Pacific Ocean and set in the Atlantic.

Fancy dress Women in Panama traditionally wear a *pollera*—a big, frilly dress with flower designs—with beautiful hairstyles held in place by gold combs and pretty pins.

BAHAMAS
★ Nassau

★ Official language: English
★ Population: 309,156
★ Currency: Bahamian dollars
★ Area: 5,382 sq miles (13,940 sq km)

HELLO (hall lo)

About 300 years ago you could hardly move in the islands of the Bahamas without kicking a wooden leg or tripping over a treasure chest. This was pirate central in buccaneering's golden days. Pirates ruled the capital, Nassau, for many years, after chasing off most of the law-abiding citizens. Today the Bahamas are better known for their laid-back lifestyle. You could visit a different island every day for eight years and not land on the same one twice—there are more than 3,100 of them!

Going for Gold

At the 2000 Olympic Games, the Bahamas was the most successful team! Why? When the results were analyzed based on how many people live in each country, the tiny Bahamas came out on top, even though it won only two medals—a gold and a silver.

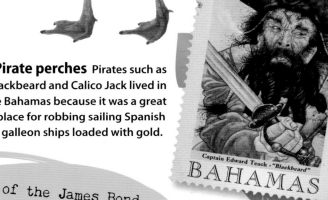

Pretty in Pink

At Inagua National Park, tens of thousands of pink West Indian flamingos gather to breed and feed.

Party time Christmas goes out with a bang, not a whimper, in the Bahamas capital of Nassau. *Junkanoo*, a massive street parade, starts in the early hours of December 26, with neighborhood teams competing for prizes.

Pirate perches Pirates such as Blackbeard and Calico Jack lived in the Bahamas because it was a great place for robbing sailing Spanish galleon ships loaded with gold.

15c

Captain Edward Teach -"Blackbeard"

BAHAMAS

Some of the James Bond movies were set in the Bahamas, including *For Your Eyes Only*, *The Spy Who Loved Me*, and *Never Say Never Again*.

Take a Big Breath

You'd have to hold your breath for five minutes and swim down more than 328ft (100m) to beat the record for diving on one breath of air in Dean's Blue Hole. The hole is—gulp!—720ft (220m) deep.

CUBA
★Havana

Humpy ride Cubans in the capital city, Havana, call their buses *camellos* (Spanish for "camels") because they have a hump toward the front.

★ Official language: Spanish
★ Population: 11,451,652
★ Currency: Cuban pesos
★ Area: 42,803 sq miles (110,860 sq km)

A traditional Cuban maraca

HOLA (oll ah)

Old cars and big cigars—you couldn't be anywhere but Cuba. This land of 4,000 islands is also home to an unlucky farmer who has been hit by lightning nine times, and an inventor who made ham and yogurt out of algae. On the Isla de la Juventud there are giant lobsters and buried pirate treasure that has never been found, but throughout Cuba you can enjoy treasure of another kind—amazing music, which seems to spill out of the windows and doors of every house and shop.

Beat it Cuban music has its roots in Spain and West Africa. Popular music styles include the salsa, rumba, conga, and the cha-cha.

Hideous History

Atomic Fright

In 1962 the world came closer than it had ever been to nuclear war during the Cuban Missile Crisis, when Russia put atomic missiles in Cuba, and the USA told Russia to take them away—or else! After a tense standoff, Russia gave in and took its weapons out of Cuba.

Scary Stuff

Dead Lucky

Former Cuban president Fidel Castro claimed he survived 638 attempts on his life, mainly from the US CIA—including poisoned cigars, a contaminated diving suit, and even a powder to make his beard fall out.

Wheely Great Old Cars

Almost half of the 150,000 American cars that were on the road in Cuba when Fidel Castro came to power in 1959 are still running. Cuba is like a giant moving museum.

Up in smoke Cuba is famous for its cigars. More than 70 million of the smelly things are exported every year!

JAMAICA
★Kingston

- ★ Official language: English
- ★ Population: 2,825,928
- ★ Currency: Jamaican dollars
- ★ Area: 4,244 sq miles (10,991 sq km)

Dreaded Hair

See what happens when you don't cut or brush your hair? These tangled hairstyles are called "dreadlocks." Many Jamaican dreadlock-wearers follow the Rastafarian (russ ta fair ee an) religion.

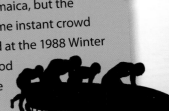

YOW WAH GWAN (Yow wa gwaan)

Hey mon, welcome to Jamaica. This hot tropical island was once thick with pirates but today is famous for its music, white sandy beaches, big matted hairstyles, and rum. Its treasures include Port Royal, also known as the "Sunken City," because much of the old town fell into the water after a huge earthquake in 1692 and is still there today. Living treasures include the beautiful doctor bird, or red-billed streamertail hummingbird, and the enormous swallowtail butterfly, as big as a dinner plate.

Sweet but sick

Ackee fruit is said to be yummy, but it can also kill you. If you eat it when it isn't ripe, it causes Jamaican Vomiting Sickness, which can lead to fits, coma, and death!

Not-So-Epic Event

Slide to Glory

There's no snow in tropical Jamaica, but the Jamaican bobsled team became instant crowd favorites when they first raced at the 1988 Winter Olympics in Canada. Hollywood even made a movie about the team, *Cool Runnings*.

Happy shack

This colorful Rastafarian house is made of wood, bamboo, and corrugated iron.

Flying underwater

The flying gurnard uses its wings to "fly" through the water in short bursts. Its bright colors are meant to scare off hungry fish.

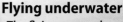

Sounds good

Some of the world's most famous modern music has come from Jamaica, including reggae, ska, mento, rocksteady, and dub.

Hideous History

Naughty Place

Back in the 1600s, the town of Port Royal was known as the "Wickedest City on Earth," full of pirates, slave traders, cutthroats, and swindlers.

Head to the clouds High up in the Macaya National Park stands the last remaining "cloud forest" in Haiti.

HAITI
★Port-au-Prince

★ Official languages: French, Creole
★ Population: 9,035,500
★ Currency: Gourdes
★ Area: 10,714 sq miles (27,750 sq km)

Fairybook houses You'll find these beautiful "gingerbread" houses in Haiti's capital city, Port-au-Prince. They were called "gingerbread" houses by American tourists in the 1950s.

BONJOUR (Bon joor)

Haiti is often called the most "African" of all the Caribbean countries, and it was the world's first black republic. It still follows lots of traditions that originally came from Africa, such as vodou (voo doo). During a vodou celebration called the *Fête Gede*, in the capital, Port-au-Prince, people flock to cemeteries to honor the dead with flowers, food, and rum. While you're in Haiti you can do as the locals do and get around on a wildly painted bus called a *tap tap*.

Who Do Vodou?

Haitian vodou is a religion based on local, West African, and Christian ideas. During a vodou service, dead spirits act and speak through living people. Some Haitians also believe in zombies.

Epic Event

In January 2010 a massive earthquake hit Haiti, destroying the capital and killing more than 200,000 people. It was described as the most devastating natural disaster of modern times.

Hideous History

When the French Revolution in 1789 outlawed slavery, Haiti's half a million slaves took control of the island, killing white sugarcane farmers and burning estates. The French sent in 70 ships and 25,000 soldiers but surrendered in 1803.

Hey, handsome Haiti's rhinoceros iguana is one of the world's largest, growing up to 4ft (1.2m). It eats mainly fruit and vegetables.

And stay out! Citadelle la Ferrière is an amazing Caribbean fort perched high on a mountain. It was built to keep the French out after Haiti gained its independence.

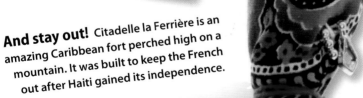

The island of Tortuga, off the coast of Haiti, became the headquarters for the pirates of the Caribbean by the middle of the 17th century.

DOMINICAN REPUBLIC
★Santo Domingo

- ★ Official language: Spanish
- ★ Population: 9,650,000
- ★ Currency: Dominican pesos
- ★ Area: 18,792 sq miles (48,670 sq km)

(see page 19)

Ahoy There
Epic Event

Christopher Columbus first saw the country in 1492, when he sailed the ocean blue. His bones are in the Columbus Lighthouse Monument, which was built 500 years later, in 1992. At night it shines out bright light beams, which can be seen 78 miles (125km) away.

DIMELO (dee mel oh)

The Dominican Republic shares the island of Hispaniola (his span yoh lah) with Haiti (see page 19). It was the first place in the Americas that Europeans settled. It has lots of waterfalls and limestone caves, and shiploads of pirates used to hide here—maybe in the caves! Today people come from all over the world to swim, relax, and play golf. When you get really hungry you can eat a soup called *mondongo*, made from tripe (cow stomach) and hoof jelly.

Hey sweetie Sugar is the country's biggest crop. They also make rum from sugarcane.

Sand castles On the beaches you might see colorful huts with thatched roofs.

Good and Evil

El Carnaval de La Vega is an old carnival that celebrates the victory of good over evil. Every Sunday in February, thousands of people romp around wearing crazy masks or scary devil costumes.

On the nose A solenodon looks like a big rat, with a long pointy snout. It has poisonous saliva. It nests in burrows and gobbles insects.

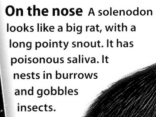

Fever pitch People here are mad about baseball, and boys dream of making the major league.

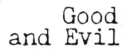

LITTLE MAN
Crazy Fact

At only 28in (71cm) tall, Nelson De La Rosa was one of the tiniest men in the world. You'll see him in a famous old film called *Island of Dr Moreau*, where he plays a man called Majai. He died in 2006, aged 38 years.

Quick step The *merengue* is the country's national dance. It's a quick dance so you'll need lots of energy, shaking your feet to instruments like drums, maracas, and accordions.

The Kalinago Genocide occurred in 1626 at Bloody Point, when the English and French killed about 2,000 native Carib people (or Kalinago). It was said the blood of the Caribs ran down the Bloody River for three days.

SAINT KITTS & NEVIS
★ Basseterre

★ Official language: English
★ Population: 40,131
★ Currency: East Caribbean dollars
★ Area: 101 sq miles (261 sq km)

Stinky Stuff

Brimstone Hill Fortress is a rambling old fortress built on an old volcano that still lets off smelly gases.

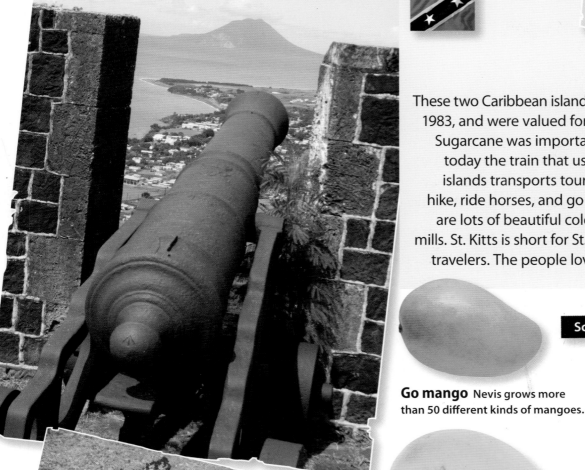

HELLO (el loh)

These two Caribbean islands were ruled by England until 1983, and were valued for their sugarcane plantations. Sugarcane was important for hundreds of years, but today the train that used to carry sugar around the islands transports tourists, who come here to relax, hike, ride horses, and go diving and snorkeling. There are lots of beautiful colonial buildings and old sugar mills. St. Kitts is short for St. Christopher, who looks after travelers. The people love cricket and music festivals.

Go mango Nevis grows more than 50 different kinds of mangoes.

Seeing stars You'll see lots of fish when you're swimming in the clear blue sea—including starfish, which are also called sea stars.

Scary Stuff

Bat Man, Frog Woman

In the dry season, the Kalinago people used to raid other islands and kidnap people for human sacrifices. They did this to keep a god called Bat Man happy. Bat Man ruled the dry season, and if he was angry, the wet season, ruled by the Frog Woman, wouldn't start and the rains wouldn't come.

A saman tree at an old sugar plantation called Romney Manor is more than 350 years old. The trunk is a massive 26ft (8m) in diameter, and the branches would cover half a soccer field.

Fun day Even the animals join in the fun during Independence Day on September 19.

ANTIGUA & BARBUDA
★St. John's

★ Official language: English
★ Population: 85,632
★ Currency: East Caribbean dollars
★ Area: 170 sq miles (441 sq km)

HOW THINGS? (how tings?)

These two islands are famous for their beautiful, soft, sandy beaches and clear water—pop videos are often filmed here. Many ships have been wrecked on the coral reefs, which are now popular with snorkelers and scuba divers. You'll hear lots of lively music here, like calypso (kal ip so) and reggae. You might see donkey and crab races, and if you're lucky you can try their favorite dessert, *duckanoo*—made from cornmeal, coconut, sugar, and spices, boiled up in banana leaves.

Read all about it People here love a good book—90% of people can read.

Scary Stuff

Oops!

The Antiguan racer, a type of snake, was being wiped out by rats, so to save the harmless little snake, mongooses (which look a bit like weasels) were brought in to eat the rats. The mongooses, however, preferred the snakes—and nearly ate them all.

High flyers Frigatebirds are seabirds that snatch fish out of the ocean. They can stay in the air for a week! Males have big red blow-up throat pouches.

Don't I know you? Many really famous people have holiday homes on Antigua, including rock guitarist Eric Clapton (left), clothes designer Giorgio Armani, writer Ken Follett, and TV host Oprah Winfrey.

Not-So-Epic Event

Up in Smoke

Redonda is an island off the coast of Antigua. In 2007 a British man tried to set up the Redonda Embassy in his pub in England, so he could smoke in it without breaking the law. But the government stubbed out his stinky plan.

A Year at the Beach

There are 365 beaches on Antigua, one for every day of the year—unless, of course, it's a leap year.

Bat man The locals are crazy about the game of cricket. The country has produced many famous players, such as Viv Richards.

DOMINICA
★Roseau

* Official language: English
* Population: 72,660
* Currency: East Caribbean dollars
* Area: 292 sq miles (754 sq km)

BON JOU (bon joo)

Dominica was the last of the Caribbean islands to be colonized by Europeans, because the native Carib people were so scary and fierce. Christopher Columbus called the island Dominica because he saw it on a Sunday (Dominica means "Sunday" in Latin). Dominica has huge, rugged, cloud-covered mountains, thick forests, steaming valleys, 365 crystal-clear rivers, and many thundering waterfalls. You better watch what you eat here—it might be smoked possum stew!

Nature Island

One third of Dominica has been protected as a national park, so its tropical rain forests are a safe home for many different birds and animals. Its waterholes are a great spot for a cool dip after trekking through the steamy jungles.

Have you seen any of the four *Pirates of the Caribbean* movies? Some of the scenes were filmed in Dominica.

Gee fizz Slight volcanic activity under the seafloor at Champagne Beach makes the water bubble, just like a glass of soda.

Amazing Animal

Don't Forget the Stuffing

Mountain chicken frogs are one of the largest frogs in the world, weighing about 2.2 lb (1kg). They are now rare, but were once a popular food, tasting a little bit like chicken.

In hot water Boiling Lake, in the Morne Trois Pitons National Park, is one of the largest hot springs in the world. Another really huge hot spring is Frying Pan Lake, near Rotorua in New Zealand (see page 194).

Spy a spout Sperm whales love living in the deep waters off Dominica, where they feast on squid and cuttlefish. Dominica is often called the "Whale-Watching Capital of the Caribbean," because other types of whales also visit regularly.

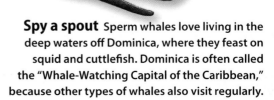

23

SAINT LUCIA
★ Castries

- ★ Official language: English
- ★ Population: 160,267
- ★ Currency: East Caribbean dollars
- ★ Area: 238 sq miles (616 sq km)

Sssssnake! When you're in the jungle, you might come face to face with a giant boa constictor.

BON JOU (bon joo)

Ancient, pointy, forest-covered volcanoes rising straight out of the deep blue ocean make St. Lucia one of the most mountainous of the Caribbean's islands. The island is still very much alive with volcanic activity and some scientists believe an eruption will wipe out much of St. Lucia within the next 100 years. But that doesn't stop the energetic St. Lucians having a good time—wherever you go on the island you'll hear music, from reggae to the traditional and popular *quadrille*.

The St. Lucia Jazz Festival gets jumping in May, with music from around the world.

Scary Stuff

Hideous History

In the 1600s, the French planted sugarcane on the island, using the local Carib people and then African slaves as laborers. Many Caribs died from deadly European diseases such as smallpox and measles, or from being treated badly.

Wooden it be good Nearby Pidgeon Island was the home of pirate *Jambe de Bois* (Wooden Leg), who used it as a base from which to raid passing Spanish ships.

Hot and Smelly

Sulphur Springs is the world's only drive-in volcano. Until recently, you could walk up to the bubbling tar pits—but you can't anymore, because the tar pits are roped off after someone fell in and got awfully burned.

What a drag Giant leatherback turtles drag themselves onto the Grande Anse beach to lay their eggs by moonlight.

SAINT VINCENT & THE GRENADINES

★Kingstown

Making a Splash

This is a great place to go swimming and scuba diving. There's plenty to see under the sea, including pipe organ coral.

★ Official language: English
★ Population: 104,574
★ Currency: East Caribbean dollars
★ Area: 150 sq miles (389 sq km)

HELLO (hall lo)

It might sound like the name of a Catholic pop group, but St. Vincent and the Grenadines is actually a string of 32 islands in the Caribbean. The area known as Tobago Cays is a tropical paradise and a great place to play pirates. If you hop over to the island of Mustique, you might spot a celebrity—some rock stars pay $150,000 a week to stay there! Not bad for a place that started out as a sugar plantation worked by slaves who were stolen from Africa.

Pirate Penalties

Parts of the *Pirates of the Caribbean* movies were filmed here. If you think it was fun being a pirate, think again! In real life, pirates were a rough lot who loved dishing up cruel punishments, such as:

Walking the plank

walking the plank – they'd blindfold you, stick a sword behind your back, and make you walk overboard

flogging – they'd whack you with nasty leather weapons, such as the cat o' nine tails

tying you to the mast – they'd suspend you high up with your arms and legs at full stretch for days

marooning – they'd leave you on a deserted island without any food or water

keelhauling – they'd tie you to a rope and throw you overboard, then pull you under the ship across razor-sharp barnacles.

Cat o' nine tails

Hideous History

Blowing Its Top

La Soufrière is a massive volcano that takes up one third of the island of St. Vincent. It last erupted in 1979. When it erupted in 1902, it killed 2,000 people.

Get bent Bananas are big business in St. Vincent and the Grenadines, accounting for 50% of the islands' income.

Lazy days The fierce Carib people and the mountainous terrain kept Europeans away for many years, but now people come here to relax.

The big beat
Here you'll hear plenty of lively Caribbean music, including calypso, reggae, soca, steelpan, and big drum (played on drums made from tree trunks).

BARBADOS
★ Bridgetown

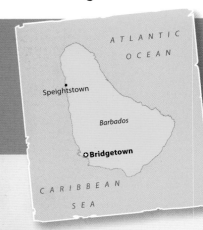

* Official language: English
* Population: 284,589
* Currency: Barbadian dollars
* Area: 166 sq miles (431 sq km)

Top Team

Barbados has produced some of the greatest cricketers in the world, including Garfield Sobers, Joel Garner, Malcolm Marshall, Frank Worrell, and Wes Hall.

Sounds fishy

Barbados is the land of the flying fish. These fish can jump right out of the water and glide for 164ft (50m). A lot of them end up on people's dinner plates—served up with a cornmeal dish called *cou-cou*.

HELLO (ha law)

The sugarcane plantations on the small Caribbean island of Barbados were once worked by slaves. Today, sugar is still a big part of life. Every year, at the end of the cane harvest, people have a huge summer festival called Crop Over, with singing, calypso music, feasting, and dancing lasting many weeks. The festival started back in 1688. When the music dies down, you might hear whistling frogs, which sound like flutes. The pop star Rihanna comes from Barbados.

What a goose! If you're taking a drive through the countryside you'll probably see a mongoose scamper across the road. They're quick little critters but they won't trouble you. Mongooses like to snack on sea turtle eggs, which is bad news for these rare animals.

The world's smallest snake, *Leptotyphlops carlae*, was found on the island in 2008. It fits on a coin and is as thin as spaghetti.

Big bird Barbados was one of the few holiday places that had a Concorde service. You'll see one of these mighty planes at the Grantley Adams International Airport in Barbados—but you won't be able to fly in it as it doesn't work anymore.

Flying Coffins

A strange mystery occurred between 1812 and 1820, in a tomb owned by the Chase family. Every time they opened the sealed tomb to bury someone, they would find that the stone coffins inside the tomb had been thrown around like toys, even though the coffins were extremely heavy.

GRENADA
★ St. George's

Sugar, spice, all things nice
Grenada is also called the "Spice Islands" because it grows beautiful food spices like cinnamon, cloves, nutmeg, and allspice berries.

- ★ Official language: English
- ★ Population: 90,739
- ★ Currency: East Caribbean dollars
- ★ Area: 133 sq miles (344 sq km)

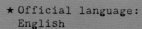

W'AP'NIN? (wop neen?)

Grenada is a small group of Caribbean islands with thick rainforests, fine beaches, and coral reefs. Christopher Columbus was the first European to sail past these islands in 1498. Grenada was ruled by the French for a long time, and then the British, and slaves once worked on its sugar and cocoa plantations. The people of Grenada are great storytellers and have lots of folktales to tell. They like to drink cocoa tea for breakfast. You can eat avocado ice cream for dessert.

Scary Stuff

Blood Sucker
Local legends tell of Ligaroo, who sheds his skin on the night of a full moon, turns into a ball of fire, and goes looking for victims so he can suck their blood.

Bodies of Water
To see the sculptures at Molinere Bay, you have to put on swimming goggles. That's because they're on the seabed. They are casts of local people.

Bug off A frangipani worm looks like a stripy snake to scare off birds.

Jab jab **good good** *J'ouvert* (joo vay) is a festival involving calypso-soca bands, called *jab jab* bands. People dress up in bright costumes or smear themselves in black paint and dance through the streets. It starts before dawn and ends just after sunrise.

Chocoholic Grenada's cocoa beans are made into yummy chocolate.

TRINIDAD & TOBAGO
★ Port-of-Spain

★ Official language:
English
★ Population: 1,229,953
★ Currency: Trinidad
and Tobago dollars
★ Area: 1,980 sq miles
(5,128 sq km)

Gentle giants Whale sharks and strange-looking manta rays patrol the waters off northwest Trinidad.

HELLO (hall lo)

People from all around the world have made their home in Trinidad and Tobago, leading to it being called the "Rainbow Country" because of the many cultures living together. The people love cricket and play it as part of the West Indies cricket team. They also love goat racing! It is just like horse racing, with goat stables and trainers, and races held on Easter Tuesday. But most of all the people love a party—the two islands often hold colorful carnivals.

Invented Here

What's that Sound?

The steelpans you hear during carnival time—and any other time—were developed in Port-of-Spain in the 1930s. They were originally made from empty oil drums. Things get pretty noisy during Panorama, the largest steelband contest in the world.

Lock up your goats The green anaconda found in Trinidad's jungles is one of the largest snakes in the world. It can grow longer than 16ft (5m) and weigh almost 220lb (100kg). It has even been known to gobble up goats!

Local currency of Trinidad and Tobago

Scary Stuff

Beware the Jumbie

Jumbie is a mischievous or evil spirit. A jumbie parasol is a poisonous mushroom, a jumbie bead is a poisonous plant, and a jumbie bird is an owl whose screech, if heard at night, is said to mean that someone will die soon.

"Greatest Show on Earth"

You can cover yourself in paint or put on a colorful costume and frolic through the streets during Port-of-Spain's amazing carnival, held just before Easter. Devils dance and whirl during three days of music madness.

Biggest Brain

Kelleston Drain, off the coast of Tobago, is home to the world's largest brain coral, measuring 10ft (3m) by 16ft (5m).

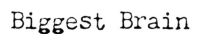

SURINAME
★Paramaribo

Colorful Past

Hundreds of years ago African slaves escaped from Suriname's coffee, cocoa, sugarcane, and cotton plantations, where they were treated badly. They hid in the forests and married people from the local tribes. Their descendants are now known as Maroons.

Historic slave quarters

★ Official language: Dutch
★ Population: 481,267
★ Currency: Surinamese dollars
★ Area: 63,251 sq miles (163,820 sq km)

FAWAKA (fa wah ka)

Suriname is the smallest independent country in South America. Back in 1667 the Dutch obtained it from the British, by trading it for some land in North America where a great city now stands: New York City! Suriname calls itself the "Beating Heart of the Amazon." Many different native Indian tribes live in its jungles. The capital city is home to people from many parts of the world and descendants of slaves from the old plantations that were scattered around the country.

Race to the sea

Suriname has one of the world's largest nesting populations of leatherback turtles. The females return to the same nesting site every year.

Sense of style
Paramaribo, the 17th-century capital, has many beautiful old Dutch, French, Spanish, and British colonial buildings.

What's cooking? Cassava is a popular root vegetable. Maroon women make yummy cakes from cassava and bake them over a fire in a large round pan.

Shocking!

The giant electric eel can grow 6ft 6in (2m) long, weigh 44lb (20kg), and generate up to 600 volts of electricity—enough to kill a grown man! It isn't really an eel, but a knife fish.

The Amazon Rain Forest is like a huge chemist shop. Native doctors, known as shamans, make medicines from jungle plants.

Fangs a Lot

The jaguar's bite is so strong it can pierce a turtle's shell. It bites through the skull of its prey, in between the ears and into the brain.

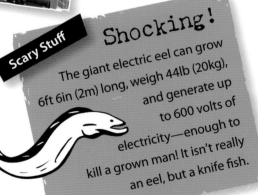

GUYANA
★Georgetown

★ Official language: English
★ Population: 772,298
★ Currency: Guyanese dollars
★ Area: 83,000 sq miles (214,969 sq km)

Crazy Fact The steeple of St. George's Anglican Cathedral soars up 140ft (43m)—very close to the heavens!

Something in the Air

Guyana's national bird, the hoatzin, keeps predators away because it stinks! It is also called the stinkbird and is closely related to dinosaurs. It has a short fat body, scruffy neck, and tiny head with a crest of spiky feathers. It grunts, croaks, growls, and hisses but hardly ever flies.

WAH GWAN? (wah gwan?)

Did you ever see the film *Avatar*? Well, Guyana has been called "Avatar on Earth." More than 80% of the country is covered in thick forest. It has about 8,000 species of plants, half of them found nowhere else on Earth. The name Guyana means "land of many waters," and the nation is also rich in gold and diamonds. An old custom is to give babies a piece of gold jewelry for good luck soon after they are born—gold bangles and earrings for girls, and a gold ring and bracelet for boys.

Pleased to eat you The red-bellied piranha is one of the most ferocious freshwater fish in the world. It's about the length of a ruler and its razor-sharp teeth strip the flesh from prey and dead animals.

You otter know this Guyana is the home of rare giant otters. They love chasing and eating fish. They're about 5ft (1.5m) long and can weigh up to 100lb (45kg).

Hideous History

The 1978 "Jonestown Massacre"

More than 900 people—including 300 children—died in a mass suicide by drinking a purple poison. They were members of a religious cult called the Peoples Temple, led by an American named Jim Jones.

Long way to fall Kaieteur Falls, at 741ft (226m), is five times higher than Niagara Falls (see page 6), and about twice the height of Victoria Falls on Africa's Zambia–Zimbabwe border. It is one of the world's most powerful waterfalls.

Biggest Drops

Once the tallest building in the world, New York City's Empire State Building is 1,454ft (443m) tall, less than half the height of the world's highest waterfall—Angel Falls.

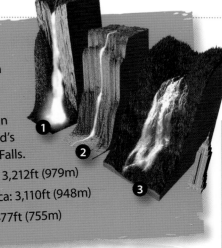

1. Angel Falls, Venezuela: 3,212ft (979m)
2. Tugela Falls, South Africa: 3,110ft (948m)
3. Kjelfossen, Norway: 2,477ft (755m)

VENEZUELA
★Caracas

★ Official language: Spanish
★ Population: 26,814,843
★ Currency: Bolivars
★ Area: 352,144 sq miles (912,050 sq km)

HOLA (oll ah)

Venezuela is named after Venice in Italy (see page 57). In 1499, Italians visited Venezuela and saw people living in houses that were built on stilts, over the water, which reminded them of the canals of Venice. Venezuela has lots of oil, as well as grasslands, cattle ranches, rain forests, and cloud forest. Ladies in Venzuela must be very pretty: the country has won 5 Miss World, 6 Miss Universe, 1 Miss Earth, and 6 Miss International beauty contests! Kids here love playing baseball and soccer.

Fallen Angel

Angel Falls is the world's highest waterfall. The water has to fall so far that most of it evaporates or is carried away as a fine mist by the wind. It's named after a pilot, Jimmy Angel, who saw it while flying overhead, looking for gold.

Like Spain, Venezuela has a town called Barcelona.

Scary Stuff

Never-ending Stormy

Seen only in Venezuela, *catatumbo* lightning is the world's biggest lightning storm. About 150 nights a year, over huge Lake Maracaibo, a dazzling 280 lightning bolts per hour light up the clouds, for up to 10 hours a night. They can be seen up to 250 miles (400km) away.

Amazing Animal

Yes Master

The bushmaster snake is one of the longest venomous snakes in the world, growing up to 10ft (3m) long. It swallows its prey head first.

Bird cave Guácharo Cave National Park has a huge limestone cave, more than 6 miles (10km) long, home to thousands of oilbirds.

Big hero General Simón Bolívar is a national hero. He freed Venezuela and its neighbors from Spanish rule in the early 1800s; the country Bolivia (see page 36) was named after him. You'll see many statues of him around Venezuela.

COLOMBIA
★ Bogotá

★ Official language: Spanish
★ Population: 45,644,023
★ Currency: Colombian pesos
★ Area: 439,737 sq miles (1,138,914 sq km)

HOLA (oll ah)

The Andes mountains split Colombia from north to south. Sitting on the Pacific Ring of Fire, Colombia has lots of earthquakes and volcanic eruptions, and it is the only South American country to have both a Pacific and Caribbean coast. Legend says there was once a tribal chief in Colombia called *El Dorado* (The Golden One), who covered himself with gold dust. *El Dorado* is also the name of a mythical lost city, loaded with gold.

Roasted bachaco ants are a great high-protein snack in Colombia. They have been de-winged, roasted, and eaten for centuries.

Matching Stones

Colombia is the world's largest producer of which of these precious gems? And in which countries would you find the other ones?

Sapphire Diamond Ruby Emerald

Answer: Madagascar has sapphires; South Africa has diamonds; Myanmar has rubies; Colombia has emeralds

Rock concert More than 500 rock figures sit in the Valley of the Statues in the Andes. Some statues are of animals such as gorillas or African elephants, and people wearing turbans. The tallest is 23ft (7m) high. They were carved as long as 5,000 years ago.

Temple of salt The Salt Cathedral is an underground church, built in a salt mine, 656ft (200m) underground in a mountain near the town of Zipaquirá. Like a fairy-tale cathedral, it seems to glow and is lit up with a blue light.

Animal or vegetable?
Colombia has the largest number of species in the world of heliconia, a plant also known as "lobster claws" or "false bird-of-paradise."

Look Out!
Colombia has one of the highest rates of kidnapping in the whole world.

Glittering treasures
More than 2,000 years ago early Colombian people started making golden objects, which you can see today in Bogotá's Gold Museum.

World's Most Venomous

Gold Poisoning
The golden poison frog is the most venomous vertebrate ever. Chickens and dogs have died from touching a paper towel that one of these frogs had hopped on. Don't touch this frog or you'll die too! The frog only uses its poison for self-defense.

ECUADOR
★Quito

★ Official language:
  Spanish
★ Population: 14,573,101
★ Currency: US dollars
★ Area: 109,484 sq miles
  (283,561 sq km)

Funky Food

Mommy, I'm Hungry

Why not snack on roasted *cuy* (guinea pig), some *tronquito* (bull penis soup), or *yaguarlocro* (potato soup made with sprinklings of blood)?

What a blast Every New Year's Eve, people make dolls from old clothes and stuff them with firecrackers and sawdust, then put on heads covered with papier-mâché masks. At midnight, the dolls are beaten up and burned so the new year will be free of trouble.

HOLA (oll ah)

Ecuador got its name because it sits on the equator. While that doesn't mean it's hot, it does have lots of hot, active volcanoes scattered around. The rugged Andes mountains run through the country, and the best way to travel over them is on llamas (see page 34). Ecuador owns the Galápagos Islands, which have many strange animals found nowhere else on Earth. One of the world's rarest marine mammals also lives in Ecuador—the pink Amazon River dolphin (see page 35).

Amazing Animal

Where Does It Keep Its Tongue?

If the tube-lipped nectar bat was a cat it would be able to drink milk from a bowl 3ft (1m) away. That's because its tongue is 1.5 times as long as its body! The bat was discovered in 2003 in Ecuador's cloud forests. It needs a long tongue to lick the nectar out of the flowers it likes to feed on.

Hat on the hop Panama hats actually come from Ecuador. The straw hats got their name because they were shipped through the Panama Canal on their way to the US.

Swimming Lizards

Found only on the Galápagos Islands, marine iguanas are the only lizards that can live in the sea.

Hideous History

In Ecuador you'll find the Lake of Blood (*Laguna Yaguarcocha*). About 500 years ago, an Inca leader conquered the native tribes around a lake. He killed all the men and boys over the age of 12 years and dumped their bodies in the lake, which turned red with blood.

World's largest and oldest
The Galápagos giant tortoise is the largest tortoise in the world, and the world's longest-living animal. Some have lived for at least 180 years. One taken to Australia by Charles Darwin in 1835 died in 2006! These big fellows can weigh more than 880lb (400kg).

Just cruising The Andean condor is Ecuador's national bird. It has the largest wingspan (10ft 6in/3.2m) of any land bird. This big bird can cruise high in the skies for hours without flapping its wings even once.

33

PERU
★ Lima

★ Official languages:
  Spanish, Quechua
★ Population: 29,546,963
★ Currency: Nuevo sol
★ Area: 496,225 sq miles
  (1,285,216 sq km)

WINCHIS (wind cheers)

Paddington Bear came from Darkest Peru, and while you probably won't see too many other bears, in the jungles you will find pumas, jaguars, crazy-looking colorful birds such as toucans, weird hairless dogs, and more than 4,000 species of butterflies. Peruvians keep guinea pigs, but not as pets—they roast them and eat them! The world's largest river, the Amazon, starts high in the Andes mountains in Peru and eventually flows through Brazil, Bolivia, Colombia, and Ecuador.

Sky lines The Nazca Lines are massive mysterious shapes carved into the desert by the native Nazca people about 1,500 years ago. The figures include birds, monkeys, animals, fish, people, and even an "astronaut." They are so big they can only really be seen from a plane.

Peruvian hairless dog

Scary Stuff

Got a Headache?

As long ago as 2000 BC, people here did brain surgery to cure sickness and fix head injuries. Brain surgery was also performed for spiritual and magical reasons, using tools made from bronze and obsidian—a hard volcanic rock with a very sharp edge.

Lost City

Built by the Inca people in the 14th century, Machu Picchu (mah choo peek choo) is a great lost city high up in the Andes. The city is made of stone, which had to be carried up the mountain. Hundreds of terraces were cut into the side, to make it easier to get around. The city was abandoned, but no one knows why.

7 ONE OF THE
NEW WONDERS
OF THE WORLD

Lake people At 12,470ft (3,800m) above sea level, Lake Titicaca is the world's highest lake that big boats can navigate. The Uros people live on the lake, on floating islands made from a grassy lake reed.

Amazing Animal

Love a Llama

Long-necked llamas are camel cousins. People ride them, eat them, drink their milk, and make wool from their fur. They burn the poo as fuel!

Hairy Killer

The Brazilian wandering spider has the most toxic venom of any spider.

Pinky's large gray matter

The pink Amazon River dolphin's brain is 40% larger than ours! Pinky grows up to 8ft 6in (2.6m) long. It is gray when young, and turns pink and then white with age.

The real macaw

Indigenous Kayapo and other tribal people wear a fancy headdress made with wild macaw tail feathers. They sometimes wear clay plates in their lips.

BRAZIL
★ Brasilia

★ Official language: Portuguese
★ Population: 198,739,269
★ Currency: Reals
★ Area: 3,287,612 sq miles (8,514,877 sq km)

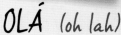

OLÁ (oh lah)

Brazil takes up almost half of South America and is home to the mighty Amazon River. You'll also find the world's largest rain forest here. A lot of the forest is being chopped down, which is really bad news for all the native tribes—and animals, insects, and plants— who live there. Brazil is rich in gold and diamonds, and the people like to dance and have a party. They are nuts about soccer, and nuts about Brazil nuts! Just watch out for the massive waves.

Oh Lord

This famous statue of Christ the Redeemer stands on top of a mountain and watches over the people of Rio de Janeiro. It is about 130ft (40m) tall and 98ft (30m) wide. It weighs 711.2 tons (635 tonnes) and has small spikes on its head to stop birds landing.

7 ONE OF THE **NEW WONDERS** OF THE WORLD

That's Swell

Twice a year, crocodiles, piranhas, and snakes go surfing, when water from the Atlantic Ocean creates huge waves in the Amazon River. These waves are 13ft (4m) high and can be heard 30 minutes before they arrive.

Party Time in Rio!

Every year, 40 days before Easter, the streets of Rio come alive with a huge party. There are colorfully decorated floats and thousands of people wearing wild costumes and dancing the samba. The main party lasts five days, but people start practicing months ahead.

BOLIVIA

★ La Paz

* ★ Official language: Spanish
* ★ Population: 9,775,246
* ★ Currency: Bolivianos
* ★ Area: 424,165 sq miles (1,098,581 sq km)

RIMAYKULLAYKI (ree mai koo lyai kee)

Bolivia is on top of the world. It has the world's highest capital city at 11,800ft (3,600m), the world's highest international airport, and with Peru (see page 34) it shares the world's highest navigable lake—Lake Titicaca. Being up so high in the Andes can make you dizzy, but locals say it helps to drink coca leaf tea. They keep warm with colorful handwoven shawls and blankets, made from llama wool. Bolivia has no coast, but even so, it has a big navy.

Road of Death

The Yungas Road may well be the world's most dangerous road, because between 200 and 300 people die on it every year. The road is carved into the mountainside, and is sometimes no wider than a car. Cars, buses, and trucks often plunge over its steep edges.

Set the table Bolivian kids are crazy about "table soccer," or foosball. You'll see them playing it on street corners, skillfully twisting the stick handles to score a goal.

Seeing is believing The bespectacled bear is the only bear in South America. It looks very wise.

Country Name Game

Bolivia was named after Venezuela's General Simón Bolivar, who freed Bolivia and other South American countries from Spanish rulers. What other countries in the world were named after people?

ANSWER: Colombia (page 32), named after Christopher Columbus; Liechtenstein (page 56), named after the royal Liechtenstein family; Saudi Arabia (page 150), named after Muhammad bin Saud; the Philippines (page 183), named after King Philip II of Spain

The real Harry Potter At the witches markets in La Paz, you'll see real-life witches casting magic spells. They sell herbs, medicines, potions, charms, jewelry, owl feathers, and dried animals.

Dancing with the devil If you go to the carnival in the old mining town of Oruro make sure you bring a raincoat. People at the carnival love to throw waterbombs and squirt foam over everyone. The carnival starts with a devil dance, where hundreds of people dress up as devils. Then everyone joins in.

Easter? Rats!

The capybara is the largest rodent. It looks like a giant, long-legged guinea pig. Each year Bolivians eat tons of capybara during Lent.

On the ball People in Paraguay love their soccer. The national team has played in seven World Cups.

PARAGUAY
★Asunción

Feasting on Flesh

Luison is the name of a hideous creature in Guarani mythology. The Guarani were the original people in Paraguay. The creature was like a wolfman, with long, dirty hair and icky-looking skin. He was said to be lord of the night—and the only thing he ate was rotting flesh.

- ★ Official languages: Spanish, Guaraní
- ★ Population: 6,995,655
- ★ Currency: Guaraníes
- ★ Area: 157,048 sq miles (406,752 sq km)

MBA'ÉICHAPA (mm ba ay cha pa)

Paraguay doesn't have an ocean border, but it has many of natural resources, forests, huge swamps, waterfalls, and plains where cowboys and cattle roam. Jaguars and tapirs prowl through its national parks. In 1893 a large group of Australians sailed here to set up an ideal society, called New Australia. While many soon returned home, their red-headed descendants still live here. Some of Paraguay's native tribes have never made contact with Europeans.

Ride in style Paraguayan cowboys travel in comfort. Their saddles are padded with soft sheep wool blankets. They are excellent horse riders.

Walk on water You could almost run across the giant waterlily pads floating in the swamps of Paraguay. They are up to 16in (40cm) across, and are very strong.

Getting the chop In the Chaco region, huge bits of forest are being chopped down—the size of 1,500 soccer fields a day. The trees are being chopped down to make more room to raise beef cattle.

CORREOS DEL PARAGUAY
₲ 0.25
PARAGUAY EN MARCHA

Half of Paraguay's people died in the War of the Triple Alliance (1864–70). Paraguay also lost lots of land to its neighbors.

Wild Thing

Many native Indian tribes still live in Paraguay. They carve amazing figures and masks from wood and use them in their rituals.

Best *mate* This cup has been carved from the hollow fruit of a plant called calabash. It is used to make a tealike drink called *mate* (mah tay).

URUGUAY
★ Montevideo

★ Official language: Spanish
★ Population: 3,494,382
★ Currency: Uruguayan pesos
★ Area: 68,036 sq miles (176,215 sq km)

Look, no teeth The giant anteater has no teeth, but its tongue can be 2ft (60cm) long! It can gobble thousands of insects in minutes. It grows up to 6ft 6in (2m) long, can weigh up to 132lb (60kg), and sleeps curled up in burrows, covered by its long, bushy tail.

HOLA (oll ah)

Uruguay is called the "Switzerland of South America" because it is so peaceful. The country has many cattle ranches, grassy pampas plains, and great horsemen called *gauchos* (gow choss), who wear handsome cowboy gear and are handy with a lasso. It also has super soccer players and is the smallest country to have won the World Cup—not once but twice, in 1924 and 1928. The largest meal of the day is lunch and many workers go home for two hours to share a huge meal with their families.

Ride 'em cowboy The *Fiesta de la Patria Gaucha* in Tacuarembó is a cowboy festival featuring rodeos, parades, and folk music. Men, women, and children dress up in their traditional *gaucho* outfits, and thousands of horses come along for the ride.

One greedy fellow The giant armadillo weighs up to 66lb (30kg), and can eat all the termites out of a single termite mound!

What's cooking? People in Uruguay love beef—everyone eats about 190lb (86kg) of meat a year. They sizzle their meat over a big barbecue pit called a *parrilla*. Grilled steak (*churrasco*) is a national dish. A beef platter called *parrillada* is also popular.

Scary Stuff

Furry Freaky

With a legspan of about 5in (12cm), the grammostola is one of the biggest spiders in the world.

World's Largest

Brawny Brainy Rat

A lucky fossil hunter in Uruguay recently found a giant skull belonging to a prehistoric rat. The mega-rodent was as big as a bull—not bad for a vegetarian.

Five Fat Fingers

Twice as high as a man, these stone fingers poke out of the sand at Punta del Este beach.

Built for speed The greater rhea is a large bird, a bit like the ostrich in Africa, the emu in Australia, and the cassowary in New Guinea. It can't fly, but can run fast—37mph (60 km/h).

Giganotosaurus

ARGENTINA
★Buenos Aires

Great Lizards

Many great dinosaur fossils have been found in Argentina. Some of the biggest dinosaurs, including *Giganotosaurus* and *Argentinosaurus*, come from here. Others include *Saltasaurus* and *Titanosaurus*.

★ Official language: Spanish
★ Population: 40,913,584
★ Currency: Argentine pesos
★ Area: 1,073,51 sq miles (2,780,400 sq km)

Duck Out for a Game

Pato is the national game of Argentina, and combines elements of polo and basketball. *Pato* is Spanish for "duck," as early games used a live duck instead of a ball. In the old days many riders fell off horses and were trampled underfoot; others were killed in knife fights when the game got heated.

HOLA (oll ah)

The name Argentina means "land of silver" because of the beautiful silver objects the early Spanish explorers found when they arrived. Argentina is the home of tango—a famous dance born in the nightclubs of the capital, Buenos Aires, more than 100 years ago. It is also the home of giant steaks, some the size of a laptop. The steaks come from cattle raised in enormous grassy lowlands called The Pampas. The inventor of the ballpoint pen, Laszlo Biro, lived in Argentina.

An ice place to visit The massive Perito Moreno glacier is 19 miles (30km) long. It is part of the Southern Patagonian Ice Field, which is the world's third-largest reserve of freshwater.

A foxy wolf The maned wolf is the largest canine in South America and looks a little bit like a fox.

The world's first animated film was made in Argentina, by Quirino Cristiani. The feature-length movie, *El Apóstol*, came out in 1917. In it, the Argentinian president used Jupiter's thunderbolts to clean up Buenos Aires. The film got lost in a fire.

Walls of water Iguazu Falls, at 269ft (82m), is higher than Niagara Falls in North America, and wider than Africa's Victoria Falls.

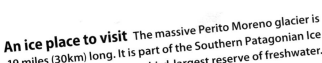
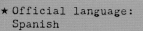

CHILE
★ Santiago

★ Official language: Spanish
★ Population: 16,601,707
★ Currency: Chilean pesos
★ Area: 292,260 sq miles (756,950 sq km)

HOLA (oll ah)

Chile is very long and very skinny and packed full of interesting things. More than 80% of the country is covered in mountains, many of them volcanoes. The El Tatio geyser field has more than 80 active geysers, which spurt hot water and steam high into the air. In the forest of southern Chile the world is turned upside down—miniature deer, called *pudu*, make their homes in giant rhubarb forests and are hunted by little wild cats called *kodkods*.

I Want my Mummy!

Thousands of years before the Egyptian mummies, the Chinchorro people in southern Chile were embalming their dead. It wasn't just for the powerful—everyone who died was mummified.

World's driest
The Atacama Desert is the driest place on Earth. In some areas it hasn't rained for 400 years! Yet plants and animals still live here because every morning thick fog brings in moisture.

Big bucks
In Chile, rodeo riding is the national sport. It is more popular than soccer. Big crowds come to watch the riders, known as *huasos* (wah sos).

Epic Event

He IS Robinson Crusoe

Alexander Selkirk was a buccaneer who got left on an island called Mas a Tierra in 1704. He lived there for four years and must have been lonely because he didn't have anyone to talk to. Daniel Defoe's book *Robinon Crusoe* was based on him.

Cute critters Guanacos (gwan ah kos) look like llamas or alpacas but are wild.

Dead Heads

Chile bought Easter Island, 2,180 miles (3,500km) away in the Pacific Ocean, from the Dutch in the 1880s. Easter Island is famous for its mysterious giant stone heads.

SCOTLAND
★Edinburgh

Wedge House in Great Cumbrae is only as wide as its front door. It has been sold to a (very skinny?) English family from Essex as a holiday home.

* ★ Official languages: English, Gaelic
* ★ Population: 5,100,000
* ★ Currency: British pounds
* ★ Area: 30,414 sq miles (78,772 sq km)

Teeny-tiny trotters The Shetland Isles are famous for knitted woolly jumpers and wee (that's Scottish for "small") ponies.

Television, telephones, fingerprinting, golf, tires, and penicillin were all invented by Scotsmen. And, of course, haggis, which no one else wanted to invent and few want to eat.

MADAINN MHATH (ma den va)

This is the country of Highlands and Lowlands, tartan kilts (worn without underpants), and wailing bagpipes. Edinburgh is the capital, but Glasgow is the biggest city. Scottish for "lake" is "loch" and one of these lochs might be home to a giant swimming snaky monster. Scots are rumored to enjoy snacking on deep-fried Mars Bars, but their most famous favorite food is haggis, a ball of minced meat wrapped in the yummy lining of a sheep's stomach.

Throwing their weight
The Scottish enjoy throwing odd things for sport. Caber-tossing is a bit like chucking a telegraph pole, while haggis-hurling is a competition to throw a meatball the farthest with least damage.

Fling your kilt In the mountainous Highlands, centuries ago, families recognized each other by their clan tartan. The government banned tartan in 1746 when the Highlanders were revolting (ugh!) and, after that, wearing tartan became a sign of rebellion.

Not so Scottish Bagpipes are not a Scottish invention— they came from Babylonia. About 200 years ago they were banned in most countries because of their "droning," but the Scots—and the Bulgarians (see page 69)—still love them.

The MacDonalds of Glen Coe invited the Campbell clan to stay the night in 1692. At midnight the guests got out of bed and murdered their hosts.

Monster or Myth?

Many people claim to have seen a giant snakelike monster in Loch Ness. This is the most famous photo of the beast, taken in 1934 by a holidaying London surgeon. Divers have trawled the loch and never found a thing. Fancy a dip, then?

IRELAND
★Dublin and Belfast

★ Official languages:
English, Irish Gaelic
★ Population: 5,978,200
★ Currency: Euros
★ Area: 32,595 sq miles
(84,421 sq km)

A bookish riddle The *Book of Kells* contains the four Gospels of Jesus. Some of the paintings in it are so tiny that they can only be seen by magnifying glass. But magnifying glasses weren't invented when it was painted. Mysterious!

Pictures for peace The people of Belfast painted the sides of their houses to show which side they supported in the "Troubles."

DIA DUIT (dee a gwit)

The Emerald Isle is home to the mythical leprechaun but not the snake (Ireland is a snake-free zone). Northern Ireland is part of the United Kingdom (see England, page 44), while southern Ireland has its own government. The Irish are patriotic (Dublin dyed its river green for St. Patrick's Day) and enjoy a good *craic* (laugh). But it's not all been a *craic* for the Irish: Northern Ireland had its "Troubles" and 1 million Irish starved in the Great Potato Famine 150 years ago.

A load of blarney If you hang over the edge of Blarney Castle and kiss the magic stone—just like Homer Simpson did—you'll get the gift of the "blarney" (be a great storyteller).

World's First

Hallowe'en started in Ireland. At Celtic New Year, the crossing point into the ghost world is very thin and bad spirits can pop through. They wander around looking for bodies to possess. Make your face and house as scary as possible, so they don't come calling.

A change of trousers
Mischievous leprechauns (shoemakers) wore red clothes until last century. Now they're always seen in green.

Ireland is the only country where windmills turn clockwise.

Picking a Giant Fight
These 40,000 blocks of volcanic lava formed 50 million years ago. Their tops make a path called the Giant's Causeway. The mythical Irish giant Finn McCool used them as stepping stones to cross the sea to fight a Scottish rival.

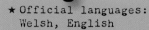

Leek   Daffodil

WALES
★Cardiff

Loompaland
Born in Cardiff in 1916 (to Norwegian parents), Roald Dahl wrote kid's books. *Charlie and the Chocolate Factory* featured Willy Wonka and Oompa Loompa helpers.

★ Official languages: Welsh, English
★ Population: 2,990,000
★ Currency: British pounds
★ Area: 8,017 sq miles (20,764 sq km)

Keep Out!
There are more castles in Wales than in any other country—most of them built to keep the English out! There are around 600 but some are just mounds of soil (watch where you're treading).

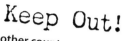

BORE DA (boy ray dah)
Welcome to Wales, a land of castles and corgis, daffodils and fiery red dragons. The Welsh graze sheep on their famous green hills, and dig under them to find coal. Road signs are all written in both English and Welsh, and one particular train station shows the longest name in the world. The leek is the national emblem, but play too much of the national sport—rugby—and you could end up with cauliflower ears. If you have a fascination with baked beans, this is the country for you.

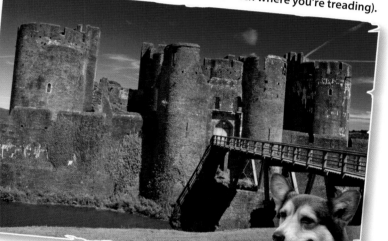

Top dogs Welsh corgis are favorites of the English royal family. Queen Elizabeth II is often seen with handbag, pearls, and a crowd of these pooches. They live in palaces, fly in private jets, and their poop is scooped by royal butlers.

Sing-along The Welsh are passionate about rugby and they also love singing—a Welsh rugby crowd can sound like an enormous male-voice choir.

RUGBY

World's Longest

LLANFAIRPWLLGWYNGYLLGOGERYCHWYRNDROBWLLLLANTYSILIOGOGOGOCH

Or is it? This Welsh village claims to have the longest name in the world, but it is said letters were added to make it longer.

Keen beans Port Talbot is home to the Museum of Baked Bean Excellence. You could gain infinite beany knowledge here...or just a lot of hot air.

Doctor Who? The modern adventures of the world's favorite time traveler are filmed in Wales. Watch out for Daleks in dark corners and Cybermen under the bed.

ENGLAND
★ London

★ Official language: English
★ Population: 51,092,000
★ Currency: British pounds
★ Area: 50,352 sq miles (130,410 sq km)

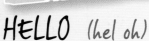

Stony stargazers Stonehenge, an eerie circle of standing stones, was built around the same time as Egypt's pyramids. Burial monument? Map of the stars? Or first ever domino topple?

Fish and chips This meal is often sold in chippies, jaunty shacks by the sea.

Eye say! You're late This huge Ferris wheel (443ft/135m high) was built for New Year 2000 but missed the date! You couldn't ride on the London Eye until March 2000.

HELLO (hel oh)

The United Kingdom is made up of England, Scotland, Wales, and Northern Ireland. When Queen Victoria (who was "not amused") sat down on England's throne in 1837, London was the largest, most important city in the world. Northern England is home to smoky industrial cities, but there are also more mysterious crop circles here than anywhere else on Earth. It rains one day in every three, but don't worry—you can stay indoors and sip tea (the English drink more cups of tea than any other nation).

Hideous History

In the 1660s England had a run of bad luck. The Great Plague (bubonic) swept the country and then London burned in the Great Fire.

Soccer crazy If you ask an Englishman, he'll tell you "soccer isn't a matter of life and death: it's far more important than that." Most cities have two teams—originally one for Catholics, one for Protestants.

Foolish Follies

The English are often described as "eccentric" (a bit mad) and this is one of the reasons why: follies. A folly is a lovely, but strange, building of absolutely no use, built around 200 years ago by posh English lords who had more money than sense.

Crazy Fact

Bearskin caps, worn by Grenadier Guards, are 18in (45cm) high and were first worn to make soldiers look taller and more scary in battle (scary to bears, anyway). The army buys 100 Canadian bear pelts a year to make the caps. One cap can last 100 years.

PORTUGAL
★Lisbon

America's "First Dog"
Bo Obama, a Portuguese water dog, lives in the White House with the American president.

Nail-biting tunes The Portuguese guitar is plucked with the fingernails, not strummed.

Tile with style
Portuguese people don't just tile their bathrooms, but the outside of the whole house.

★ Official languages: Portuguese, Mirandese
★ Population: 10,707,924
★ Currency: Euros
★ Area: 35,556 sq miles (92,090 sq km)

OLÁ (oh lah)

Five hundred years ago Portugal was on top of the world. It ruled a huge empire and was famous for its daring explorers and trading ships. Unfortunately, Portugal is now one of the poorest countries in Europe (although its trees produce two thirds of the world's corks). But let's not feel too sorry for this fallen superpower…it's still got the world's tastiest ham, great holiday beaches, and famous custard tarts—and the American president loves his Portuguese water dog.

Amazing Animal

Picky Pigs

Warm up the sandwich-toaster—the black-footed pigs of Portugal and Spain produce Jamon Iberico, supposedly the best-tasting ham in the world. These pigs are fussy eaters—they feast on the acorns that grow here and aren't as fat as other pigs.

World's best custard tarts? These are for eating, not throwing. They are said to be the best custard tarts on the planet.

Fishing frenzy The Portuguese discovered America before anyone else—they just didn't bother to land while they fished for cod off Newfoundland.

Valiant Vasco

Portugal bred many famous explorers during its Age of Discovery. Vasco da Gama discovered a route by sea from Europe around Africa to India, making the Portuguese Empire even bigger.

SPAIN
★ Madrid

★ Official language: Castilian Spanish
★ Population: 40,525,002
★ Currency: Euros
★ Area: 194,897 sq miles (504,782 sq km)

If you ask someone who first sailed around the world, they may say it was Spaniard Ferdinand Magellan in 1522. Actually, he was Portuguese but sailed for Spain. He got killed in the Philippines halfway round, but one of his ships did finish the journey.

HOLA (oll ah)

This is Spain, famous for brave bull-fighting toreadors, castanet-clacking flamenco dancers, a mustache-twirling surrealist artist, and possibly the "most spectacular building in the world." It's only 9 miles (15km) across the sea to Africa (grab your rubber ring) and the North African Moors ruled this land for nearly 1000 years, leaving spectacular castles behind. If you don't want to fight the bulls, run with them. (And, if you don't want to eat the tomatoes, throw them at your friends.)

Run with the bulls This is when Spanish bulls get their revenge for all those bullfights. Brave (or crazy?) people gather in the narrow walled streets of Spanish towns and try to out-run these angry bovines.

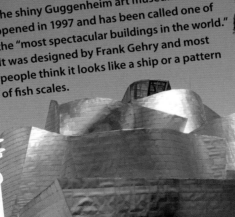

Come for dinner! The Alhambra Palace was built about 700 years ago by the Moors. The last sultan of Granada invited local chiefs to a banquet here, and then killed them all.

A Work of Art

The shiny Guggenheim art museum in Bilbao opened in 1997 and has been called one of the "most spectacular buildings in the world." It was designed by Frank Gehry and most people think it looks like a ship or a pattern of fish scales.

Lolly lover Salvador Dali is best known for his surrealist paintings of melting watches, but he also painted the logo for Chupa Chups.

Play with your food!

La Tomatina has to be the world's messiest festival. About 112 tons (100 tonnes) of overripe tomatoes are tipped from the backs of trucks into the crowd. People squish the fruit into each other's faces and are then hosed down by the local fire brigade.

The Torre de Hercules is the oldest working lighthouse on Earth. It was built in the 1st century by the Romans and flashes every 20 seconds. (That must be a good lightbulb.)

Bye-bye Cows!

In 1957 an Andorran farmer realized his snowy sloping fields were better for skiing than grazing animals!

ANDORRA
★ Andorra la Vella

★ Official language: Catalan
★ Population: 83,888
★ Currency: Euros
★ Area: 181 sq miles (468 sq km)

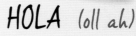

Epic Event

Charlemagne, King of the Franks, made Andorra a country in the 9th century. Some people say the Andorrans forged the signed treaty to get independence.

HOLA (oll ah)

This tiny country is the sixth smallest in Europe. But what it lacks in size, it makes up for in…money! The citizens pay no tax so a lot of wealthy people move here. Andorra is famous for ski hills and posh shops. It has more than 2,000 shops—more than one for every 40 people (which is a LOT). Since 1278 Andorra has paid a yearly fee (the *pestia*) to France or Spain, who take it in turns to protect the country if someone attacks. Let's hope they're keeping track of whose turn it is.

Crazy Facts

• Every adult in Andorra can read and write, and everyone has a job.
• The people here live second-longest of anyone on Earth (the longest-living people are from Osaka, Japan).
• Four fifths of Andorra's money every year comes from tourists.

Sky-high living The Pyrenees are the mountains between Spain and France. Andorra is in the Pyrenees and its capital city is the highest in Europe. It has no airport—to get here you drive for three hours from Spain or France.

Trees, not skis! Andorra's name comes from the Moorish *Al-Darra*, which means "thickly wooded." Hmmm…many of those woods have now been cut down to make ski slopes.

47

FRANCE
★Paris

★ Official language: French
★ Population: 64,057,792
★ Currency: Euros
★ Area: 212,935 sq miles (551,500 sq km)

BONJOUR (bon joor)

Welcome to France, one of the largest countries in Europe and home to the most famous bicycle race on the entire planet. France is also home to a whopping 500 different kinds of cheeses and the only Disneyland in Europe. This is the place where frogs' legs are served for dinner, and nervous garden snails hide under leaves. As a people, the French are known to have a passion for fashion, a flair for art, and a fierce pride in their nation, language, and culture. *Vive la France!*

Hideous History

'Teen Queen Got the Chop!

In 1793 Queen Marie Antoinette and her hubby, Louis XVI, came to a nasty end when the people revolted and chopped off their heads with a guillotine. Revolting!

Step 1, Step 2... Step 1,665

Phew! But the view from the top of the Eiffel Tower is worth climbing all those stairs. This famous landmark was built in 1889 for the Paris World's Fair.

Oh so chic! The French sense of style is admired the world over. Many of the world's most famous fashion designers are French.

What are you wearing? The Tour de France bicycle race works by different colored jerseys: the day's best sprinter wins the green jersey; the best climber wins the polka dot jersey; and the overall leader gets to wear a yellow jersey.

Maze of skeletons
The creepy Catacombs under Paris are where poor citizens buried their dead when the graveyards were full.

What's that smell?
"Pungent" is a polite way to describe Époisses de Bourgogne, a French cheese that is often called the "world's smelliest." It's so stinky it's banned on public transportation.

That's not fair! Monte Carlo Casino is where the rich and famous gamble away their money. But the citizens of Monaco aren't allowed to gamble, or even visit the Casino (unless it's to vacuum the carpets or clean the bathrooms).

MONACO
★ Monaco

★ Official language: French
★ Population: 32,965
★ Currency: Euros
★ Area: 0.8 sq miles (2 sq km)

FRANCE
Port de Monaco
Mediterranean Sea

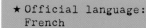

Epic Event

Watch Out for the Monk

In 1297 Francois Grimaldi sneaked into Monaco dressed as a monk, with a sword hidden under his robes. He whipped out the sword, let in his soldiers, and the Grimaldi family has ruled ever since.

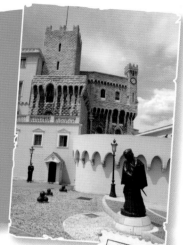

Princess Grace Grace Kelly was a famous American film star who married Prince Rainier Grimaldi and became a real princess. She died in 1982, after a car accident on a winding road.

USA 29 GRACE KELLY

BON GIURNU (bon joor noo)

Everything about tiny Monaco screams wealth: you can gamble a million dollars at Monte Carlo Casino or race your Formula One car through the steep streets; yachts are anchored in the glittering harbor; and the royal family is one of the world's most glamorous. This city-state (everyone lives in the very-small-but-perfectly-formed city) is only 0.8 sq miles (2 sq km), which makes it the world's second-smallest country—but one of the richest. Start saving your pocket money.

Crazy Facts

- It takes only 56 minutes to walk across this whole country.
- Monaco has more police for every citizen than any other country.
- Monaco's flag is the same as the flag of Indonesia (see page 181).

Real-life film set
Three James Bond movies have been filmed here: *Casino Royale*, *GoldenEye*, and *Never Say Never Again*.

Take a break!
Monaco's Port Hercules is named after the mythical hero, who stopped here to take a breather from thumping foes with his gnarly club.

Rev It Up!

The annual Formula One Grand Prix around Monaco is one of the oldest car races in the world. It takes six weeks to set up the circuit and three weeks to remove it.

NETHERLANDS

★ Amsterdam

NORTH SEA
Groningen
Amsterdam
The Hague
Eindhoven
BELGIUM
GERMANY

★ Official language: Dutch
★ Population: 16,715,999
★ Currency: Euros
★ Area: 16,033 sq miles (41,526 sq km)

Love Those Flowers

The Dutch are crazy for tulips and grow and sell more bunches than any other country. During World War II many Dutch people had little or no food and survived by eating tulip bulbs.

Wind and water There are about 1,180 windmills in the Netherlands. They use wind power to pump water away from farmland.

HELLO (hal low)

Water, water, everywhere! Netherlands means "low country" and half this land lies only waist-height above sea level (perhaps ankle-height if you're Dutch, the world's tallest nationality). In the 17th century the Dutch had a Golden Age when they were top of the class in art, science, and exploring— New York was originally called "New Amsterdam." Because their country's so flat, the Dutch love cycling…they own twice as many bicycles as cars.

Clever clogs These were worn by farmers, who spent all day up to their ankles in water-logged fields.

World's tallest The Dutch are the world's tallest nationality. When the average Dutchman visits the Democratic Republic of Congo (see page 116), he towers 17.3in (44cm) over the Mbuti people who live there.

Netherlands: 6 ft 0.4in (1.84 m)

Mbuti people: 4ft 7in (1.4m)

Funky Food

Carrots weren't always orange. They used to be black, purple, red, or white. The Dutch bred them orange 500 years ago for their royal family, the House of Orange.

Amsterdam Hiding Place

Amsterdam is famous for its canals and the very tall, skinny houses that are built along them. In one of these tall houses the young Jewish girl Anne Frank and her family were hidden by friends from the Nazis in a secret apartment behind a bookcase.

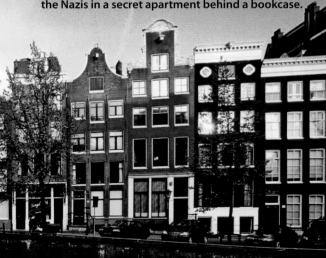

BELGIUM
★Brussels

Chocolate heaven More chocolates are sold in Brussels National Airport than anywhere else on Earth. (Forgotten to buy holiday presents? Get a box of sweets.) Praline chocolates were invented in Brussels in 1912.

★ Official languages
Dutch, French, German
★ Population: 10,414,336
★ Currency: Euros
★ Area: 11,787 sq miles
(30,528 sq km)

Yes, he is weeing!
Manneken Pis is a world-famous piddler. Every few days the locals put a different outfit on him. Is it because he keeps wetting his trousers?

BONJOUR (bon joor)

Belgium has three national languages, but none of them is "Belgian." If you know any Walloon, you can speak it here. The Belgians love beer (although not as much as the Czechs, see page 75) and invented chocolates and French fries, which really should be called "Belgian fries." Europe's first skyscraper was built here in 1932 and the lights of Belgium's highway system are the only man-made thing visible from the moon (yes, that's right—not the Great Wall of China, see page 186).

Crazy Fact

In Belgium it's rude to keep your hands in your pockets while you talk to someone.

Castles Galore

The Royal Palace of Brussels looks like London's Buckingham Palace but is half as long again. Every other year a grand flower display is held here. The Belgians love palaces and castles and have more than 3,000—some greedy villages even have two castles.

Invented Here

A Crashing Entrance

In 1760 Joseph Merlin, a Belgian inventor, decided to go to a masked ball wearing his newest creation, a pair of boots with metal wheels on them. For some reason, he chose to play the violin at the same time. He rolled across the room at top speed, and crashed into a huge mirror on the other side.

Best-selling Belgian
Georges Rémi, using pen name Hergé, wrote these comic books about young reporter Tintin and his dog, Snowy. More than 350 million books have been sold.

AUSTRIA
★ Vienna

Strudel (like "poodle") This yummy sweet layered pastry is filled with apple or sour cherries.

★ Official language: German
★ Population: 8,210,281
★ Currency: Euros
★ Area: 32,383 sq miles (83,871 sq km)

SERVUS (see ah vass)

Warm up your yodeling voice and lace up your mountain boots because nearly two thirds of this country is covered by the Austrian Alps (where the hills are alive with the sound of nuns singing). Austria is well known for skiing and strudel-making (not both at the same time, unless you're very clever) and its beautiful capital, Vienna. This country has also produced a heap of classical composers and a fantastic plastic candy dispenser (just tilt back the head).

Hohensalzburg Castle The first brick of this huge castle was laid in 1077 and building went on for centuries. In the 20th century it became a prison, and then a fortress for keeping prisoners of war.

Hideous History

The Hapsburgs, who ruled the old Austrian Empire, were so worried about contaminating the family tree with "common blood" that they sometimes married their relatives. There were significant medical results, including a deformed mouth called the "Hapsburg lip."

Scary Stuff

The Eisriesenwelt ice caves are nicknamed "World of the Ice Giants." In 1879 explorers discovered a maze of underground caves 26 miles (42km) long. The local people knew about the caves but were too terrified to go inside—despite the ice, they thought this was the entrance to Hell.

The Hills Are Alive...

If you've ever wanted to sing loudly and twirl around on a grassy hillside, feel free to do it here—this is where the famous 1960s film *The Sound of Music* was set.

AUSTRIA'S TOP 5
Composers to Know

1. Joseph Haydn
2. Wolfgang Amadeus Mozart (no, he's not a werewolf!)
3. Franz Liszt
4. Johann Strauss Jr.
5. Franz Schubert

Flip the lid
PEZ dispensers were invented here, in 1927, to hold mints. The name comes from the first, middle, and last letters of *pfefferminz* (peppermints).

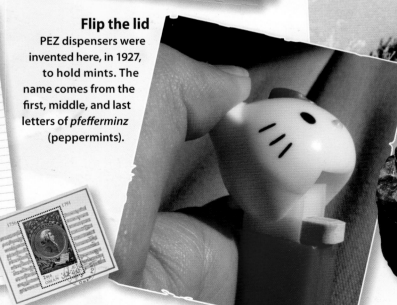

World's biggest emerald This green whopper, carved out of a single emerald crystal in 1641 for Hapsburg King Ferdinand III, is on display in Vienna's Imperial Treasury. To find out about the world's largest producer of emeralds, Colombia, see page 32.

To find out about the world's largest producer of emeralds, Colombia, see page 32.

Leaning Tower of Suurhusen This less famous tower beats the one in Pisa, Italy (see page 57), for leaningness!

(see page 57)

GERMANY
★ Berlin

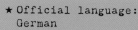

★ Official language: German
★ Population: 82,329,758
★ Currency: Euros
★ Area: 137,787 sq miles (356,866 sq km)

Amazing Animal

German dachshunds, or "sausage dogs," are the world's most effective fox chasers. (Because their sausagey bodies fit perfectly down fox holes?)

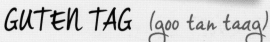

GUTEN TAG (goo tan taag)

Step into a land of fairy-tale castles, super-fast highways, and a famous dividing wall. Germany has the second-largest population in Europe, but thick dark forest still covers much of the land. Many famous storybook characters were dreamed up in Germany, and so was your friendly garden gnome. There are more than 1,500 kinds of sausages to be sampled, and plenty of "sausage dogs" to admire (just don't get the two confused).

That wall must fall! A huge wall once divided Germany into East and West. In November 1989 it was torn down, and Germany became one nation again. For another great wall, go to China (see page 186).

go to China (see page 186)

World's First

The first garden gnome was made here in the mid-1800s. He wasn't alone for long—now he has pals all around the world.

Stop, go! East Germany had its own particular style of traffic lights. You can buy T-shirts, flip-flops and even candy that feature this cute German couple.

Neuschwanstein Castle

This fairy-tale castle in Bavaria was built for eccentric King Ludwig II. It took 14 carpenters 4½ years just to finish the woodwork in his bedroom! Sleeping Beauty's castle in Disneyland is based on this castle.

GERMANY'S TOP 5
Stops on the Fairy-tale Road

1. Schwalm River woods: *Little Red Riding Hood*
2. Castle Sababurg: *Sleeping Beauty*
3. Hamelin: *Pied Piper of Hamelin*
4. Bremen: *The Town Musicians of Bremen*
5. Statue of the Little Goose Girl in Göttingen: near where the Brothers Grimm worked

LUXEMBOURG
★ Luxembourg

★ Official languages:
  French, German,
  Luxembourgish
★ Population: 491,775
★ Currency: Euros
★ Area: 998 sq miles
  (2,586 sq km)

MOIEN (moy yen)

This is the special Grand Duchy of Luxembourg—special because it's the only Grand Duchy left in the world. It has ancient medieval towns, but it's also Europe's modern communications whiz, with 34 TV stations and a love of cell phones. The world's sixth-smallest country makes up for lack of size by speaking a lot of languages…business is done in French, German is taught at school and used on TV, but the natives speak Luxembourgish into their beloved cell phones.

Epic Event

Once a year the lively people of Echternach dance in the streets to honor St. Willibrord, the monk who founded the town in 698. It's no surprise that they're proud—he's Luxembourg's only saint.

Scary stuff
Luxembourg's fortress is one of the best-defended castles in the world. Beneath it lie 13 miles (21km) of secret underground passages for sneaking around.

Luxembourg has the most cell phones per person of any country in Europe.

No Ruin Now

The 1,000-year-old Vianden Castle is one of the most awesome in Europe, but 30 years ago it was a ruin. Its careless 19th century owner sold bits of it until only rubble was left.

No to violence
This sculpture was made in 1980 after Beatle John Lennon was shot. It inspires people to put away their guns (or tie them in a double reef knot).

All the fun of the fair
Luxembourg's national fair started in 1340. They didn't have Ferris wheels then…just lots of exciting farm animals to stare at!

Crazy Fact

Tune In, Teens!
Radio Luxembourg broadcast from here between 1933 and 1992. It played all the "tuneless" pop music that parents hated (Elvis Presley, The Beatles, punk) every night from 6 p.m. to midnight. Teenagers listened in under the bedclothes.

Invented Here

Swiss Army Knife

So many tools in one little knife…
tweezers, toothpick, can opener,
screwdriver, scissors, nail file, saw, hook,
magnifying glass, pen, fish scaler, and
kitchen sink (oops, where did that come from?)

SWITZERLAND
★ Bern

★ Official languages:
  German, French,
  Italian, Romansch
★ Population: 7,604,467
★ Currency: Swiss francs
★ Area: 15,937 sq miles
  (41,277 sq km)

Who's Horn?

The Matterhorn is one of the world's most famous mountains. No one knows who it was named after, but lots of proud families called "Matter" live in the valley below.

GRUEZI (grea atsie)

This small Alpine country (think snowy mountains and grassy valleys) is famous for skiing, not fighting. Switzerland hasn't taken part in a war since 1814—not even the two World Wars. Even today, Switzerland still doesn't like to join in with the gang—it's in the middle of Europe but hasn't joined the European Union and doesn't use the Euro for money. Swiss clocks are famously reliable—they need to be, because it's said that all Swiss trains and buses run on time.

Swiss cheese

Invented Here

Velcro was created when a Swiss inventor took his hairy dog for a walk in 1948. The dog came home covered in grass seeds. The hooks on the seeds gave the owner an idea for a new fastener.

Money in the safe Because Switzerland stayed neutral in both World Wars, it was a safe place to keep money while other countries fought. Rich people from all over the world left their money in Swiss banks.

Cuckoo! The Germans invented cuckoo clocks but the Swiss made them into "chalet" (house) clocks. Little people pop out to tell you you're late.

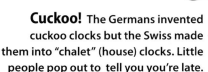

St. Bernard If you were buried under a snowy avalanche, wouldn't you like to be dug out by a big snuffly dog with bloodshot eyes?

Daisy ringing Wondering what that noise is on the mountainside? Bell-ringers? Mad xylophone players? No, it's cows wearing bells so farmers can find them.

55

LIECHTENSTEIN
★ Vaduz

★ Official language:
German
★ Population: 34,761
★ Currency: Swiss francs
★ Area: 62 sq miles
(160 sq km)

Europe's Wealthiest

Money, Money, Money
Liechtenstein is the world's smallest (and richest!) German-speaking country. Liechtensteiners are the second-richest people in the world, beaten for wealth by the residents of Qatar (see page 154).

Top teeth
This country is the world's largest maker of false teeth. That's something for everyone to smile about.

GRUEZI (grea atsie)
This wealthy Alpine country is made up entirely of mountains (no wonder the national soccer team struggles—their pitch must be on a terrible slope). The Liechtenstein family worked for the Hapsburgs of Austria (see page 52) and Emperor Charles VI gave this little bit of land to his servant Anton Florian Liechtenstein in 1719. Liechtensteiners love their "zfood"—breakfast is *zmorga*, lunch is *zmittag*, and dinner is *znacht*.

Flaming Swiss
The walls of Liechtenstein's Vaduz Castle are 13ft (4m) thick. You might think that would keep it safe, but the Swiss burned it down in 1499. (In those days the Swiss still liked a good fight, see page 55.)

World's First
Marco Büchel is the first skier to compete in *six* Winter Olympics. That's 24 years of Olympic skiing.

EUROPE'S TOP 5
Smallest Countries

5. Malta: small
4. Liechtenstein: very small
3. San Marino: teeny tiny
2. Monaco: ridiculously microscopic
1. Vatican City: *how* small? (See page 59.)

Giant-slayers Liechtenstein's soccer team is so bad that a book was written about it—it's the only team to lose to San Marino, and it lost all 20 World Cup qualifiers without scoring a goal. Then it stunned giants Portugal with a 2–2 draw.

Stuff that! Liechtenstein is the world's largest producer of sausage skins.

Crazy Fact

Liechtenstein is doubly landlocked, so you have to travel through two other countries to get to the ocean. There is only one other doubly landlocked country in the world: what is its name?

Answer: Uzbekistan (see page 160)

ITALY
★ Rome

Basta Pasta!

This means "enough pasta" and is not something the Italians often say. They each eat 80lb (36kg) of pasta every year.

Funky Food

"Pizza" is one of the few words that is understood in almost every country of the world. Pizza was "invented" in Naples in the 1860s—why so many Italian restaurants are called Pizza Napoli.

Speed freaks Italy is famous for luxury sports cars: Ferrari, Maserati, Alfa Romeo, and Lamborghinis—the police force's favorite!

★ Official language: Italian
★ Population: 58,126,212
★ Currency: Euros
★ Area: 116,348 sq miles (301,340 sq km)

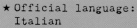

CIAO (chow)

The Roman Empire ruled the world for 500 years and built thousands of roads that all "lead to Rome." This is the land of pasta and gelato, the sleepy siesta (a little nap after lunch) and buzzing Vespa, war-loving Caesars and battling gladiators, and the world's most beautiful sinking city. The Romans also invented lavatories (teachers like to stress how "civilized" this was, forgetting to mention that everyone wiped their bottom with the same wet sponge on a stick).

Crazy Fact

Leaning Tower of Where?

Everyone's heard of the Leaning Tower of Pisa, but the world has many other leaning towers. Can you name some?

Answer: Tower of Suurhusen, Germany; Tiger Hill Pagoda, Japan; Leaning Temple of Huma, India; Capital Gate Tower, UAE (this was built to lean)

Colossal fun (for some) The Colosseum was *the* place to be in Roman times (although perhaps more fun for the audience than the performers). This is where gladiators battled against each other and wild animals.

7 ONE OF THE NEW WONDERS OF THE WORLD

Early gelato In AD 62 the Roman emperor Nero sent his servants to the mountains for ice. His cooks mixed it with a fruity topping—the world's first ice cream sundae?

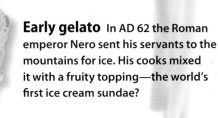

Venice

This city sinks slightly each year. Where other cities have roads, Venice has canals. *Gondolas* (thin boats) and *vaporetti* (water buses) ferry people around.

Vespa

SAN MARINO
★ San Marino

★ Official language: Italian
★ Population: 30,324
★ Currency: Euros
★ Area: 24 sq miles (61 sq km)

San Marino declared it would not take sides during World War II. How could that work, when it's right in the middle of warring Italy? The Italians thought it might pass secrets to the enemy, so they cut all phone lines into the country!

Multitalented These are the Guards of the Rock, the fortress guards who are San Marino's police officers and also defend the country.

CIAO (chow)

San Marino is often overlooked as a country, but it really is one. This little patch of hilly land is near the city of Rimini in eastern Italy. In AD 301 a stonecutter was sent to Rimini to rebuild the city walls. He was bullied for being a Christian and escaped to the top of a nearby hill, where he built a stone church tower and started his own city. More than 1,000 years later Napoleon offered to make San Marino larger—the citizens said "no thanks" in case they drew attention to their quiet country. Clever!

Tre Monti (Three Towers)

Three towers are built on the three peaks of Monte Titano. They feature on the flag and coat of arms and in the national chocolate wafer cake—the *Torta di Tre Monti*.

World's Worst

Sporting Embarrassments

- San Marino's soccer team is usually placed last in the world rankings. It once lost 13–0 to Germany.
- San Marino has never won a single Olympic medal.

Make sure you have a good time here. Over half this country's income comes from tourists.

Peaceful place This country is so peaceful that its official name is The Most Serene Republic of San Marino.

What's in a Name?

A person who comes from San Marino is called a Sammarinese.

Coat of arms

LIBERTAS

World's Oldest

This is the world's oldest sovereign state. It was founded in AD 301 by Marinus of Arbe, a Christian stonecutter working in Rimini.

REPUBBLICA DI S. MARINO   LIRE 3

Rude nudes? Michelangelo's most famous work is the ceiling of the Sistine Chapel. He spent four years lying on his back on scaffolding to paint these scenes from the Bible. After Michelangelo's death, underwear was painted on many of the naked people in his frescoes.

VATICAN CITY
★ Vatican City

★ Official languages: Italian, Latin
★ Population: 826
★ Currency: Euros
★ Area: 0.17 sq miles (0.44 sq km)

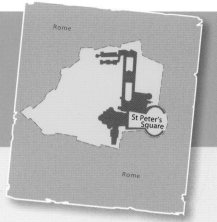

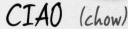

Pope John or Joan?
It is said that in the 9th century a woman dressed in man's clothes and became Pope John. She was Pope for three years, but then gave birth during a procession— a bit of a giveaway for the crowd.

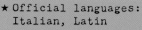

CIAO (chow)

The world's smallest country is in the middle of Rome and has only about 800 citizens, but its head of state is the Pope and, when he speaks, around 1 billion Catholics listen carefully. This tiny walled city became an official country in 1929. Even though it only takes a few minutes to walk across Vatican City, its museums hold so many works of art that they stretch along 9 miles (15km) of corridors. If you looked at each painting for just one minute it would take four years to see them all.

Vatican City has a bank machine that gives instructions in Latin.

Crazy Fact

The Pietà is the only work in the world that Michelangelo signed. It is kept behind bulletproof glass after it was attacked by a mad geologist with a hammer in 1972. Bits of marble, including Mary's nose, flew off and passersby grabbed pieces as souvenirs.

Groovy guards
They might look as if they're about to leap onto a trapeze or pull a rabbit out of a hat, but these are Vatican City's colorful Swiss Guards. They've kept the Pope safe since 1506.

Not-So-Epic Event

On May 13, 1981, a Turkish gunman, Mehmet Ali Agca, shot Pope John Paul II in St. Peter's Square in Vatican City. The Pope had four bullet wounds and lost a lot of blood, but he survived. Since then, Popes travel in special Popemobiles that have bulletproof glass on all sides.

World's Smallest
Vatican City is only 0.17 sq miles (0.44 sq km), which makes it tinier than the average American shopping mall. All water, food, and power have to be imported (usually from Italy—just across the road).

Pope mail, not snail mail Vatican City has its own postal service. The clever Romans noticed that Vatican mail is a lot quicker than Italian mail, so they buy Vatican stamps and post letters here.

MALTA
★ Valletta

MEDITERRANEAN SEA

Gozo
Mgarr

Valletta
Rabat

★ Official languages: Maltese, English
★ Population: 405,165
★ Currency: Euros
★ Area: 122 sq miles (316 sq km)

Carne vale This means "meat allowed" in Italian and was the traditional feast before 40 days of Lent. Today, Malta's carnival means five days of fun (and dressing up as Darth Vadar).

BONGU (bon joo)

This nation of islands has a storybook history. For three centuries the valiant Knights Hospitaller lived here and the capital Valletta is said to be "built for gentlemen, by gentlemen." After Napoleon chucked the Knights out of Malta in 1799, they went back to building hospitals. Malta has churches galore, the oldest man-made standing stones on Earth, and several hospitals! The favorite drink here is Kinnie, made from herbs and sour oranges (but the national food is *not* Maltesers).

Christian Bodyguards

One thousand years ago the Knights Hospitaller worked at a Jerusalem hospital for Christian pilgrims (pilgrimage was a dangerous business in those days). They offered their services to travelers as armed bodyguards and soon became a well-known army, based in Malta.

The Maltese Cross This symbol of the Knights Hospitaller has now become the symbol of Malta. Each of the star's eight points has a different meaning, such as bravery and loyalty...and being cross?

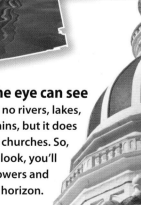

Across the water Now the Maltese leave their country by boat or plane, but thousands of years ago there was a bridge of land linking Malta to Sicily.

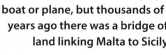

World's Oldest

The Tarxien Temples were built around 5000 BC, making them the oldest standing stones on Earth. Yes, that *is* older than the Pyramids and Stonehenge!

Far as the eye can see Malta has no rivers, lakes, or mountains, but it does have over 350 churches. So, wherever you look, you'll spot bell towers and domes on the horizon.

SLOVENIA
★Ljubljana

Sour Grapes

Slovenia has a 400-year-old vine. (It started growing when Shakespeare was writing.)

Jason's dragon The symbol of Ljubljana city is the dragon. Legend says that heroic Jason sailed up the Danube River with his band of Argonauts. A ferocious dragon attacked them here and, after a brave fight, Jason managed to slay it.

Slovenia has more tractors per person than any other country on Earth. (And a lot of happy farmers and plowed fields?)

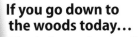

If you go down to the woods today… The dark scary forests of Slovenia (and almost half this country is covered by forest) are home to about 400 brown bears.

SLOVENIA
★Ljubljana

★ Official language: Slovenian
★ Population: 2,005,692
★ Currency: Euros
★ Area: 7,828 sq miles (20,273 sq km)

ZIVJO (zee vyoh)

This is a land of forests and caves, well-trained horses, and traffic jams of tractors. In those forests you can hear the roar of wild bears, the scream of a mythical dragon, and the squeaks of some very scared dormice. When they're not enjoying kransky sausages (or feasting on dormice), Slovenians celebrate the Salt Makers' Festival, Cabbage Festival, and Bean Day. And they're not scaredy cats: a Slovenian was the first person to ski down Mt. Everest (see Nepal, page 169).

Funky Food

All Together Now…

Lipizzaner horses were bred here for the Hapsburgs of Austria (see page 52) to ride into battle. They are now most famously ridden in formation at Vienna's Spanish Riding School.

Predjama Castle Robber baron Erazem Lueger lived here and used the secret tunnels under the castle to escape and go robbing.

Dormice have been eaten in Slovenia for centuries, and their fur used for (very small?) clothes. Dormice feasts gave the hungry peasants a big feed. Yum.

CROATIA
★ Zagreb

★ Official language: Croatian
★ Population: 4,489,409
★ Currency: Kunas
★ Area: 21,851 sq miles (56,594 sq km)

BOK (bohk)

Croatia's national animal is the weasel, but its most famous is the Dalmatian. In the countryside here are lavender fields and truffle-hunting dogs. This country brought neckties into fashion and its beautiful white stone was used to build one of the world's most famous buildings. With Slovenia, Bosnia and Hercegovina, Serbia, Montenegro, and Macedonia, Croatia was part of the former Yugoslavia, which split into independent countries in the early 1990s with terrible civil wars.

World's Largest Truffles are one of the world's most expensive foods and the world's largest truffle was found here in 1999. It was the size of a pineapple.

Evidence of war Dubrovnik has been fought over many times, most recently during the Siege of Dubrovnik in 1991. There is a chart near the city gate showing which buildings were destroyed, but from high up you can easily tell which were rebuilt by their new, brightly colored roofs.

Lucky toe Diocletian's Palace in Split is built of white Croatian stone (the same bright white stone that was sent to the USA to build the White House). Outside its gate is a statue with a nicely polished big toe. The toe is shiny because Croatian legend says whoever rubs it will have good luck.

Spotted Here

Cruella De Vil's favorite dogs come from the Dalmatian Coast. They're also known as Dubrovnik Hunters, or Plum Pudding Dogs.

Invented Here

Who would've thought the Croatian army had contributed to the fashion world? In the mid-1600s Croatia's dandy soldiers worked in Paris, wearing their uniform neckties. The fashionable French loved them! And so, the *cravat* was born.

Checkerboard The red and silver squares on Croatia's coat of arms aren't for playing chess—they represent ancient Red Croatia and White Croatia.

BOSNIA & HERCEGOVINA
★Sarajevo

Stećci Bosnia has 60,000 of these medieval tombstones. They are engraved with patterns and pictures, but no one knows exactly why.

- ★ Official languages: Bosnian, Croatian, Serbian
- ★ Population: 4,613,414
- ★ Currency: Konvertibilna markas
- ★ Area: 19,767 sq miles (51,197 sq km)

HEJ (hay)

This land of mountains and rushing rivers is where history was made when World War I was started with an assassination in 1914. Its decorated tombstones have puzzled for centuries, but a recent prankster didn't puzzle anyone for long with his "discovery" of Bosnian pyramids. Bosnia and Hercegovina was part of the former Yugoslavia and fought a terrible war of independence from 1992 to 1996. Signs of its struggle can be seen across the land, especially in Sarajevo.

Epic Event

Archduke Franz Ferdinand was assassinated in Sarajevo in 1914 by a patriotic Bosnian. His death started the planet's bloodiest conflict: World War I.

Sarajevo roses
Craters left in the Sarajevo pavements by explosions were filled with red resin after the war. These "roses" are the city's signs of remembrance.

Crazy Fact

Ever heard of Tutankhamen of Bosnia? Probably not. In 2006 a Bosnian "explorer" claimed to have found pyramids with burial chambers in Visoko. It was later discovered that he had reshaped the local hill to look like a Mayan pyramid.

Call the dentist!
Bosnians don't sweeten coffee with sugar—they dip sugarcubes in the cup and eat them whole.

Bridge of Hope

In 1993 the 500-year-old Mostar bridge was destroyed by Croatia. After the war, many countries chipped in funds to rebuild it brick by brick, using local materials.

Hideous History

The city of Sarajevo was under siege from 1992 to 1996—the longest siege of a modern capital city. More than 1,500 children were killed. The band U2 recorded the song "Miss Sarajevo" in support of the capital city.

SERBIA
★ Belgrade

★ Official language: Serbian
★ Population: 7,379,339
★ Currency: Serbian dinars
★ Area: 29,913 sq miles (77,474 sq km)

Spray art
Belgrade holds many art exhibitions, but sometimes the paintings are sprayed on the walls of local buildings!

World's Top Producer

Heavenly Red Berries

Serbia is the world's largest raspberry grower—95% of the world's *top-quality* raspberries come from here. So who's growing the world's squishy, moldy, sour raspberries, then?

ZDRAVO *(zz drah voh)*

Serbia is old! It contains two of the oldest cities in Europe (Starčevo and Pločnik) and its capital is one of the oldest too, although it has only been known as "Serbia" since 2006. Visit here if you enjoy raspberries, but not if you're scared of peacocks. If a Serbian friend wants to tease you, they'll call you a *kornjaca*—a "turtle"! The Serbian version of carol singers are *Koledari*: young men who dress up and sing...with one of them dressed as a pregnant woman.

Free as a bird Belgrade's City Forest has peacocks roaming wild (dodging the stray cats and dogs).

Prince Michael Street The buildings along Belgrade's main street are protected by law. They might look a jumble, but the houses show architecture from all different times.

What's in a Name?

If you hear someone being called "Johnny" in Serbia, then they're probably named Nikolas. Weird? The nickname for Nikolas is Nijo. The Serbians think it's a great idea to mix those letters and come up with "Joni."

Old White Town

Belgrade is one of the oldest capital cities in Europe—it was first settled in the 3rd century BC by the Celts. Its name means "white fortress" or "white town."

Party time For a week in June 2010, Vrnjacka Banja was World Carnival City Capital.

Montenegro's Tara River Canyon is 0.8 miles (1.3km) deep—Europe's deepest.

The world's deepest canyons are:
1. Yarlung Tsangpo, Tibet: 3.7 miles (6km)
2. Colca Canyon, Peru: 2.5 miles (4.16km)
3. Grand Canyon, USA: 1.1 miles (1.83km)

Tara is deeper, but Nevidio Canyon, also in Montenegro, is the world's most difficult. Its name means "never seen" because no one managed to climb into it until 1965.

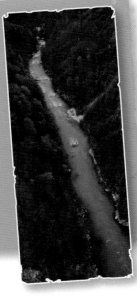

MONTENEGRO
★ Podgorica

★ Official language: Montenegrin
★ Population: 672,180
★ Currency: Euros
★ Area: 5,333 sq miles (13,812 sq km)

ZDRAVO (zz drah voh)

Welcome to Europe's "baby" country, created in 2006 when it split from Serbia to become the sixth piece of the former Yugoslavia. Montenegro means "black mountain" and this land was once covered in thick dark forest—Biograd Forest is the only patch of rain forest in Europe. Europe's deepest canyon is here and the town of Cetinje has the continent's most rainy days. Montenegro causes problems for mapmakers because its name is too long to fit on such a small country.

Old Olives In the town of Bar is an olive tree that's more than 2,000 years old. And it's still growing olives!

Cave Church

The Monastery of Ostrog is built into a steep cliff, using the cliff caves as rooms in the building. Here you can confess sins in three different faiths: Muslim, Serbian Orthodox, and Catholic.

Quick victory Just two weeks after Montenegro became a country in 2006, its national team won the Water Polo World Cup.

Speedy delivery In 1903 Montenegro was the first country in Europe to deliver mail by car—the car also happened to be the first one in Montenegro.

Just One Big Hotel...

Sveti Stefan was once a fishermen's island, connected to the mainland by a thin sandy land bridge. In the 19th century 400 people lived here. By 1954 fishing wasn't so popular, only 20 people were left, and the whole village was turned into the world's first hotel-town. Marilyn Monroe and Claudia Schiffer have spent holidays here.

ALBANIA
★ Tirana

★ Official language:
Albanian
★ Population: 3,639,453
★ Currency: Leke
★ Area: 11,100 sq miles
(28,748 sq km)

Raising an eyebrow?
In Albanian *vetullushe* means "a goat with brown eyebrows." That's just one of 30 different Albanian words for eyebrows. This facial-hair-obsessed language also has 27 words for "mustache."

What's in a Name? Gjirokastra changes its name depending on what its citizens are doing. First it was called "City of Silver," then in medieval times it became "City of Wailing" because the Albanians wail for their dead. (Not a happy time for the city then?) Now it's "City of Stone," because that's what the town roofs are covered with.

TUNGJATJETA *(tune jat yet ah)*

The Albanians call their home *Shqiperia*, which means the "land of eagles," and that's what's on the flag. This country once had a ruler called King Zog and its local languages are Tosk and Gheg. If you like breaking school rules, be careful here—the government has a list of 1,262 rules for citizens, including 38 on how to behave with guests. It's easy to be misunderstood in Albania, where nodding your head means "no" and waggling it sideways means "yes." Yes, no, whatever!

Bobble head The traditional white felt hat worn by Albanian men is called a *qeleshe*. In the north the cap is short, like half an eggshell. In the south it's a tall cone. And in some places it has a bobble on top.

Stuffed peppers

Crazy Fact
An eccentric Englishman called C. B. Fry held the world long jump record in 1913 (he could also jump up backward onto a mantelpiece and land perfectly). After World War I he was asked to become King of Albania, but he said no.

Bunker down Communist leader Enver Hoxha thought everyone wanted to invade his country. In 1981 he had concrete bunkers built as lookouts all over the land.

Two fingers only If you can't play the guitar you might prefer the *çiftelia*— it has only two strings.

Calling All Window Cleaners!
It's easy to see why Berat was given the name "City of a Thousand Windows."

GREECE
★Athens

★ Official language: Greek
★ Population: 10,737,428
★ Currency: Euros
★ Area: 50,949 sq miles (131,957 sq km)

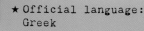

World's most famous building? The Parthenon on top of the Acropolis is one of the most famous and most copied buildings in the world. It was built of white marble in 438 BC by Pericles and had a statue of Athena inside. It was also used as a great big bank for storing ancient Greek money.

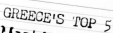

GREECE'S TOP 5
Mythical Monsters

1. Medusa: a stony gaze and snakes for hair
2. Harpies: flesh-eating bird–women
3. Minotaur: head of a bull, body of a man
4. Cerberus: three heads!
5. Cyclops: who needs more than one eye?

Medusa

Yo-yo Invented here over 3,000 years ago!

KALIMERA (ka lee me rah)

Modern Greece is just a tiny part of the ancient Greek Empire that ruled the world from 750 BC to 30 BC (although slaves made up over half of its population). Thousands of English words come from Ancient Greek, along with the Olympic Games. If you're wondering why so many things are painted blue here, it's because the superstitious Greeks think blue protects from evil. (And don't worry if they spit after paying a compliment—they're just keeping away the "evil eye.")

What's in a Name?

Possible Confusion?

The Greek words for bread and toilet seat are the same: *kolóura*. The same word also means life preserver. Be careful what you call for if you fall overboard.

What's in a name? Gods Athena and Poseidon agreed that whoever gave this city the best gift would have it named after them. Poseidon gave Athens the gift of water; Athena gave an olive tree. Guess who won!

Going to war in a dress? They might not look like it, in dresses and pompom shoes, but these are soldiers. This is the traditional dress of the Klephts, ancient warriors of the Greek mountains.

Santorini

This volcanic island lost its center in a huge eruption in 1645 BC. The semicircular cliff that is left is the huge rim of the volcano. Legend has it that this may have been the lost city of Atlantis.

The Greek national anthem has 158 verses.

MACEDONIA

★ Skopje

★ Official languages: Macedonian, Albanian
★ Population: 2,066,718
★ Currency: Macedonian denars
★ Area: 10,700 sq miles (27,713 sq km)

ZDRAVO (zz drah voh)

This country has produced some of the world's most famous leaders, including Alexander the Great and Egypt's Cleopatra, and the saintly nun Mother Teresa, who looked after the poor in India. Here are mountain slopes for skiing, ancient cities, and deep cool lakes. Like its neighbors, Macedonia was part of Yuogoslavia until 1991, so Communist–era housing blocks are built next to ancient bathhouses with copper domes and Ottoman mosques with minarets.

Amazing Animal

Lake Ohrid (horrid?) is the home of the European eel, which swims there from its birthplace thousands of miles away in the Sargasso Sea. The eel lives in Lake Ohrid for 10 years, then returns to the Sargasso to have babies and die. The baby eels then do exactly the same thing. What a life!

Woof, woof

It might not look scary now, but this tiny Yugoslav Shepherd will grow up tough enough to fight off a pack of wolves.

Mountainous Macedonia
This country has two different mountain ranges and 16 of Macedonia's mountain peaks are higher than 6,560ft (2,000m).

Scary Stuff

Stone Dolls

Legend says that a man couldn't choose which of two women to marry, so he decided to secretly marry both. The second bride saw the first wedding happening and cursed everyone there, turning them to stone. Now 120 giant pillars stand at Kuklica, waiting for the wedding cake.

Yes, I'm Great!

Alexander the Great was the son of King Philip of Macedon and became the most famous ruler of the Greek Empire. He wasn't modest... He was the first Greek ruler to put his own face on coins, instead of the face of a Greek god or goddess.

Egyptian link

The Ptolemys, rulers of Egypt for centuries (think Cleopatra), were originally from Macedonia.

BULGARIA
★ Sofia

Sofia? Or Scotland? Along with Scotland (see page 41) and Ireland, Bulgaria is one of the three countries that play bagpipes as their national instrument.

★ Official language: Bulgarian
★ Population: 7,204,687
★ Currency: Leva
★ Area: 42,811 sq miles (110,879 sq km)

Optical illusion? Bulgarian houses really do get bigger as you go upstairs. For 200 years these upwardly expanding wooden houses have been built on stone bases to try to protect them from earthquakes.

ZDRASTI (zz dra stee)

Bulgaria is one of Europe's oldest countries and the oldest one that's kept its original name. This land was founded in AD 682 by the Bulgars. In the 8th century its leader, Emperor Tervel, was proclaimed "Saviour of Europe" for defeating the invading Arab army. This is a land of ancient treasures (sometimes dug up by factory workers). Bulgarian sheet music was sent into space on US Voyager 1 as part of a collection of humankind's finest artifacts—let's hope alien intelligence likes folk music.

Crazy Fact

Happy Grandma Day!

On March 1 a Bulgarian might give you a red and white *Martenitsa* to welcome spring. Wear the doll on your wrist until you see a fruit tree in flower, then tie it to the tree and leave it there.

Bulgarian Peter Petrov invented the world's first digital wristwatch.

Black and Blue

The Black Sea coast is where Bulgarians make their sandcastles. It's easy to see the water is blue, not black, but it can be dark and stormy. The Greeks called this the "Hostile Sea" because it was so difficult to cross.

Hidden in the rock The Sumela Monastery is carved right into the cliff wall. Frescoes of biblical scenes are painted inside, outside, and even on the rock around the building.

Not-So-Epic Event

The Panagyurishte Treasure is a 13-lb (6-kg) stash of 23-carat gold. The nine objects were made in the 3rd century BC and dug up in 1949 by three poor brothers who worked at a nearby factory. Not so poor now!

69

ROMANIA
★ Bucharest

★ Official language:
  Romanian
★ Population: 22,215,421
★ Currency: Romanian lei
★ Area: 92,043 sq miles
  (238,391 sq km)

Painted Eggs

For Easter, the Romanians hollow out chicken eggs and paint them in red (for Jesus' blood), black (for Jesus' suffering), and yellow (for light).

Moving on Romany gypsies traditionally live in horse-drawn caravans and there are still 750,000 horse carts in everyday use here.

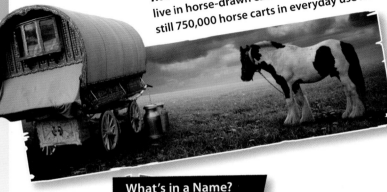

BUNA ZIUA (boo nuh zee wah)

Hmmm...who's the world's most famous Romanian? Olympic-champion teenage gymnast Nadia Comăneci? Johnny Weissmuller, the film star who played Tarzan? No, when Romania is mentioned, most people think of cold dark castles and Count Dracula, the world-famous coffin-sleeping, sunlight-hating, blood-guzzling vampire. In reality, Dracula wasn't a vampire, he was just a Romanian prince who liked to skewer his enemies with sharp spikes and watch them die. So that's ok then.

What's in a Name?

The city of Bucharest is named after Bucur—but who on Earth was Bucur? He could have been a prince, outlaw, fisherman, shepherd, hunter, or airline pilot (no, sorry, forget that last one!) depending on which legend you believe.

Drumming for Freedom

Bucharest has the world's largest government building, built by its greedy Communist leader just before he was overthrown in 1989. These six drummers, suspended on wires from a crane, played a show in front of the building when he'd gone.

World's Largest

Blood-sucker

By far the most famous Romanian is Dracula of Bran Castle. (Romania also has a ruined Castle Dracula, but this is not where the evil one lived.) Vlad Dracul was known as Vlad the Impaler for his bad habit of impaling enemies on spikes. He was turned into a blood-sucking vampire by Bram Stoker in his 1897 book.

Good neighbors Moldovans make the astrakhan *Ushanka* hats that their Russian neighbors wear to keep their ears warm. (*Ushanka* means "ear hat.")

Sweet Sunflower

Halva is a popular sweet in many countries, but in Moldova the fields are full of sunflowers and the seeds are used to make halva.

MOLDOVA
★Chisinau

★ Official language: Moldovan
★ Population: 4,320,748
★ Currency: Moldovan lei
★ Area: 13,070 sq miles (33,851 sq km)

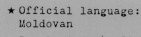

BUNA ZIUA (boo nuh zee wah)

This is a land of sunflowers and watermelon fields, where wine-making is taken very seriously and the roadsides are dotted with religious symbols. Moldova, named for a dog who drowned, is one of the poorest countries in Europe. It was part of the huge Russian Empire from 1912 until the empire started to break up in 1991. But the Moldovans still do their neighbors a favor by making the famous astrakhan hats that keep Russian ears warm—sometimes in wild colors!

Perfect Can you draw a perfect circle? The Moldovans built this stone fortress in a perfect circle in 1543.

The Moldova River gave this country its name. The river was named by Prince Dragos for his dog Molda, who drowned in it after a long and exhausting hunt.

Cross drivers This country is crowded with religious statues and crucifixion scenes on roadsides.

Keen on Color

The blue, white, and gold church of All Saints in Chisinau is one of the most brightly colored in the world. For other wild paint jobs see Belarus (page 77) and Russia (page 81).

Wine-making is BIG in Moldova—it has the world's biggest wine cellar, with room for 2 million bottles.

UKRAINE
★ Kiev

★ Official language:
  Ukranian
★ Population: 45,700,395
★ Currency: Hryvnias
★ Area: 233,032 sq miles
  (603,550 sq km)

PRYVIT (pri veet)

Glittering Kiev, also known as Kyiv, is the beautiful capital of this land, where Cossacks once terrified their enemies (with their fast dancing?) and spiders are seen as a good luck charm. This country is called simply "Ukraine," not "The Ukraine," although it does have another name: the "Breadbasket of Europe," because it grows so much wheat. The blue and yellow flag shows a blue sky over a yellow wheat field. Woolly mammoths once roamed here (and were made into neat little houses).

Crazy Fact

It's good luck to find a spider or spider's web on Christmas Day. So, guess what clever Ukrianians decorate the Christmas tree with? Yes, spiders are more popular than tinsel here.

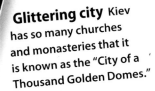

Glittering city Kiev has so many churches and monasteries that it is known as the "City of a Thousand Golden Domes."

Funky Food

Not So Kiev
Chicken wrapped around garlic and herb butter and coated in breadcrumbs is called Chicken Kiev. It wasn't invented in Kiev, but in a Moscow dining club.

How many mammoths does it take to build a house? Ancient houses made from the bones of woolly mammoths were discovered here in 1965. The huts were built of bones and tusks and covered with dried skin. That's a mammoth building job!

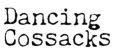

Dancing Cossacks

These fearsome Ukrainian warriors fought the Tartars, but are now best known for their lively dancing and baggy trousers.

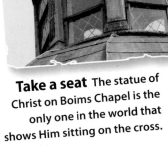

Take a seat The statue of Christ on Boims Chapel is the only one in the world that shows Him sitting on the cross.

Visitors here are greeted with bread and salt. Bread represents hospitality and salt means friendship.

HUNGARY
★ Budapest

Dog or moving rug? The Hungarian Komondor, with its bizarre stringy hair, is sometimes called a mop dog. It is often used as a guard dog—perhaps it mops intruders to death?

- Rubik's cube: can you solve this puzzle?
- Noiseless match (what noise?)
- Krypton electric bulb
- Biro: Laszlo Biro updated the ballpoint pen and gave it his own name

★ Official language: Hungarian
★ Population: 9,905,596
★ Currency: Forints
★ Area: 35,918 sq miles (93,028 sq km)

Spicy stuff Dried peppers are ground into paprika and used to flavor the Hungarians' favorite dinner—goulash.

SZIA (zee yah)

This country was named for Attila the Hun (who actually came from the Urals of Russia, see page 81). The Huns were a fearsome mob who rampaged across Europe in the final days of the Roman Empire. Budapest's thermal springs mean there are medicinal baths all over this city—a good place to relax after fighting a Hun. If you buy a Hungarian a bunch of flowers, take care to count the number of blooms. Odd numbers of flowers are given only at funerals!

Just the place for a nice hot bath Budapest has more thermal springs running under it than any other capital city.

World's Largest

Hungary's currency used to be the pengo. In 1946 Hungary issued a 1,000,000,000,000,000,000 (1 quintillion) pengo bank note—the world's highest ever denomination.

Great Aunt Turul? Legend says that Attila was descended from this powerful mythological bird. The Turul is often shown carrying the Sword of God—a very clever bird then!

Attila's Land?

Attila the Hun, who invaded most of Europe 1,500 years ago, gave his name to Hungary. The Huns had an unusual parenting style—they slashed their baby sons' faces so they would grow up to look frightening. They also invented stirrups, so that they could stand up on horses and terrify the enemy with their scarred faces.

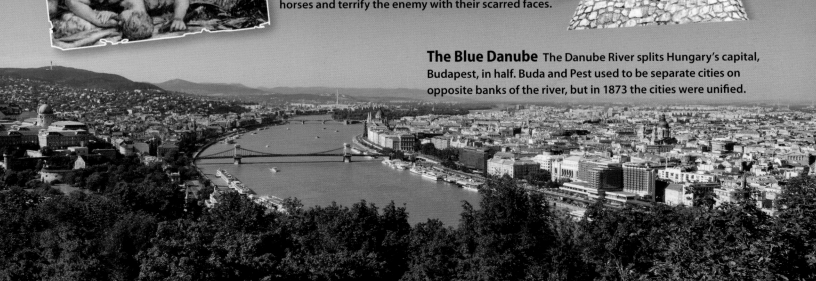

The Blue Danube The Danube River splits Hungary's capital, Budapest, in half. Buda and Pest used to be separate cities on opposite banks of the river, but in 1873 the cities were unified.

SLOVAKIA
★ Bratislava

★ Official language: Slovakian
★ Population: 5,463,046
★ Currency: Euros
★ Area: 18,933 sq miles (49,035 sq km)

AHOJ (a hoy)

This small country made up part of Communist Czechoslovakia and its landscape is a mixture of ancient castles and Communist buildings—and some very unusual statues. The Slovaks love ice hockey (they make more hockey pucks than any other country) and claim American pop artist Andrew Warhola (aka Andy Warhol with the soup cans) as their most famous countryman. The world's largest stalagmite is hiding in a cave here, growing upward very, very, *very* slowly.

What's in a Name?

Slovakia and Slovenia tripping you up? If you're confused, take pity on the soccer commentator who embarrassed himself several times when they played each other in an important soccer game. Both call their (very similar) languages "Slovenski."

Ready, Jump!

Stefan Banic, a Slovak inventor working in the US, patented the parachute in 1914. Daringly, he jumped from a 41st-story window to demonstrate it.

Funky Food

Slovakia's traditional Christmas Eve meal is carp. The fish are sold live and often swim around in the bath for a couple of days before they're killed and cooked. Just try not to get too fond of your new pet!

A clue for burglars Bratislava Castle has four corner towers and one is bigger than the others—that's the one the Crown Jewels are in.

World's Largest

The world's biggest stalagmite is in Krásnohorská Cave.

Watch your head! This bronze statue is peeping out of a manhole. He has his own traffic sign ("Man at Work") because careless drivers have almost decapitated him twice.

Star Wars? No, it's not an alien spaceship but a restaurant on top of a 1970s bridge in Bratislava. The locals do call it the UFO though.

Short of decorating ideas? What about human bones? The little church at Kutná Hora features the skeletons of up to 70,000 people, artistically arranged over the walls and ceilings.

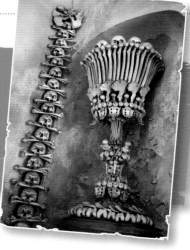

CZECH REPUBLIC
★Prague

★ Official language: Czech
★ Population: 10,211,904
★ Currency: Koruny
★ Area: 30,451 sq miles (78,867 sq km)

Puppet or person?
The Czechs have a tradition of puppet-making. Some are so realistic you might find yourself chatting to them in the street.

Golden City
The beautiful city of Prague on the Vltava River has many nicknames, including "Mother of Cities," "City of a Hundred Spires", and "Golden City." Prague is built on both sides of the Vltava, with 20 bridges joining its banks.

AHOJ (a hoy)

With Slovakia, this country gained its independence in 1993. Its capital, Prague, is one of Europe's most beautiful cities, with cobblestone streets and a fairy-tale castle watching over it. The Czechs enjoy puppet shows and are world-champion beer drinkers (they drink 560 cupfuls per person, every year). If you like potatoes, you'll love it here...they're served mashed, roasted, fried, in salads, soups, and dumplings. When you need a rest from potatoes and beer, try pork and sauerkraut.

Przewalski's Horse
The world's last species of "wild" horse hadn't been seen since 1966 in its native Mongolia. Prague Zoo breeds these rare horses and releases them back into the wild.

That's astronomical!
The Prague Orloj doesn't just tell the time—it shows months, signs of the zodiac, and the Sun's position.

The Lennon Wall Since 1980 young Czechs have painted graffiti about John Lennon and words of Beatles songs on one Prague wall. The government paints over the graffiti but it quickly reappears.

POLAND
★Warsaw

★ Official language:
  Polish
★ Population: 38,482,919
★ Currency: Zloty
★ Area: 120,728 sq miles
  (312,685 sq km)

CZESC (chesht)

For two years (1955–57) Poland's Palace of Culture and Science was the tallest building in Europe. Now it's the 187th tallest—which might be why the Polish feel a bit upside down these days. The Poles love dumplings and doughnuts and encourage lucky storks to nest in their homeland. Here you won't find many gravestones over 50 years old—you get buried and 40 years later your old bones are dug up and someone new gets your spot. You can only stay buried if you're very famous!

Funky Food

Mardi Gras (Fat Tuesday) is the Tuesday before Lent, when Christians traditionally fast. Poles eat huge quantities of doughnuts to use up all the fat and eggs in the house. It's the same idea as English Pancake Tuesday and German *Fetter Dienstag*.

Love those bears!
The United Buddy Bears stopped off in Warsaw in 2008 on their world tour to promote peace and love between countries.

Fast food Pierogi are little dumplings that can be filled with almost anything: cheese, sauerkraut, mashed potato, cabbage, meat, wild mushrooms, blueberries, or strawberries.

Amazing Animal

Coming Home to Roost

Every April Poland welcomes visitors—a huge flock of white storks arrives to nest here. The Poles see storks as a sign of good luck and put up special platforms for them to build nests on. Stork nests are so big that sparrows and starlings often sneak in there too.

Where's the plane?
The Wieliczka Salt Mine has been worked for 800 years. During World War II the Poles hid an airplane factory in here, 1,000ft (300m) underground.

The Polish enjoy competitive mushroom picking!

Feeling Topsy-turvy
This upside-down house was built as a life-size sculpture to describe how Polish people feel now that Communism has gone from their country and life is changing so quickly. Visitors to the house often complain of dizziness, so it's working well!

Crazy Fact
Smingus Dyngus Day
On Easter Monday Polish boys are allowed to throw water at anyone they like. In the past they carried buckets, but now they use water pistols. Any girl who gets soaked will marry in the next year.

BELARUS
★ Minsk

Weave that! The Belarusians can weave pieces of straw into just about anything!

tanding out from the crowd
he "Red Church" is very different from e buildings around it. It was built by a ch Belarusian family in 1910 after the ath of two of their children. During viet times it was used as a cinema.

* ★ Official languages: Belarusian, Russian
* ★ Population: 9,648,533
* ★ Currency: Belarusian rubles
* ★ Area: 80,155 sq miles (207,600 sq km)

VITAJU (vit ah joo)

Belarus has had a difficult time in history, mainly because of its geography, caught between Communist Russia and Poland. It has been independent of Russia since 1991. Here you'll find ancients forests home to Europe's largest animal, but that are also full of wooden crosses to remember sad times in the country's history. Now Belarus is wrestling its way to a happy independent future and its people can weave their straw creations in peace at last.

Nearly Lost Forever

Belarus is home to the wisent, Europe's biggest animal. In 1915 the German army arrived here and hunted the wisent for food. The Polish army defeated them in February 1918, just one month after the last wisent was eaten. Luckily there were enough in captivity to breed.

Remember the brave
Minsk has many war memorials— half of its population was killed in World War II and most of the city was destroyed when the Russians recaptured it.

Wrestle free
The Belarusians, both men and women, are champion wrestlers.

What's in a Name?
Belarus means "white Russian." No one is sure if this comes from the country's snowy places, or its people's white clothing.

Much loved Mir
Mir Castle, built to protect this fertile area of Europe, has become the symbol of brave Belarus.

Independence Square
When Belarus was part of the Russian Empire, this was called Lenin Square. The enormous government building and the huge statue of Soviet leader Lenin in front of it were built by the Communists.

LITHUANIA
★ Vilnius

★ Official language: Lithuanian
★ Population: 3,555,179
★ Currency: Litai
★ Area: 25,213 sq miles (65,300 sq km)

Coat of arms

LABAS (lah bahs)

According to geographical computers, Lithuania's captital, Vilnius, is at the very center of Europe. This is the incredible shrinking country—during the 14th century, Lithuania was the largest nation in Europe (what are now Belarus, Ukraine, and parts of Poland and Russia once all belonged to the Grand Duchy of Lithuania). That seems a very long time ago. For all its wonderful past, Lithuania now holds a sad world record: it's the country with the highest suicide rate.

Watch out for witches
As well as the HIll of Crosses (below), this country now has the Hill of Witches. Witchy wooden sculptures started appearing here in 1979.

Favorite Dishes
- *Saltanosiai* (cold noses): dumplings stuffed with bilberries were given this name because they are blue.
- *Cepelinai* (potato zeppelins): patties shaped like zeppelin airships.
- *Vederai*: intestines stuffed with meat and potato (the Lithuanian version of a sausage!).

Dream city Legend says that Vilnius was built in the 1320s when Lithuania's Grand Duke dreamed of an iron wolf that howled "with the voices of 100 wolves." This meant he should build a city "as mighty as their cry." (Either that, or stop eating wolfburgers at bedtime.)

Fair trade The Kaziukas Fair has been held for hundreds of years for local artists and craftspeople to sell their wares.

Crazy Fact
Christmas Eve
Don't load the dishwasher after this 12-course vegetarian feast—the food must be left on the table all night so that the spirits of dead loved ones can come to eat, too.

The Hill of Crosses
Crosses first started to appear on this hillside in the 14th century. When Lithuania was under the control of Communist Russia, its people put up crosses as a sign of resistance. Three times, in 1961, 1973, and 1975, the crosses were burned down and the hill bulldozed, but they quickly reappeared.

Get your skates on! Ice hockey is the most popular sport in this chilly northern country. It's been played here since 1909.

LATVIA
★ Riga

★ Official language: Latvian
★ Population: 2,231,503
★ Currency: Lati
★ Area: 24,938 sq miles (64,589 sq km)

Map labels: BALTIC SEA · ESTONIA · Valka · RUSSIAN FEDERATION · Riga · Liepaja · Daugavpils · LITHUANIA · BELARUS

Amazing Animal

Two-spot Ladybug

Latvia's national insect protects plants from parasites and is loved all over the country. Its Latvian name, *marite*, is for the ancient goddess of Earth, Mara.

LABDIEN (lab dee en)

In Latvia's beautiful capital, Riga, you'll find that the walls really do have ears (and eyes, and whole faces!). Here is the famous Riga Cathedral, often called the Riga Dome, although it has no dome. On the banks of the stormy Baltic Sea winters can be cold and the people of Riga hold the world record for knitting the longest woolly scarf (105ft/32m), in the Latvian flag colors of red and white, of course. Latvians love ice hockey, and they like to celebrate with a nice plate of cheese!

Someone's Looking at You

Ever had the feeling you're being watched? These Art Nouveau buildings are about 100 years old. The idea was to give builders creative freedom, just like artists have.

Turaida Castle This 1214 tower burned down in 1776 and was a ruin until the Latvians completely rebuilt it in the 1970s.

Funky Food

Go Wild with Cheese

The Latvians celebrate *Jāņi*, their traditional festival of summer's longest day, with a plateful of caraway cheese.

Musical monster In Riga Cathedral you can sing along with one of the world's biggest organs—it has 6,828 organ pipes. (Some people call this cathedral the "Riga Dome," but *Doms* is Latvian for cathedral.)

ESTONIA
★ Tallinn

★ Official language: Estonian
★ Population: 1,299,371
★ Currency: Euros
★ Area: 17,463 sq miles (45,228 sq km)

Estonia's answer to the Leaning Tower of Pisa (see page 57): the Leaning House of Raekoja Square. One side of the house was built on the old town wall, the other on sinking wooden blocks.

Crazy Fact

TERE (ter e)

Welcome to Estonia, home of the world's wife-carrying champions. This is the smallest of the three Baltic States (with Latvia and Lithuania) and was named after the Ests who lived here in the 1st century. Almost half this land is forest and more meteorites per land area have crash-landed here than anywhere. Estonia is the least religious country on Earth—only 14% of its people believe in a god—but for 75 years its church had the world's tallest tower.

Jagala Falls Estonia's largest waterfall is often called the "Niagara Falls of the Baltic." In winter it sometimes freezes over.

Scared of the dark? Almost half of this country is covered in thick dark forest.

Champions

The Estonians are the wife-carrying champions of the world. This contest is held every year in nearby Finland. The winner gets to drink his wife's weight in beer.

Tallinn's tall tower For 75 years Estonia had the world's tallest building. Between 1549 and 1625 the spire of St. Olav's Church was higher than any other building on Earth. In 1625 it was struck by lightning and burned down. As you can see, luckily it's been rebuilt!

World's Most

That's Meteoric!

Estonia has the most meteorite craters of any country.

Skype was invented in Estonia.

RUSSIAN FEDERATION
★ Moscow

First in space, too
Russia launched the first dog in space (1957) and first man in space (1961).

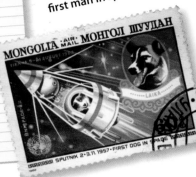

★ Official language: Russian
★ Population: 140,041,247
★ Currency: Russian rubles
★ Area: 6,601,668 sq miles (17,098,242 sq km)

What's in a Name?

Great...or Not-so-great?

Russia was once ruled by tsars and tsarinas who were given flattering and not-so-flattering names: Ivan the Great, Peter the Great, Catherine the Great...and Ivan the Terrible. If you were a Russian leader, what would you be called?

PRIVET (pree vyet)

Russia is the world's largest country and it holds so many records for "biggest", "highest," "coldest," and "first" that it puts the rest of Europe to shame. Not content with all these firsts on Earth, Russia raced the USA to be the first into space and Yuri Gagarin was the first man to orbit Earth on April 12, 1961. For hundreds of years the Russian Empire was ruled by tsars, good and bad. During most of the 20th century it was called the Soviet Union, and its people lived under Communist rule.

The people's palace?
This isn't really a palace: it's Moscow's Metro station. Its beautiful sculptures and chandeliers were ordered by Stalin, to remind the Russians "what privileged lives they lead."

No parts for dogs
At Moscow's House of Cats, talented felines are the stars of the show. They perform tricks on stage—making dogs jump through rings of fire, perhaps?

Thanks a Lot!
This amazing building on the right of Red Square is St. Basil's Cathedral. It was built 500 years ago by Ivan the Terrible and has nine famous, brightly painted "onion domes." The story goes that, when it was finished, Ivan had the architect blinded so that he could never build anything as wonderful for someone else.

FINLAND
★Helsinki

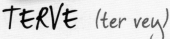

★ Official languages:
  Finnish, Swedish
★ Population: 5,250,275
★ Currency: Euros
★ Area: 130,559 sq miles
  (338,145 sq km)

TERVE (ter vey)

This is a country of islands (a whopping 179,584 of them) and lakes (an even-more-whopping 187,888 of them). The Finns like to sweat in a hot sauna, then roll in the snow—for fun! Northern parts of Finland, Sweden, Norway, and Russia are called Lapland, which is where the reindeer-farming Sami live. In this land there are entire weeks when the sun never sets. The Finns drink more coffee than anyone on Earth—maybe so they can stay awake for all those weeks.

Get strumming
The world 'air guitar' championships are held here each year.

Invented Here
Ice-skating is one of the world's oldest sports. Around 1000 BC the Scandinavians started to use elk bones as skating blades. Ancient skis found in bogs in Finland are about 5000 years old.

Hide and Seek

The Sami of Lapland were one tribe who never fought Genghis Khan (see page 187) because they always hid when he and his Mongol troops came plundering!

(see page 187)

Crazy Fact

Night-lights

It's a popular tradition in Finland to light bonfires on midsummer's eve, June 20 or 21, to mark the Northern Hemisphere's longest day.

Letters to Santa Korvatunturi mountains in far north Finland is where Father Christmas lives. His postcode is 99999 Korvatunturi, but all mail sent to this address is delivered to Santa Claus Village at Rovaniemi.

Not so crowded Finland is the fourth most sparsely populated country in Europe (after Iceland, Russia, and Norway): there are only 40 Finns per sq mile (16 per sq km) of this land.

Storybook castle Olavinlinna is the world's most northerly medieval castle. It features as Kropow Castle in The Adventures of Tintin (see page 51).

(see page 51)

There are nearly 2 million saunas in Finland.

Funky Food

Swedes are crazy for meatballs with lingonberry sauce and mashed potatoes; rolled-up herrings called *rollmop*; and dumplings filled with blueberries, liver, and blood (yes, blood!)

SWEDEN
★ Stockholm

★ Official language: Swedish
★ Population: 9,059,651
★ Currency: Swedish kronor
★ Area: 173,860 sq miles (450,295 sq km)

Goths galore?
Visby on the island of Gotland was the home of the ancient Goths. (A tribe known for pale makeup and black nail polish, perhaps?)

HEJ (hey)

You've arrived in Viking territory. Along with Denmark and Norway, Sweden made up the homeland of the fiercest race of people the world has probably ever seen. Vikings plundered Europe, taking land and capturing people to sell as slaves. Today's Swedes are completely different: happy to dance along to ABBA, enjoy a plate of *rollmop* herrings, and then drive off in the Volvo to go shopping at Ikea. When you visit this country, try to resist stealing the road signs!

Prize with a bang
The Nobel Prize is given each year to people across the world who have achieved greatness. The prizes were founded by Alfred Nobel, a Swede who invented dynamite in 1866.

Dragon heads The biggest, most fearsome warships of the Viking fleets had carved prows.

Crazy Fact

One of the most popular souvenirs that tourists take home from Sweden is a "moose-crossing" road sign. Lots of these go missing from Swedish roadsides every year. Imagine trying to fit that in your suitcase…

Invented Here
ABBA; Volvo cars; Ikea; H&M; Pippi Longstocking

Turn the Heating Up!
The Ice Hotel in Kiruna started out as a simple igloo and becomes more elaborate every year. Yes, every year it's rebuilt after it melts in the summer.

DENMARK
★ Copenhagen

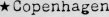

★ Official language: Danish
★ Population: 5,500,510
★ Currency: Danish kroner
★ Area: 16,639 sq miles (43,094 sq km)

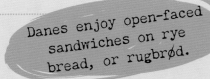

Danes enjoy open-faced sandwiches on rye bread, or rugbrød.

Pedal power The Danish government loves cycling so much it leaves free bikes around.

HEJ (hey)

This is true Viking country. The Danes ruled Europe from AD 800 to 1200 with their flaming torches and dragon-headed longboats. Viking leaders kept their names simple: Eric the Red, Harald Fairhair, and Harald Bluetooth. (What happened to Kevin Yellowsnot?) Today, the Danes choose bicycles over longboats and LEGO over warfare. They do still rule Greenland and the Faroe Islands, which the King of Norway lost to Denmark in a poker game.

Crazy Fact ## Jelling (Not Jelly)

Jelling stones are like Viking gravestones. King Gorm the Old made one in the 10th century for his wife. His son, Harald "Bluetooth" Gormsson, put one up in memory of his parents. Now they are showing damage from 1,000 years of Danish rain, so there is a national competition to decide how to protect them. Umbrellas?

Super Vikings
For about 400 years, Viking longboats were feared across Europe, and Denmark was Europe's superpower.

Crazy Fact

Did you know "The Little Mermaid" is almost 175 years old?! Hans Christian Andersen published the fairy tale way back in 1837.

No Green in Sight
Greenland, the world's largest island, was discovered by Eric the Red in the 10th century.

Copycat Walt Disney visited Copenhagen's Tivoli Park and loved it so much he decided to build something similar in the USA: Disneyland.

Invented Here
LEGO was invented in Denmark. If you stacked about 40 billion LEGO bricks, the tower would reach the Moon.

Mush! Mush! When the Vikings first found Greenland, they also discovered its huskylike dogs—perfect for pulling sleds over snow.

Thrilling Killers

Killer whales spend three months of each year swimming off northern Norway, eating herrings. You can go snorkeling with them...just don't wear your herring suit.

NORWAY

★Oslo

★ Official language: Norwegian
★ Population: 4,660,539
★ Currency: Norwegian kroner
★ Area: 125,021 sq miles (323,802 sq km)

Northern Lights

The aurora borealis is one of nature's best shows. These glowing lights in the sky are caused by Earth's magnetic field and can be seen in far northern lands. Centuries ago, people thought they were a message from the gods.

HEI (hey)

One third of Norway is above the Arctic Circle. This is a land of mountains and fjords, high waterfalls, and the most spectacular natural light show ever. Sea eagles and killer whales hunt these icy waters, and remote islands are home only to seals and polar bears. There were killers here 1,000 years ago—this was Viking country. The Norwegians are more friendly now: the Christmas tree in London's Trafalgar Square is a present every year from the people of Oslo.

Hideous History

Oslo became the capital in 1299, but in 1350 three quarters of its population was wiped out by the Black Death (bubonic plague).

Epic Event

Norwegian Roald Amundsen became the first person to reach the South Pole, on December 14, 1911. He was racing Englishman "Scott of the Antarctic" and beat him by 35 days. Robert Scott and his party perished on the Antarctic ice shelf, and Amundsen became famous for eating his sled dogs!

The Torghatten Troll Legend says that a troll was chasing a beautiful girl and shot an arrow at her. The Troll King threw his hat in the way to save her. His hat turned into the mountain with a hole in it—Norway's Torghatten.

Party time! Norwegians commonly wear embroidered folk costumes, known as *bunads*, for weddings and various festivals, especially the May 17 Constitution Day celebrations.

Claws under the ice The red king crab grows up to 6ft (2m) wide and is, not surprisingly, the world's largest crustacean. The females have 10,000 babies each year, so more than 20 million crabs now live under this ice.

Mountain coral Fjords are made by glaciers moving (very, very slowly!) and carving out deep valleys that fill with icy water. Coral reefs have been found in some deep Norwegian fjords!

ICELAND
★Reykjavik

★ Official language:
  Icelandic
★ Population: 306,694
★ Currency: Icelandic
  kronur
★ Area: 39,769 sq miles
  (103,000 sq km)

HALLO *(hal lo)*

This chilly northern land is where Earth's molten heat comes bursting to the glacial surface in bubbling hot water springs or belching volcanoes. Iceland is Europe's most sparsely peopled land, and in winter it's dark here for all but a few hours each day. The Icelanders stoke up on special *Thorramatur* meals to get them through the cold months. (And they can always while away a dark hour at the Iceland Phallological Museum, which has a penis specimen from every animal in the country.)

Farthest north
Founded in 1786, Reykjavik is the northernmost capital city in the world.

Not so bad The angler-fish looks ugly but tastes delicious. Its meat is called "the poor man's lobster."

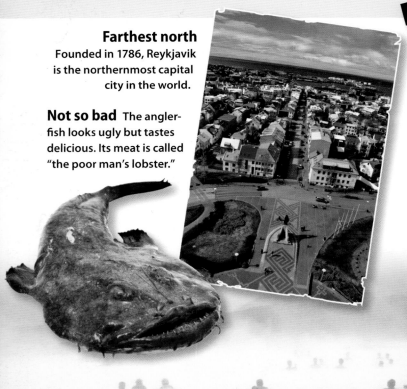

Epic Event

In April 2010 the Icelandic volcano Eyjafjallajökull erupted, sending black ash 5.6 miles (9km) into the air. Flights were stopped all across Europe for five days.

Stoking up From January to March the Icelanders eat a special diet called *Thorramatur:* smoked meat, burned sheep's heads, dried fish, and smoked shark. They find it perfect for keeping them cheerful during the dark days.

Ice and fire Glaciers cover more than one tenth of Iceland. Many of them are on volcanoes.

Amazing Animal

If you spent all your life in Iceland, this is the only horse you'd ever see. Icelandic horses were brought here by the Vikings over 1,000 years ago and now no other horses are allowed, in case they weaken the Icelandic "bloodline." Once a horse has left Iceland, it's never allowed to come home.

In Hot Water

Iceland's hot springs can spurt geysers of boiling water 230ft (70m) into the air. They are named after the country's Great Geysir, the first ever seen by Europeans. (We don't know if the Europeans were burned and confused, or if they got out the tea bags to make a nice hot drink.)

Puffed out
About 10 million puffins live in Iceland.

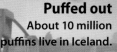

MOROCCO
★Rabat

On their big day, brides in Morocco decorate their hands, arms, and legs with tattoos made from henna, a reddish brown dye that comes from the henna plant.

Arabian knights Armed men on horseback take part in a spectacular war exercise called a *fantasia*. They do amazing acrobatic tricks and fire their muskets into the air while riding at full gallop.

Funky Food

Morocco's favorite drink is mint tea. It's usually served in a pretty, colorful glass.

★ Official language: Arabic
★ Population: 34,859,400
★ Currency: Moroccan dirhams
★ Area: 172,414 sq miles (446,550 sq km)

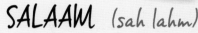

SALAAM (sah lahm)

Morocco is a kingdom, ruled by King Mohammed VI. You can join a camel safari through sand dunes in the Sahara desert, ride a donkey through old Berber villages, or watch brave, hypnotizing snake charmers. It is an ancient land overflowing with grand palaces and beautiful mosques. Moroccans love a bargain and the country's markets have for centuries been selling an amazing range of goods, from gold to ostrich feathers to rugs and even, long ago, slaves!

Monster Minaret

Hassan II Mosque in Casablanca has the world's highest minaret at 689ft (210m). A minaret is a type of spire. Ulm Minster, in Germany, has the world's tallest church steeple, 528ft (161m) high.

Potted history Tagines are traditional clay cooking pots. They are often hand-painted.

On the move People who live in the Sahara desert are nomads, which means they never stay in one place for very long.

Colorful Places

Chefchaouen is often called the "Blue City" because many of its houses are painted blue! Marrakesh is called the "Pink City" because many houses are pink.

Souks and the city You'll find treasures in markets called souks.

Objects of great beauty Moroccans use beautiful tiles to decorate their homes and mosques. Many put striking Berber carpets on their floors.

ALGERIA
★ Algiers

★ Official language: Arabic
★ Population: 34,178,188
★ Currency: Algerian dinars
★ Area: 919,595 sq miles (2,381,740 sq km)

Living in a fort The five *ksour* (walled villages) of the M'Zab Valley are together called the Pentapolis. Their design dates back to the 10th century.

The town of Ghardaïa is famous for its carpets (maybe some are magic?). It even has a carpet festival!

SALAAM (sah lahm)

Algeria is very hot and dry—much of it is covered by the Sahara desert, a huge playground for antelopes, gazelles, hyenas, lizards, and snakes. You can take a trip in a four-wheel drive vehicle through the vast ocean of sands that stretch off to the horizon. Algeria also has a long coastline, so you might see dolphins, porpoises, and whales. In summer, a hot, dry wind called the Sirocco blows into coastal cities, carrying desert sand and dust with it.

Amazing Animal

The fennec is the world's smallest fox. It may be tiny, but its huge ears keep it cool by releasing excess body heat. It sleeps underground when the sun is up and hunts at night.

Men in Blue

The Tuareg nomads are sometimes called the "Blue People of the Desert" because the blue dye from their clothes rubs off on their skin! They carry goods across the Sahara desert on their camels and live in tents. They love holding big camel races during their festivals.

High cuisine Goats love the taste of argan berries, but to get to them, they have to climb into the argan tree.

Long way from home You'll find a little bit of Rome at Djémila. The Roman invaders built a forum, temples, basilicas, grand arches, and houses in the mountain town more than 2,000 years ago.

Hideous History

The French set off an atomic bomb in the middle of the Sahara in 1960. They called the bomb the Blue Jerboa (*Gerboise Bleue*), after the desert's small hopping mouse, the jerboa (see page 89). They called the second and third bombs the White and Red Jerboas, after the colors of the French flag. Blue, white, red—KABOOM!

Tiny jerboas are great jumpers. They look like mice but have massive ears and a tuft on their long tail. They sleep in burrows in the day and hop around at night.

TUNISIA
★ Tunis

* Official language: Arabic
* Population: 10,486,339
* Currency: Tunisian dinars
* Area: 63,170 sq miles (163,610 sq km)

Out with a bang
At the Sahara Festival in the village of Douz you'll see musicians in robes, and men on camels and horses showing off their riding skills.

Couscous

SALAAM (sah lahm)

Tunisia's Cape Blanc is the most northern part of Africa. There are golden beaches in the country's north, but the south is covered by the Sahara desert, where some *Star Wars* movies were filmed. People in Tunisia like to eat fish and a grain dish called couscous—but watch out, their food is hot and spicy! The Phoenicians, Romans, Vandals, Byzantines, Turks, Spanish, and French have passed through here for 3,000 years, leaving their stories in mosaics.

Said who? Sidi Bou Saïd is a lovely seaside village. Most of its buildings are painted blue and white. You can buy traditional puppets in the markets.

In 218 BC General Hannibal from the Tunisian city of Carthage drove 37 elephants, 38,000 soldiers, and 8,000 horsemen over the Alps of Spain (see page 46) and France (see page 48) into Italy (see page 57), almost defeating the Roman Empire.

Star Wars is Born
These fantastical mud and clay houses starred in the *Star Wars* movies. Ksar Hadada was used as a location for *Star Wars: The Phantom Menace*. In the movie it was called Mos Espa, a town on the planet Tatooine. The town of Ksar Ouled Soltane was used as the Slave Quarters Row of Mos Espa, where Anakin Skywalker lived as a boy.

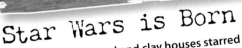

Lucky hand Tunisians use charms and symbols such as the Hand of Fatima to ward off the "evil eye" and bring good fortune. Fish are also symbols of luck.

LIBYA
★ Tripoli

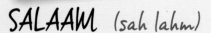

★ Official language: Arabic
★ Population: 6,310,430
★ Currency: Libyan dinars
★ Area: 679,362 sq miles (1,759,540 sq km)

On the rocks The rocky monoliths at Jebel Acacus rise straight out of the Sahara. If you go here you'll find rock paintings and carvings that are 12,000 years old.

Great panes One proud family has gone all out to decorate their window.

SALAAM (sah lahm)

Nearly all of Libya—95%—is covered by the Sahara desert, so don't forget your camel! Some of the great sand "seas" in the desert are the size of small European countries, but they also contain an oasis or two where you'll find water to drink and some trees to lie under in the shade. Luckily Libya has a large coastline on the Mediterranean Sea, so you can have a dip in the ocean. It is also rich in oil. There are ruins of ancient Roman and Greek cities to explore.

Saved by sand Shifting sands covered the Roman city of Leptis Magna in the 11th century, preserving it from erosion. The city was uncovered in the 20th century.

Crazy Fact

Libya is the only country that has a single-colored, patternless flag! It's a green flag, because green is the national color.

Happy feet Traditional Libyan shoes are pointy, bright, and pretty, although they are a little impractical.

World's Hottest

The highest shade temperature ever recorded was 136°F (57.8°C) in the town of Al Aziziyah on September 13, 1922.

What a Relief

Oasis towns such as Ghat, Ghadames, and Ubari were watering holes for the camel caravans that trudged through the desert.

EGYPT
★ Cairo

The Nile river is the world's longest river, running 4,132 miles (6,650km). Ancient Egyptians used it for transportation and to water their crops. Egyptians still use beautiful old wooden sailing boats called *feluccas* to get about on the Nile river.

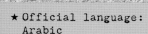

★ Official language: Arabic
★ Population: 83,082,869
★ Currency: Egyptian pounds
★ Area: 386,662 sq miles (1,001,450 sq km)

Precious kitties Cats were sacred in ancient Egypt because they killed cobras, as well as mice that ate people's vital crops. Some were even mummified after they died, just like people! One tomb held 80,000 cats and kittens.

Egypt had two of the seven Ancient Wonders of the World: the Great Pyramids and the Lighthouse of Alexandria. Can you name the other five?

Answer:
• Hanging Gardens of Babylon, Iraq
• Statue of Zeus at Olympia, Greece
• Temple of Artemis at Ephesus, Turkey
• Mausoleum at Halicarnassus, Turkey
• Colossus of Rhodes, Greece

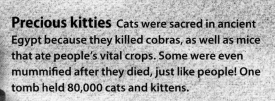

MARHABA (muh hub ah)

Egypt is the home of the Great Pyramid of Cheops, a massive tomb built from 2 million blocks of stone. It was the tallest building on Earth for almost 4,500 years! Nearby is the Great Sphinx, which has the head of a person and the body of a lion lying on the ground with its big paws stretched out. It is very mysterious. Egypt has lots of ancient buildings, statues, and treasures, but many were carried off by grave robbers and by invaders, who sold them to museums around the world.

Beautiful in Death

The gold death mask of Tutankhamen is made of solid gold, inlaid with glass and precious stones. The vulture and cobra on his headdress are supposed to protect the pharaoh after death. He lived more than 3,000 years ago, from about 1341–1323 BC.

In 2011 hundreds of thousands of Egyptians in towns and cities across the country held peaceful protests against the country's president, Hosni Mubarak, booting him out of office.

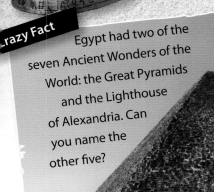

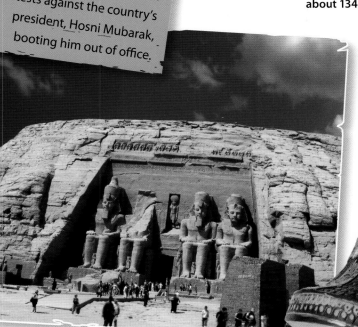

Dam, we have to move! The temples of Abu Simbel, built in the 13th century BC for Pharaoh Ramesses II and his queen, Nefertari, were moved in 1968 when the Aswan Dam was built.

Final pharaoh
Cleopatra was one of history's most famous women. She was the last pharaoh of ancient Egypt. She liked to have baths in donkey's milk. She died when she let an asp, or Egyptian cobra, bite her.

SUDAN & S. SUDAN
★Khartoum and Juba

★ Official languages:
Arabic, English
★ Population: 41,087,825
★ Currency: Sudanese
pounds
★ Area: 967,500 sq miles
(2,505,813 sq km)

SALAAM (sah lahm)

Most of Sudan is hot and dry—the Nubian Desert covers 154,000 sq miles (400,000 sq km) of the country. Nomads live in the desert, herding camels and sheep. Sudan also has huge wetlands because the Nile river, for more than half its length, flows through the country. Although Sudan has lots of oil under its deserts, it is still poor, mainly because its people have been fighting each other for a long time. In July 2011, South Sudan became an independent country.

Take note The odd-looking secretary bird, which can kill a snake by whacking it on the ground, got its name from the feathers that stick out of the back of its head. It looks like those old-fashioned secretaries, who used to tuck pens behind their ears.

World's Biggest The Sudd Marshes are the world's biggest inland wetlands. In the rainy season they fill up and cover an area the size of England.

Dark days in desert Haboobs are huge sand storms that sweep across the desert. They can be up to 62 miles (100km) wide. They block out the sun as they roll along, turning day into night.

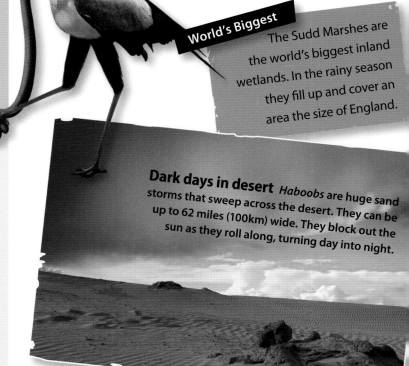

Pyramid Selling

The people of Sudan have long links with Egypt. In fact while Egypt is well known for its pyramids, Sudan has more than 200—twice as many as Egypt. Can you name some other countries with pyramids?

Answer: Countries include Spain, Greece, USA, Peru, Brazil, Bolivia, Japan, Guatemala, Mexico, Indonesia, Tahiti, Samoa, and Turkey.

Hideous History Since Sudan's independence from Britain in 1956, a civil war in the Darfur region has killed hundreds of thousands of people.

Wild Whirl

Sudan's Whirling Dervishes work themselves into a trance as they twirl around in their famous dance, to the beat of rhythmic drumming.

Hooves and feathers Sudan is a great place to see wildlife. It has some of Africa's biggest herds of animals, including 800,000 kob antelope, 4,000 Nile lechwe (an antelope), 250,000 Mongalla gazelles, and 2,800 ostriches.

CHAD
★ N'Djaména

Lake on the run

Lake Chad is one of Africa's biggest lakes, but it is rapidly shrinking. The people who live around the shallow lake are sucking water out of it to grow crops and keep animals alive. However, the hippos and crocodiles who live there seem right at home in the shifting waters.

★ Official languages: Arabic, French
★ Population: 10,329,208
★ Currency: Coopération Financière en Afrique Centrale francs
★ Area: 495,755 sq miles (1,284,000 sq km)

Sitting pretty Seen from the air, this walled village makes a nice pattern on the flat, dry landscape.

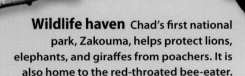

SALAAM (sah lahm)

Chad is called the "Dead Heart of Africa" because it is mostly desert and so far from the sea. The top third of the country is covered by the Sahara desert, which gets very hot during the day, even in winter. But it is not all dry and dust—Chad also has a huge lake, Lake Chad, and several big rivers, which means lots of different animals can live here. The Tibesti Mountains were once volcanoes, and even now the inside of the planet is spewing out through geysers and hot springs.

Wildlife haven Chad's first national park, Zakouma, helps protect lions, elephants, and giraffes from poachers. It is also home to the red-throated bee-eater.

To the point The Toubou people are desert warriors who live in the Tibesti Mountains. Even the women carry daggers. Their ancestors were the original Ethiopian troglodytes, or people who lived in caves.

Crazy Fact

Like Bolivia (page 36), Switzerland (page 55), Niger (page 94), and Afghanistan (page 164), Chad is a "landlocked" country, which means that it doesn't have a coast. No sea to see!

Cool Camels

Hundreds of camels escape the searing heat of the desert by taking a dip at a waterhole on the Ennedi Plateau. The Nile crocodiles that live in the water don't mind sharing.

NIGER
★ Niamey

* ★ Official language: French
* ★ Population: 15,306,252
* ★ Currency: Communauté Financière Africaine francs
* ★ Area: 489,191 sq miles (1,267,000 sq km)

SANNU (san oo)

Although Niger does not have a coastline, it does have a very unusual sea—it is a sea of sand dunes that stretch across the country to the Chad border. The sand sea is called the Erg of Bilma and its dunes look like towering waves rolling across the land. While most of the country is now desert, thousands of years ago it was very much greener—amazing rock paintings and carvings show large towns and ancient people herding sheep and goats through lush grasslands.

Dust buster There are many dinosaur remains in the Sahara desert in Niger. A bizarre dinosaur named *Nigersaurus* had a long neck and a square, broad mouth containing 500 teeth for grazing. It looked a little like the head of a vacuum cleaner.

Family affair Fishing is such an important source of income and food for many people in Niger that whole families get involved in bringing in the day's catch.

Slavery was only declared illegal in Niger in 2003!

Hi there handsome W National Park only has a small name, but it has a big number of animals, including warthogs, lions, elephants, and monkeys.

Scary Stuff

Best Left Alone

The ghost town of Djado was once a slave-trading station. It is surrounded by smelly swamps and no one lives in the houses except scorpions and snakes.

Looking Good

During the *Cure Salée* (Salt Cure) festival, Wodaabé men take part in a special ceremony in which they put on traditional costume, fancy hats, and makeup to try to win a wife.

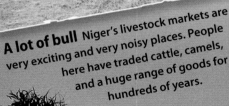

A lot of bull Niger's livestock markets are very exciting and very noisy places. People here have traded cattle, camels, and a huge range of goods for hundreds of years.

MALI
★ Bamako

Howdy doodee When the Dogon people pass someone in their village, they go through a long greeting ritual, asking about every member of their family—even if they saw the same person earlier in the day!

Elephants in trouble
The desert elephants of Mali are the most northern elephants in Africa, but their living space is shrinking as their habitat is being destroyed by farming.

★ Official language: French
★ Population: 12,666,987
★ Currency: Communauté Financière Africaine francs
★ Area: 478,841 sq miles (1,240,192 sq km)

Hot and pointy
The town of Hombori is one of the hottest places on Earth, with an average temperature of 86°F (30°C) day and night! Nearby are amazing rock formations called the Needles of Gami.

I NI BARA (ee nee bah rah)

Many years ago Mali was a very rich country because it sat on major African trade routes. Today it is quite poor, but it is still rich in culture. You can listen to the famous music of Mali at the Festival in the Desert, which draws musicians from around the world. In Mali's deserts there is an area called the Pink Dune, which people used to believe was the home of sorcerers. Mali is also where you'll find the legendary town of Timbuktu (tim buck too).

Old school One of the oldest universities in the world is in Timbuktu. It was built in the 1320s. Many of its original books about astronomy, mathematics, medicine, and law are still there today, almost 700 years later.

azy Fact

In the 1500s stories swept Europe about the fabulous riches to be found in the city of Timbuktu. The stories excited explorers, who set off to find the city.

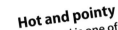

World's Largest Mud Church

The Grand Mosque at Djenné is the largest mud-brick mosque in the world. It is a popular place for locals to sell colorful handicrafts.

MAURITANIA
★ Nouakchott

- ★ Official language: Arabic
- ★ Population: 3,129,486
- ★ Currency: Ouguiyas
- ★ Area: 397,956 sq miles (1,030,700 sq km)

Flying visit More than 2 million birds fly from Europe, Siberia, and Greenland to breed in Mauritania's national parks. One plucky bird that makes the long trip south is the Eurasian spoonbill.

SALAAM (sah lahm)

Mauritania is constantly on the move. Much of it is covered by desert sand dunes which are always being blown around by the wind. It is one of the largest countries in Africa, but much of Mauritania has very few people living in it because it is so dry and sandy. Some of the people who lived in Mauritania thousands of years ago made their homes in caves, and even today some people have caves as part of their houses. Mauritania has a long coast, so people eat plenty of fish.

World's Longest

On the Rails
The world's longest train carries iron ore almost 435 miles (700km) from the town of Zouérat to the coast. The train is 1.9 miles (3km) long. You can catch a ride on top of a wagon, or be boring and travel in a normal train carriage.

Here's Looking at You
Called the "Eye of Africa," the Guelb er Richat is a huge hole in the ground, about 31 miles (50km) across. It can be seen from space. It could have been caused by a massive meteorite hitting the ground, or lava rising up from beneath Earth's surface.

Amazing Animal

Snappy Surprise
The waterhole at Matmata is in the middle of a desert. Don't jump in here to cool off or you might be dinner for the world's last desert crocodiles.

Going under The town of Oualata has some of the oldest stone houses in Africa, but it is slowly being swallowed up by the desert.

Rock on Ben Amira is the world's second-highest rock monolith. It is 2,077ft (633m) high. Only Uluru in Australia is bigger (see page 193).

Crazy Fact
Almost 20% of the people in Mauritania are slaves, even though slavery is illegal

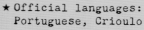

CAPE VERDE
★ Praia

Shell of a place You can watch loggerhead turtles slowly drag themselves up the beach and lay eggs in deep holes in the sand.

★ Official languages: Portuguese, Crioulo
★ Population: 429,474
★ Currency: Cape Verdean escudos
★ Area: 1,557 sq miles (4,033 sq km)

OLÁ (Oh lah)

There were no people living on the islands of Cape Verde when Portuguese sailors set up a town there in 1462, but there were plenty of strange animals found nowhere else in the world. That's because Cape Verde was cut off from the rest of Africa for thousands of years. It was sometimes attacked by pirates and was a big slave-trading port—sadly for many slaves it was the last piece of Africa they saw. The people who live there now come mainly from Europe and Africa.

Sound advice Don't forget to bring your dancing shoes when you visit Cape Verde. Local people love getting dressed up and dancing in the streets during the country's many festivals, such as Boa Vista and the São Vicente Creole Carnival.

Hot Headed

The people of Chã das Caldeiras don't seem to care that the volcano Pico do Fogo is still active—they've made their home inside its crater!

Hideous History

Gourd ideas A calabash gourd is a melon that grows on a vine. You can eat them, but many Cape Verdians dry them, then use them as a container or a musical instrument.

Cape Verde means "Green Cape," but it hasn't always been green. In the 100 years after 1773, three major droughts killed about 100,000 people (nearly half the population).

Amazing Animals

Because Cape Verde was cut off from the rest of Africa, many of its birds and animals are found only on these islands, including this big gecko called the Cape Verde giant gecko. It likes to gobble up small birds and insects.

Blown away The country has its own hurricanes! Cape Verde–type hurricanes form in the Atlantic Ocean and are usually the largest and most intense storms of the hurricane season.

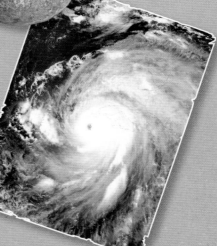

97

SENEGAL
★ Dakar

★ Official languages: French, Wolof
★ Population: 13,711,597
★ Currency: Communauté Financière Africaine francs
★ Area: 75,955 sq miles (196,722 sq km)

NAKA MU (nuh kaa mooh)

Senegal sits on the western bulge of Africa and teems with different types of animals and birds. Its national animal is the lion, which you can see in the country's parks, along with many different monkeys like the red colobus monkey, which hangs around in trees, and our close cousins the chimpanzees, which roam around the savannas. Senegal has plenty of great musicians and storytellers. There are many nice beaches, pretty towns, and sleepy little fishing villages to explore.

Funky Food People in Senegal love to eat *Ceebu jen* (cheh boo jen), a tasty dish of fish, rice, and vegetables. They also like to fry up fish balls and serve them with tomato sauce.

Musical style Senegal's famous musical style *mbalax* mixes Western music with the traditional drumming and dance music of Senegal. The *sabar* is the name of a traditional drum. Youssou N'Dour is a well-known modern performer of the *mbalax* style.

Long drive In 1979, driving a Range Rover, Frenchmen Alain Génestier and Joseph Terbiaut won the first Paris–Dakar Rally, an off-road race open to professional and amateur drivers.

In a Flap

It's standing room only between November and April at Djoudj National Bird Sanctuary. That's when more than 3 million tired birds call in on their way south from Europe. Pink flamingos, pelicans, ducks, and waders all pay a visit.

Splash of pink Retba Lake is known as the "Pink Lake" because of its amazing color, caused by salt and a strange bacteria.

Crazy Fact

Mystery Stones

The stone circles in Senegal and Gambia are four large groups of stone on the Gambia River. Some stones weigh up to 10 tonnes (11.2 tons). They stand on top of an old burial site, but no one's really sure why they are there.

Hello there The Senegal parrot is a pretty little fellow and a popular pet.

GAMBIA
★ Banjul

Wrestlemania! Gambians love wrestling and it's one of the oldest traditional sports in the country. The winner is the first one to throw their opponent to the ground.

★ Official language: English
★ Population: 1,782,893
★ Currency: Dalasis
★ Area: 4,361 sq miles (11,295 sq km)

Risky business
Imagine bathing with 100 crocodiles! That's what Gambians do in the Kachikally Crocodile Pool. Many believe its waters have healing powers. The crocs are said to be tame, but who would take the chance?!

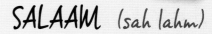

SALAAM (sah lahm)

Tiny Gambia packs a lot into its little size. The Gambia River flows right through its middle, so much of the country is quite fertile. Today the country is still home to many different tribes, and a lot of people still live in traditional villages and grow their own food. Many slaves passed through Gambia on their way to the Americas. Gambia only has a short coast, but people from overseas like to come here on holidays to soak up the hot sun and swim in the refreshing surf.

Hideous History

After the British ended its slave trade here, in 1807, they stationed troops at Fort James to stop slavers from other countries. The fort that once held slaves became a place that tried to stop slavery.

Strings attached These people are playing a *balafon* (xylophone), and also *koras,* which are stringed instruments made from melons.

> Gambia is the smallest country in mainland Africa.

Amazing Animal

The Gambian pouched rat grows up to 3ft (1m) long and gathers nuts in its cheeks, just like a chipmunk does. It is very friendly and makes a great pet.

Animals Everywhere

Kiang West, Gambia's largest national park, is home to an amazing variety of animals, including bush babies—which can leap up to 15ft (4.6m)— as well as baboons, warthogs, marsh mongooses, crocodiles, and hyenas.

99

GUINEA-BISSAU
★ Bissau

* Official language: Portuguese
* Population: 1,533,964
* Currency: Communauté Financière Africaine francs
* Area: 13,948 sq miles (36,125 sq km)

ABALA (uh buhl ah)

Welcome to one of Africa's most beautiful countries. Guinea-Bissau still has vast ancient forests full of wild animals, and the islands off the coast have plenty of lovely places to swim. On some of these islands men get dressed up and dance furiously to try to attract a wife. To get around, all you have to do is hop on a *toca-toca*, which is a type of minibus. The locals like to share their food, but be careful if they offer you a bite to eat—they sometimes feast on roasted monkeys!

Hungry jumbos Forest elephants are smaller than savanna elephants, but still spend 19 hours a day eating. They can scoff down 220lb (100kg) of food every day!

Crazy Fact

Going Green

Almost three quarters of Guinea-Bissau's land is still forests. That's more than any other country in Africa except Gabon.

Getting ahead This young dancer on the Bijagós Islands, off the coast of Guinea-Bissau, wears an unusual hat, hoping it will attract a potential wife.

Amazing Animal

Red river hogs like to munch on the carcasses of dead animals. The hogs have bright red fur, black porky legs, and a tufted white stripe along the spine.

Salty Hippos

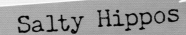

If you go surfing at Ilhas de Orango National Park you'll have to share the waves with a herd of adventurous saltwater hippos, who love to drop in uninvited.

Going nuts!
Cashew nuts are a major crop grown in Guinea-Bissau.

Dress-up day
These youngsters are proud to show off their beautiful traditional clothing.

Scary Stuff

The Conakry Monster was a huge blob that washed up on the coast of Guinea in 2007. It looked like a giant crocodile, with an armored back, thick fur, a long tail, and four paws. It turned out to be just a big smelly bit from a long-dead whale.

GUINEA
★Conakry

★ Official language: French

★ Population: 10,057,975

★ Currency: Guinean francs

★ Area: 95,698 sq miles (247,857 sq km)

SENEGAL
MALI
GUINEA-BISSAU
Siguiri
Kindia
Conakry
Kankan
SIERRA LEONE
ATLANTIC OCEAN
LIBERIA
CÔTE D'IVOIRE (IVORY COAST)

BONJOUR (bon joor)

Guinea pulses with music, which is usually a blend of Western and African rhythms. Local people like to play the *kora*, a stringed instrument with a big, fat bottom. There are plenty of lovely places to walk, but it's a good idea to take an umbrella, because Guinea is one of the wettest countries in Africa. When the sun is shining there are nice beaches to swim at. Sheep and goats wander around the streets of the capital, Conakry, causing frustrated drivers to honk their horns at them.

Hammer a tune A *balafon* looks a bit like a xylophone, with wooden keys. It sometimes has dried melons underneath to boost the sound. The Sosso Bala is supposed to be the first *balafon* ever made. It was built more than 800 years ago.

What's in a Name?

Guinea pigs didn't come from Guinea—they came from the Andean areas of South America, such as Ecuador (see page 33), Peru, and Colombia. They were domesticated 7,000 years ago. One theory is that they came to Europe via Guinea and picked up the name on the way.

Monkey Business

Male chimpanzees in Guinea's forests try to woo the ladies by stealing papayas from nearby farms. They then share the tasty fruit with the female chimps of their choosing. Guinea is one of the best places in West Africa to see chimpanzees in the wild.

World's Wettest

Conakry, in Guinea, is the wettest capital city on Earth. It receives 14ft (4.3m) of rain a year.

Go with the flow The Fouta Djallon plateau, which receives 5ft (1.5m) of rain each year, is the source for the Niger, Gambia, and Senegal rivers.

Amazing Animals

If you see something yellow flying in Guinea's forests and parks, it could be a flittering golden butterfly, or a sunny bird like the yellow-billed stork or the yellow-casqued hornbill flapping around.

SIERRA LEONE
★ Freetown

GUINEA

• Makeni

○ Freetown

Bo •   • Kenema

LIBERIA

ATLANTIC OCEAN

★ Official language: English
★ Population: 6,440,053
★ Currency: Leones
★ Area: 27,699 sq miles (71,740 sq km)

Sierra Leone is one of the top 10 diamond-mining countries. Most of its diamonds are mined by hand, which means anyone with a sieve can try to find the precious gems and strike it rich!

OWDIBODY *(low de body)*

Sierra Leone is very beautiful and has long white beaches washed by a shimmering ocean. There are plenty of wild animals in the nation's only national park, Outamba-Kilimi, where you can see elephants thundering through the scrub and hippos soaking in the waterholes. There are tropical rain forests throughout the country. The people are very friendly and are keen to welcome more visitors. The country produces a lot of diamonds and gold.

Happy little hippos
Tiwai Island is home to cute pygmy hippopotamuses. The little fellows grow to only about 32in (83cm) high. Bathtime is their favorite time.

Slave home Centuries ago thousands of slaves were shipped from Sierra Leone all around the world. Some of them returned to Freetown, which was built in 1787 as a safe home for freed slaves.

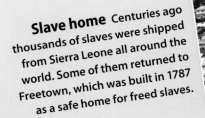

Hideous History
More than 50,000 people were killed between 1991 and 2001 in Sierra Leone's bloody civil war. Rebels often cut off the limbs of their victims, using sharp knives. There were also reports of cannibalism. Several countries, with the assistance of the United Nations, helped the people of Sierra Leone end the war. A new, peaceful government runs the country now.

That's the spirit
Genies are spirits in African cultures. To the Mende people of Sierra Leone, genies might try to possess people. Some believe genies can be kept away with magic.

How the Leopard Got Its Spots

Children in Sierra Leone learn the story of how the leopard got its spots. Leopard often visited his friend Fire and would beg Fire to visit his home. Fire always said no. But one day Fire did visit Leopard. Sadly, Leopard's house was destroyed and Leopard and his wife were scorched by the flames. And that's why leopards have blackened spots on their fur.

Jungle Zoo

If you sneak quietly through Sapo National Park you might come face to face with a handsome golden cat. The park is famous for its pygmy hippos, which love to wallow in waterholes. Elephants, Liberian mongooses, leopards, African civets, zebras, gray parrots, chimpanzees, African fish eagles, and monkeys have also made their homes in the park's forests.

LIBERIA
★Monrovia

★ Official language: English
★ Population: 3,441,790
★ Currency: Liberian dollars
★ Area: 43,000 sq miles (111,369 sq km)

HELLO (hel oh)

The name Liberia means "liberty" or "freedom." The country was given this name when it was set up as a home for people who were once slaves. In the old days, young people took part in secret ceremonies before they became grown-ups. Traditional ways are still important to many people today. Liberia has sandy beaches, quiet lagoons, and thick rain forests that are home to all kinds of creatures. It also has a huge rock called Blo Degbo, which looks like a human face!

Crazy Fact

Liberian warlord Joshua Milton Blahyi was better known as General Butt Naked during the First Liberian Civil War in the 1990s. He led his troops naked, except for shoes and a gun, believing that his nudity would protect him from bullets. It is also said that he used to kill people as a sacrifice before a battle.

Amazing Animal

The rare Liberian mongoose tries to hide away because people like to hunt it. It likes to snuffle around in lowland areas and riverbanks in the forest.

Love of liberty Liberia was founded by freed American and Caribbean slaves in 1847. Its capital, Monrovia, was named after the US president James Monroe.

Can't beat it

Traditional Liberian music uses drums, West African rhythms, and long, wavering voice calls.

CÔTE D'IVOIRE (IVORY COAST)
★ Yamoussoukro

★ Official language: French
★ Population: 20,617,068
★ Currency: Communauté Financière Africaine francs
★ Area: 124,504 sq miles (322,463 sq km)

Using brains for brains
The clever chimpanzees in Taï National Park have worked out how to jam sticks into the skulls of dead colobus monkeys to scoop out the brains. They also use the sticks as tools to get ants out of nests and honey from beehives.

I NI SOGOMA (ee nee so yom ah)

Ivory is the tusks of elephants and it was once very precious. Ivory was made into all sorts of objects, including pool balls and piano keys! A huge amount of ivory was once traded from this coastal region of Africa, which is how this country got its name. Now the elephants are protected, although poachers (people who kill animals illegally) still shoot some. The country's official language is French, but because of the many tribes living here, 60 native languages are also spoken.

Magic masks
Many tribal people like to remember dead family members by making masks that are symbols of their souls. Putting on a mask is said to give the wearer special powers. Some of the masks represent gods.

What's brewing?
Côte d'Ivoire is among the world's largest producers of cocoa, coffee beans, and palm oil (seeds, below).

What's in a Name?
The country picked up its name because of the ivory traded in the area.

Other parts of Africa have been called:
• Grain Coast
• Gold Coast
• Slave Coast

Leopards spot monkeys
Monkeys that come down from the trees during the day to find food have to keep a close eye out for leopards, which reckon they make a tasty treat.

World's Largest Church
The Catholic Basilica of Our Lady of Peace is the largest church in the world. It was built in the 1980s and covers 322,917 sq ft (30,000 sq m).

Saw-scaled vipers kill more people each year than any other snake in Africa. When threatened, the snakes rub their scales together to make a sound like water sizzling on a hot plate.

BURKINA FASO
★ Ouagadougou

★ Official language: French
★ Population: 15,746,232
★ Currency: Communauté Financière Africaine francs
★ Area: 105,869 sq miles (274,200 sq km)

MALI
NIGER
Koudougou • ◌ Ouagadougou
• Bobo-Dioulasso
BENIN
CÔTE D'IVOIRE (IVORY COAST)
GHANA
TOGO

BONJOUR (bon joor)

Burkina Faso used to be called Upper Volta, but its new name makes much more sense because there was never a Lower Volta. Burkina Faso is near the equator and is very dry in the dry season and very wet in the wet season. You can ride a camel in the desert and sleep out on the sand, or you can wander through thick forests, keeping an eye out for animals. If you are paddling a canoe across Lake Tengrela, watch out for hippos—they get very cranky when disturbed!

Fried fun
You'll find people frying balls of dough to sell on the streets of Burkina Faso's towns. If you're brave you can try frogs too!

Men in masks
The colorful masks made by the Mossi people are used in celebrations, festivals, and during funerals to honor the dead.

Ride on People from Burkina Faso love riding motor scooters, which they call mobylettes. Bicycles are popular, too.

The country used to be called Upper Volta because of the three rivers that flow across it—the Black Volta, the White Volta, and the Red Volta. *Volta* is Portuguese for "twist."

In the wild The country has the greatest variety of animals in western Africa, including hippos, buffalo, monkeys, crocodiles, giraffes, antelopes, and the region's largest elephant population.

Take a Peak
The Peaks of Sindou are sandstone rock formations that rise straight out of the surrounding plain. They are sacred to the local people.

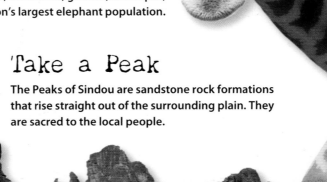

GHANA
★ Accra

★ Official language:
  English
★ Population: 23,832,495
★ Currency: Cedis
★ Area: 92,098 sq miles
  (238,533 sq km)

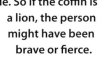

Death as in life The Ga-Adangbe people carve coffins that reflect something about the dead person who will be going inside. So if the coffin is a lion, the person might have been brave or fierce.

ETE SEN (eh tah sang)

Ghana is a golden country. The Ashanti are one of the groups of people who live here and they were once very rich and powerful because they traded gold. Today the country is still rich thanks to its gold mines. But it is rich in natural beauty, too. There are thick forests inland, where you can walk among the tops of the trees on a canopy walk. Or you can search for shells on sandy beaches in the hot sun. If you're brave you can even try their hot pepper soup.

Not-So-Epic Event

All Arms

Prince Octopus Dzanie competed in the boxing event at the 2008 Beijing Olympic Games, but lost to the 2007 Pan American champion, Idel Torriente from Cuba.

Never walk alone If you take a stroll through Mole National Park, make sure you go with an armed guard—there are lions, leopards, and buffalo out there! Hartebeests, on the other hand, have to rely on their speed to escape hungry predators.

Good as Gold

The Ashanti people had a golden past. They produced some of the most beautiful gold work in Africa. They lived in an area that Europeans called the "Gold Coast."

Water power Lake Volta, the world's largest artificial lake, is formed by the Akosombo Dam, which holds back the Volta River. The force of the water flowing makes electricity.

Princes Town, at the very bottom of Ghana, is the closest town on Earth to 0° longitude and 0° latitude.

Sad memories
Elmina and Cape Coast castles are forts in very pretty spots right next to the ocean, but slaves were kept there before being shipped overseas. Elmina Castle was built in 1482.

TOGO
★ Lomé

You can buy spooky voodoo medicines such as monkey and snake heads in the markets of the capital, Lomé. Voodoo is also practiced in Togoville, a fishing village that has fetishes in the streets. A fetish is an object that is considered holy or that people think has a special power.

★ Official language: French
★ Population: 6,019,877
★ Currency: Communauté Financière Africaine francs
★ Area: 21,925 sq miles (56,785 sq km)

BURKINA FASO
Dapaong
Kara
BÉNIN
GHANA
Atakpamé
Lomé
ATLANTIC OCEAN

NILYENIA (nee yen yah)

Togo is only tiny but it has so much of Africa to offer to visitors, and a little bit of Europe, too. There are all sorts of amazing animals here, and because the country is so small it is easy to wander around and see them all. The ocean off the coast of Togo has plenty of interesting animals in it as well. The nation's capital, Lomé, was once called the "Paris of West Africa," and it still has wide streets, just like the French capital (see page 48). The country is also home to about 40 different tribal groups.

Sleepy tree
People in Togo make sure they get a good night's sleep by stuffing their pillows and beds with the soft, fluffy fiber from the seeds of the kapok tree.

Going batty
Scary-looking bats are everywhere in Togo. There are dozens of kinds, with strange names like naked-rumped tomb bat or halcyon horseshoe bat.

Just the tonic Before making a traditional tonic, visit the *marché des féticheurs* (fetish market). It stocks all the ingredients, such as porcupine skins, donkey skulls, warthog teeth, serpent heads, parakeet tails, and chameleons (right).

Mud Castles
About 65,000 Tamberma people live in fortified mud-tower houses in the region of Koutammakou. Groups of families live in two-story compounds that look like little castles.

REPUBLIQUE DU TOGO POSTES

BENIN
★ Porto Novo

★ Official language:
French
★ Population: 8,791,832
★ Currency: Communauté
Financière Africaine
francs
★ Area: 43,484 sq miles
(112,622 sq km)

KUDEU (koo day oh)

Benin is the home of voodoo, which sees spirits in natural objects such as rocks and water. Voodoo came to the Americas with African slaves and the Hollywood movies turned it into something spooky. If you don't like snakes, better give the Python Temple in Ouidah a miss—they might curl one of the slithery reptiles around your neck. Benin is also famous for its lively music, which is sure to get your toes tapping. Lions, elephants, and crocodiles will also keep you hopping.

Scary Stuff
Get on Your Goat

Benin is the birthplace of voodoo. Every year the city of Ouidah holds a noisy festival, which begins with the slaughter of a goat. About 60% of Benin's people practice voodoo.

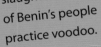

Hideous History

In the ancient kingdom of Dahomey, which is now Benin, people were killed every year to supply dead kings with new servants and to make sure the kings remained happy. Humans were also sacrificed during times of war, when pests destroyed food, or when there were big floods.

Tight squeeze If you catch a taxi in Benin you might have to share it with a farmer's crops or their animals!

Amazing Animals

Many strange creatures live in the river that flows through Pendjari National Park, including this freshwater butterfly fish. The national park is also famous for its many different kinds of birds. Almost one quarter of Benin's land has been set aside as national parks or reserves.

Faces of the past
Old Benin art, made for its royalty, featured beautiful carved wooden masks, and ivory armlets inlaid with brass and carved with fish and the heads of Europeans.

High-rise Village

The villagers of Ganvie took big steps to escape the bloodthirsty Dahomey tribe. They built their village on stilts in Lake Nokoué. The Dahomey tribe believed a water demon lived in the lake and wouldn't go near the place.

Nollywood The Nigerian film industry is known as Nollywood. It is the world's second-largest producer of movies after India. It makes about 2,000 films every year—more than five a day!

NIGERIA
★Abuja

★ Official language: English
★ Population: 149,229,090
★ Currency: Nairas
★ Area: 356,669 sq miles (923,768 sq km)

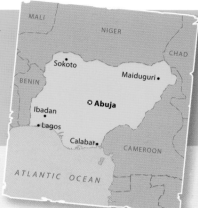

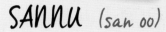

Nigerian mantis The praying mantis gets its name from the way it holds its front legs, as if it's saying a prayer.

Scary Stuff

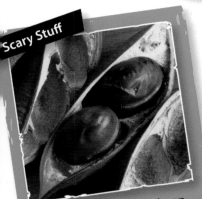

The poisonous calabar bean was once used in Nigeria's outlawed "ordeal by bean." People accused of witchcraft or a crime had to eat the bean and died a horrible death.

SANNU (san oo)

About 150 million people live in Nigeria. That's more than any other country in Africa. Many elephants also live here in the lush green forests. Nigeria is one of the largest oil producers in the world, but sadly the oil wells have polluted the country's waterways and ruined farmland. Every year the Yoruba people take part in a *gelede*, which is a witch festival. If you get an email from someone in Nigeria promising you lots of money, don't believe them—it is just a trick!

Fishing frenzy Fishing folk don't use lines at the Argungu Fishing Festival. Up to 35,000 people leap into the river with nets, trying to snare the largest fish.

Most Twins

If you have always wanted a twin sister or brother, you might just get one if you were born in the town of Igbo-Ora. It has the highest rate of twin births in the world. Then again, if your sister or brother gets on your nerves, it might be best if you don't go there.

Wreckers and robbers Benin City, which is in Nigeria, was destroyed by the British in 1897. The British also took some of the country's ancient artworks and sold them around the world.

109

CAMEROON
★ Yaoundé

★ Official languages: French, English
★ Population: 18,879,301
★ Currency: Coopération Financière en Afrique Centrale francs
★ Area: 183,568 sq miles (475,440 sq km)

BONJOUR (bon joor)

Cameroon is known as "Africa in Miniature," as if all the best bits of the continent have ended up in the one place. There are many different people—including pygmies who live in forests. It also has many different wild animals, such as elephants, giraffes, and big cats. Volcanoes rise straight out of the sea, and there are rain forests and deserts. The people love to dance and they hold many different celebrations that give them the chance to show off their dancing skills.

Giant Leap

The Goliath frog is the largest frog in the world. It can grow up to 33cm (13in) long and weigh 3kg (6.6lb). But there are not many left because people like to eat them!

Epic Event

Deadly Burp

Cameroon has volcanic lakes. In 1986 one of them, Lake Nyos, belched out carbon dioxide, killing about 2,000 people and 3,000 cows.

Bomby place
The Musgum people live in houses shaped like bombshells. The huts are made of squashed sun-dried mud and grass.

Soccer stars Cameroon was the first African country to reach the quarter-finals of the soccer World Cup, in 1990. It has won the African Cup of Nations four times.

Scary Stuff

Keep It in the Family

The Bamileke people keep the skulls of their ancestors, because they believe their spirits live in them. Carved masks are also popular and are usually worn during funerals and festivals.

Park with plenty Cameroon's most popular tourist destination is the Waza National Park, home to elephants, giraffes, and antelopes such as the topi.

Big bug The Goliath beetle is the world's largest and heaviest beetle. It can grow up to 4.7in (12cm) and weigh 4oz (125g).

EQUATORIAL GUINEA
★ Malabo

The country's most famous swimmer is Eric Moussambani, nicknamed "Eric the Eel." He came last in the 100-meter freestyle race at the 2000 Sydney Olympics—but the crowd really loved him!

★ Official languages: Spanish, French
★ Population: 633,411
★ Currency: Coopération Financière en Afrique Centrale francs
★ Area: 10,831 sq miles (28,051 sq km)

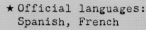

Poo monkeys Bioko Island was once called Fernando Poo after the first European man to visit. It has many rare monkeys living in its thick forests.

M'BOLO (um bol oh)

People who come from Equatorial Guinea are called Equatoguineans. The country gets plenty of rain and is rich in forests. Most people here are very poor, even though the country has good oil reserves. It is one of the few mainland African countries where Spanish is an official language. The capital city, Malabo, is actually on Bioko Island, so Equatorial Guinea is the only country in Africa where the nation is on the continent, but its capital is on an island!

Hideous History

The nation's first president, Francisco Macias Nguema, was thought to have supernatural powers. He amassed a huge collection of human skulls to scare everybody. In 1975 he had 150 people killed to the sound of a band playing "Those Were the Days."

Drumming up Dinner

In Equatorial Guinea, a bongo is not a type of drum, but a striped antelope with big horns. It lives in thick forest. It sometimes ends up on people's dinner plates, along with prickly porcupines.

Amazing Animal

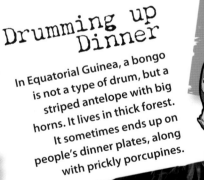

Playtime At Christmas time, the government gives 500,000 toys to Equatorial Guinea's children.

Shy and Mighty

Forest elephants have made a comfortable home in Monte Alen National Park. They're a bit smaller than other elephants and quite shy. Their tusks are straighter and a bit pinker than those of other jumbos.

CENTRAL AFRICAN REPUBLIC

★Bangui

★ Official language: French
★ Population: 4,511,488
★ Currency: Coopération Financière en Afrique Centrale francs
★ Area: 240,536 sq miles (622,984 sq km)

Gorillas in our midst The Dzanga-Sangha Forest Reserve has about 2,000 gorillas living in it—more than almost any other place in the world. It is also home to large herds of forest elephants.

BARA ALA (Bar ah la)

Many people think that the Central African Republic is the "real" Africa. It is off the beaten path and has plenty of great, scary wildlife, such as lions, buffalo, and elephants. There are vast grasslands, called savanna, where the wild things hunt, but in the south you'll see thick rain forests that echo with the cries of forest gorillas and chimpanzees and the growls of leopards. Even the rivers are swarming with life, including fish, hungry crocodiles, and smelly old hippos.

Hideous History

In 1972 Jean-Bédel Bokassa made himself president for life of the Central African Republic. He was accused of being a cannibal and feeding his enemies to lions and crocodiles in his personal zoo. He got kicked out in 1979.

To the point The Aka people are nomadic pygmy people. Aka teenagers get each of their top four front teeth filed to a sharp point. Some girls also get their bottom four front teeth pointed as well. Ouch!

Don't Go Here Alone

The Manovo-Gounda St. Floris National Park is a savanna, or grassland, with plenty of wildlife, including leopards, lions, and cheetahs.

Crazy Fact

Many Central Africans have a "totem" animal, whose spirit is passed on from generation to generation. They are never allowed to eat that animal.

Amazing Animal

A blue duiker antelope is only 14in (35cm) tall at the shoulder and weighs 8.8lb (4kg). Its brown coat has a slight blue tinge and the animal has tiny horns. It's a popular dinner item for hungry forest pygmies.

Don't strike a match People in many villages in the Central African Republic live in grass huts.

SÃO TOMÉ & PRÍNCIPE
★ São Tomé

Caught sport
Many people come here to try to catch big fish, such as marlin or sailfish. They catch them for sport and let them go again.

In 1919 an important experiment was held on the island of Príncipe. It is said to prove that Albert Einstein's famous "theory of relativity" was correct. Scientists did this by watching the relative position of the stars near the Sun during a total solar eclipse.

Big Dog
Cão Grande (Big Dog) peak, on São Tomé, is a thin rock tower that was once part of a volcano. It is about 2,133ft (650m) tall and rises out of thick jungle. The top is often shrouded in cloud.

Motorcycle taxis are a popular way of getting around because they are cheap and fast.

Crazy Fact
If you're walking along the beach, local children might come out of the jungle that creeps down to the sand and show you how to pick coconuts.

★ Official language: Portuguese
★ Population: 212,679
★ Currency: Dobras
★ Area: 372 sq miles (964 sq km)

SEJA LOVADU (sej ah low var doo)
If you like chocolate, you'll love São Tomé and Príncipe. They are called the "chocolate isles" because so much cocoa is grown here. Portuguese settlers started growing cocoa, sugarcane, and coffee on the islands more than 500 years ago. They brought African slaves to work on the plantations. The two islands are part of an extinct volcanic mountain range so they have steep mountains on them. Even though they have Africa's second-smallest population, they have four local languages!

S. TOMÉ E PRÍNCIPE
Db. 800

Safe drink Up to 20% of the country's people can't easily access clean water.

GABON
★ Libreville

★ Official language: French
★ Population: 1,514,993
★ Currency: Coopération Financière en Afrique Centrale francs
★ Area: 103,347 sq miles (267,667 sq km)

M'BOLO (um bol oh)

Welcome to Gabon—a sea of green in an often dry continent. Rain forests cover 85% of the country and more than 10% is set aside as national parks. Most of the country is undeveloped, so you'll find its forests, savannas, and waterways are home to an amazing array of wildlife, including chimpanzees, elephants, hippos, and hundreds of species of fish and birds. Its beaches are lovely—but be careful of the gorillas that like to lie on the golden sand and soak up the sun!

Crazy Fact

Seeing Things
The iboga plant is used in ceremonies as a medicine by the Babongo and Mitsogo people. It can cause hallucinations.

Horny hisser The Gaboon viper has a pair of horns on its snout, long fangs, and is very, very poisonous.

Funky Food

The pangolin protects itself with armor plating, like an armadillo does. But that doesn't stop people eating it.

Here's looking at you
Giant floating heads keep an eye or 10 on spectators who have turned out to watch this Gabon cultural festival.

Rainbow lizard Red-headed rock agamas are lizards that change color depending on the temperature. They're brown when it's cool, but their body turns blue and their head red-orange when it's hot!

Gran in the cupboard
The Fang and Kota people wear wooden tribal masks during traditional ceremonies. They keep the bones of their ancestors in wooden boxes and were known to be cannibals.

Scary Stuff

There are still many sorcerers and witch doctors working their magic in Gabon. Death is often explained as the work of an evil spirit, or of someone skilled in casting spells.

REPUBLIC OF CONGO
★ Brazzaville

Hang on Baby gorillas can hang on to their mother's fur and ride on her back at four months old.

Scary Stuff

The Mokele-mbembe is known as the Loch Ness Monster of the Congo. According to a pygmy legend it is a long-necked reptile that likes to swim and can kill elephants!

★ Official language: French
★ Population: 4,012,809
★ Currency: Coopération Financière en Afrique Centrale francs
★ Area: 132,047 sq miles (342,000 sq km)

LOSÁKO (los ah ko)

The Republic of Congo is a wild place. Pygmy tribes still live in its thick jungles—just as they have done for hundreds of years, living off the land and hunting for a fabulous collection of wildlife. The jungles are also home to Africa's largest population of lowland gorillas, and to millions of blood-sucking insects. In the cities and towns, table soccer is popular, so if you fancy your chances, take on a local kid! In World War II, Congo was the center of a French movement against the Nazis.

Sing sing sing It is said that every Congolese person learns to sing. Singing has long been used to make work less boring. There are songs about fishing, planting, and how to use a hoe, paddle a canoe, or pound cassava (a type of root) to make food.

Forget Email
People in Congo send messages using drums, called *ngoma*, with special rhythms for death, birth, marriage, or the arrival of someone important.

How about a kiss?
Lovebirds come from Congo and are popular pets around the world because they like to smooch each other. They will also form good relationships with their owners.

Amazing Animals

Well Bred
The Bateke people breed dogs and cats. The *chien bateke* is a small, lean hunting dog with a short gray coat. The *chat bateke* is a large house cat, the same color as the dog.

115

DEMOCRATIC REPUBLIC OF CONGO
★Kinshasa

★ Official language: French
★ Population: 68,692,542
★ Currency: Congolese francs
★ Area: 905,355 sq miles (2,344,858 sq km)

Wiping out the relatives
Bonobos and chimpanzees are our closest relatives, but they are in danger of dying out. This is the only place in the world where they are still found in the wild.

LOSÁKO (los ah ko)

The Democratic Republic of Congo (Zaïre) straddles the equator. For many years its leaders were not very nice. They stole big amounts of money and let the people go hungry. In the 1800s the British and Germans fought a battle here, which ended quickly when the British were attacked by a swarm of angry bees! Mt. Nyiragongo is an active volcano that has a lava lake in a crater in its top. Strangely, the country has more thunderstorms than anywhere else in the world.

Not-So-Epic Event

Rumble in the Jungle
One of the most famous boxing fights took place in Kinshasa on October 30, 1974, when boxer Muhammad Ali fought George Foreman for the World Heavyweight title. Ali won.

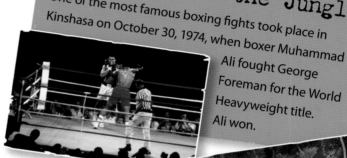

Scary Stuff
The first outbreak of the deadly Ebola virus took place on August 26, 1976, in Yambuku. Mabalo Lokela, a 44-year-old teacher, became the first recorded case. The virus is usually deadly and causes bleeding from the eyes, ears, and nose.

Stripy bottom
The okapi has stripes like a zebra, but is related to the giraffe. Its tongue is so long it can wash its eyelids and clean out its ears!

World's shortest people The Mbuti people of the Ituri forest are pygmy hunter-gatherers—and the shortest people on Earth! Their average height is 4ft 7in (1.4m). They still gather plants for food and use bows to hunt small animals.

Pythons big and small
The ball python (right) is a small, beautiful, harmless python. The African rock python, one of the world's biggest, can grow up to 20ft (6m) long.

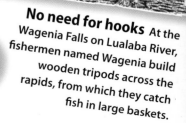

No need for hooks At the Wagenia Falls on Lualaba River, fishermen named Wagenia build wooden tripods across the rapids, from which they catch fish in large baskets.

Very Long Sleep

The tsetse (teet see) fly carries a germ that causes "sleeping sickness." From 1900 to 1920, the disease killed more than 250,000 people.

UGANDA
★Kampala

★ Official language: English
★ Population: 32,369,558
★ Currency: Ugandan shillings
★ Area: 93,065 sq miles (241,038 sq km)

OLYOTYA (ol lee o tee uh)

Uganda is home to the highest mountain range in Africa—the Mountains of the Moon in the Rwenzori National Park. The country has more bird species than any other country in Africa because migrating birds stop here on their way south. A good way to get around is on a *boda-boda*, which is a bicycle with an extra seat stuck on the back. The start of the Nile river flows through a small hole in a rock at Murchison Falls.

Melting away The Rwenzori Mountains were once covered by 43 glaciers. Now, because of global warming, half of them have melted. The Nile river starts in these mountains.

Idi Amin, the country's ruler in the 1970s, was known as the "Butcher of Uganda," but some of his bizarre titles were "King of Scotland," "Conqueror of the British Empire in Africa in General and Uganda in Particular," and "Lord of All the Beasts of the Earth and Fishes of the Sea." He killed 500,000 people.

Growing up Half of Uganda's population is under 15 years of age.

What a sight The marabou stork is so ugly it's almost cute! It eats rotting flesh. It uses its sawlike bill to cut up the dead animals. It has a bald head, so all the blood and guts don't get stuck in its feathers!

Dead Kings

Four former rulers lie in the Tombs of Buganda Kings at Kasubi. The main circular dome is made from wood and has a thatched roof. It was built where the old hilltop palace of the kings used to stand.

Bwindi Impenetrable National Park has half the world's mountain gorillas. There's just one gorilla for every 20 million people.

KENYA
★Nairobi

- ★ **Official languages:** English, Kiswahili
- ★ **Population:** 39,002,772
- ★ **Currency:** Kenyan shillings
- ★ **Area:** 224,081 sq miles (580,367 sq km)

JAMBO (jum bo)

Kenya has huge wildlife parks containing thousands of animal species. Its vast plains are a great spot to go on safari—you'll see more animals than you can count! It has savanna, hills, forests, and river systems, but Kenya also shares Lake Victoria with Uganda and Tanzania. Lake Victoria is one of the world's largest freshwater lakes. Some of the very first people in the world came from Kenya. Giant crocodile fossils that are more than 200 million years old have also been found here.

Epic Event

Every year more than 1.8 million wildebeest and 500,000 zebras migrate across Kenya in search of food.

Meeting the king
Kenya's a good spot for a *Lion King* experience. You are sure to spot the "king of the beasts."

Funky Food

Samburu people eat blood taken from living animals. They have many ways of preparing blood and can make a whole meal out of it!

Leaping into Adulthood
Maasai people do an *eunoto*, or jumping dance, during a coming-of-age ceremony, which can involve 10 days of singing and dancing.

Safari in the city
Nairobi National Park is the only place in the world where you can go on a real safari with a backdrop of towering skyscrapers. It is just 4.3 miles (7km) from the city of Nairobi.

Scary Stuff

Killing Spree
The Tsavo man-eaters were a pair of hungry lions. For nine months in 1898 they attacked a railroad campsite at night, eating about 100 workers.

SOMALIA
★ Mogadishu

Writing's on the wall The Laas Geel cave paintings are about 10,000 years old. They are some of the oldest rock art in Africa. The paintings show people worshipping cows, which are wearing ceremonial robes.

★ Official language: Somali
★ Population: 9,832,017
★ Currency: Somali shillings
★ Area: 246,201 sq miles (637,657 sq km)

Amazing Animal

The giraffe-necked antelope is a great survivor, perhaps because its long neck lets it nibble on the leaves of trees other animals can't reach.

MA NABAD BAA (mar nar bard bah)

Somalia has the longest coastline of any African country, bordering the Indian Ocean for more than 1,860 miles (3,000km). Perhaps that's why so many pirates come from Somalia! It is also famous for bloody wars and terrible droughts. But Somalia also has some amazing animals and ancient rock paintings, and is the home of camels—the much-loved "ships of the desert." The north of the country has some lovely beaches and amazing ancient treasures.

World's Top Producer

The Good Oil

Somalia is the world's leading maker of frankincense, which is valued for its fragrant oil. Frankincense was carried by the Three Wise Men.

Lives in ruins Parts of beautiful Zeila were built more than 1000 years ago by Muslim rulers.

Scary Stuff

Somali pirates take over ships and then demand a big ransom from the ship's owner. Apparently many of the pirates are fishermen whose fishing grounds have been poisoned by toxic waste.

Old Humpy

Ancient Somalis domesticated camels about 5,000 years ago. The camels then spread to ancient Egypt and North Africa.

ETHIOPIA
★Addis Ababa

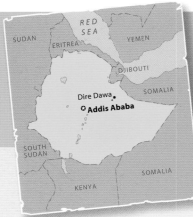

★ Official languages:
  Amharic, Oromiga,
  Tigrinya, Somali,
  plus three others
★ Population: 85,237,338
★ Currency: Birr
★ Area: 426,373 sq miles
  (1,104,300 sq km)

No Need to Build

Churches in the holy city of Lalibela are carved straight into the rocky hills. Many pilgrims visit the city.

TEANASTELLEN (tee nah steh lehn)

This is where it all began—humans that is. The bones of our ancestors were found here and are more than 200,000 years old. It is believed that people then spread slowly throughout the world. Today, women from the Karo tribe have deep scars cut into their bellies to make them look beautiful—before they are allowed to marry. Crocodiles sunning themselves at the "Crocodile Market" on the shore of Lake Chamo don't care whether they look beautiful or not!

Teenagers give lip Mursi women still wear lip plates. As teenagers, girls have their bottom lip pierced and a clay lip plate inserted. As their lip stretches, larger and larger plates are inserted.

Funky Food

Coffee is a popular drink in Ethiopia and was discovered here when a 9th-century goatherder noticed the perky effect the plant had on his flock.

Bleeding heart The gelada baboon lives in the Simien Mountains. It is called the bleeding-heart baboon because of the bright red patch on its chest.

Stopped by sand Ethiopian wolves originated here 100,000 years ago. They did not make it farther into Africa because they weren't able to cross the deserts surrounding Ethiopa.

Crazy Fact

Abebe Bikila was a two-time Olympic marathon champion from Ethiopia. He was the first black African to win a gold medal in the Olympics, winning in Rome in 1960. He ran the race barefoot!

Dry beginnings
The first people might have come from the Afar Depression, 500ft (150m) below sea level.

Crazy Fact

Dancing with the Dead

The nomadic Afar people celebrate dead people at an annual festival called Rabena.

Underwater wonderland

Djibouti's coastline is ringed with coral. There are more than 200 species of coral, some found nowhere else in the world.

Amazing Animals

Huge whale sharks gather between October and January in the Bay of Tadjoura, where they breed and feed on tiny plankton.

DJIBOUTI
★ Djibouti City

★ Official languages: French, Arabic
★ Population: 516,055
★ Currency: Djiboutian francs
★ Area: 8,958 sq miles (23,200 sq km)

MARHABA (muh hub ah)

Djibouti was once called the "Valley of Hell" by Europeans because it was so hot and dry. Much of it is below sea level. But it can also be very wet. Cyclones from the Indian Ocean create heavy rains and flash flooding. You can find underwater exhibitions from the Red Sea at the country's tropical aquarium. Djibouti was once a French territory and there are still many French people here, including soldiers from the Foreign Legion.

Green oasis

This horned cow lives in Djibouti's only national park up in the Goda Mountains. Unlike other parts of Djibouti it is green and it sometimes rains.

World's Saltiest

Even if you can't swim, it would be hard to drown in Lake Assal. It's the world's saltiest lake, and all that salt makes people float. Its shores are 508ft (155m) below sea level, Africa's lowest point on land.

Walking on the Moon

Part of the original *Planet of the Apes* movie was filmed at Lake Abbe—a salt lake on the border of Djibouti and Ethiopia. It has limestone chimneys 164ft (50m) high. The Afar people live on its shores.

Djibouti has the most urbanized population (85%) in Africa.

Flock of pink Colorful flamingos live on Lake Abbe.

ERITREA
★ Asmara

★ Official languages: Tigrinya, Arabic, Tigre, Afar, Kunama
★ Population: 5,647,168
★ Currency: Nakfas
★ Area: 45,406 sq miles (117,600 sq km)

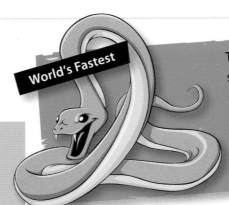

World's Fastest

The black mamba is the fastest snake in the world, able to slither at 12mph (20km/h). It is also the longest poisonous snake in Africa, averaging about 8ft 2in (2.5m), and sometimes over 13ft (4m).

SELAM (sel ahm)

Eritrea was the world's first country to turn its coast into an environmentally protected zone. Elephants are native to Eritrea, and ancient Egyptians used to get their elephants from here. They used them in battles because the jumbos were so big and their skin was so tough. The southern coast is perhaps Eritrea's most dramatic yet most inhospitable landscape, because of its volcanoes and bubbling mud pools. The Danakil Depression is one of the hottest places on Earth.

On the move
The Tigre people are nomadic Muslims and make up about 65% of Eritrea's population.

Hideous History

From May 1998 to June 2000, Eritrea was at war with its neighbor Ethiopia. Although both countries were very poor, they spent hundreds of millions of dollars on the fight. Tens of thousands of people were killed. One good thing is that fishing in the Red Sea stopped during the war, and the fish increased in big numbers!

Capital of style Asmara, the capital, looks like a film set from an early Italian movie because of its beautiful Art Deco buildings. The center of the port city of Massawa contains hundreds of old Islamic buildings.

Feeling blue Male humphead wrasse can grow to 6ft 6in (2m) long. As the fish ages, its hump gets bigger.

I Sea Red

The Red Sea is not actually red, and no one really knows where its name came from. It is very warm and very salty. Many corals and fish—including 40 types of sharks!—live in it.

In 1994, over about 100 days, almost 800,000 people were murdered in a conflict between the nation's Hutu and Tutsi people.

RWANDA
★Kigali

★ Official languages: Kinyarwanda, French, English
★ Population: 10,473,282
★ Currency: Rwandan francs
★ Area: 10,169 sq miles (26,338 sq km)

Mini Africa Akagera packs all of Africa into one national park. There are lakes, waterfalls, forests, and plenty of wild animals, such as elephants, zebras, buffalo, lions, topis, gazelles, impalas, baboons, giraffes, leopards, crocodiles, hippos…

Pick of the crop Plantains look like bananas, but don't be fooled—they are not very sweet and have to be cooked before they are eaten.

MURAHO (moo rah hoe)

Rwanda is known as the "Land of a Thousand Hills"—you'll be able to climb mountains in the middle of the country. Some of them are volcanoes. If you want to get to the mountains you could catch a taxi-velo, which is a bicycle with a skinny seat for passengers. Rwanda is peaceful now, but in 1994 many Rwandans were killed when two groups fought each other for more than three months. You might still see *imigongo*, an ancient type of art made from cow poo!

Dance Parties

Male Intore dancers leap high into the air when they perform. They were once fierce warriors. Female Intore dancers perform a type of ballet that is very graceful.

Making do A soccer ball made from rope is better than no soccer ball at all.

Gorillas in trouble The Virunga Mountains help protect the few mountain gorillas still alive in the wild. There are also eight volcanoes in the mountains.

Secret stash Rwandan women carry many things around in baskets, including secret messages they don't want anyone else to see!

BURUNDI
★ Bujumbura

★ Official languages:
  Kirundi, French
★ Population: 8,988,091
★ Currency: Burundi
  francs
★ Area: 10,745 sq miles
  (27,830 sq km)

BWAKEYE (bwok eye)

It was in Burundi that explorer Henry Stanley finally came across Dr. David Livingstone and said the famous words, "Dr. Livingstone, I presume?" People in Burundi often build their huts from grass and mud in the shape of a beehive. Chimpanzees live in the forests and like to monkey around, although there are no national parks or reserves protecting the animals. Cows are symbolic in Burundi—they are a sign of wealth.

Scary Stuff **Angry, Angry Hippo**

Hippos love wallowing and splashing around in the water. Don't get too close though, because they have a very bad temper and can bite hard!

Animals licked
People from all over the world collect Burundi's pretty postage stamps.

A tiny stream that flows from the top of Mt. Kikizi eventually joins the mighty Nile river.

Growing business About 800,000 people in Burundi earn a living by growing coffee.

Big Bang Theory

The famous Royal Drummers of Burundi beat big drums made from hollowed tree trunks covered with animal skins. Their skills are passed down from father to son.

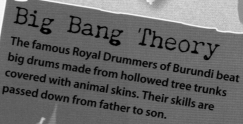

Not-So-Epic Event

In 2005 the government banned people from having real Christmas trees—but only because they didn't want people chopping down trees.

Something fishy
Lake Tanganyika is the world's longest freshwater lake. It has more than 350 fish species swimming in it, and even has beaches!

In 1979, a 164-ft (50-m) trail of the earliest human footprints was discovered in the Kibish region of Tanzania.

TANZANIA
★ Dar es Salaam

- ★ Official languages: Swahili, English
- ★ Population: 41,048,532
- ★ Currency: Tanzanian shillings
- ★ Area: 365,755 sq miles (947,300 sq km)

Crater full of critters
Ngorongoro Crater was once a giant volcano. It is now home to a wide variety of wildlife, including zebras and lions.

JAMBO (jum bo)

Tanzania is a country that's larger than life. It is the home of the Serengeti Plain, across which millions of wildebeest thunder every year during the great migration. In its borders, you'll find Lake Victoria, the largest tropical lake in the world. Tanzania has a huge elephant population as well as large cats, especially lions and cheetahs. Cheetahs are the world's fastest land animals and can reach 52mph (84km/h) in three seconds from a standing start—about the same as a Ferrari!

Close to home
Mums like to carry their babies around in colorful slings, called *kangas*. The baby stays safe and mum's hands are free for when she works.

No less a flamingo
Lake Natron is the largest breeding site for the threatened lesser flamingo. Its salty marshlands help keep predators away.

Can't Beat This Peak
Mt. Kilimanjaro, at 19,341ft (5,895m), is the highest mountain in Africa. It's an old, snow-capped volcano.

The world's shortest war happened in Zanzibar, in Tanzania. Known as the Anglo–Zanzibar War, it took place on August 27, 1896. It was over in less than an hour.

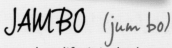

Kilimanjaro

MOZAMBIQUE
★ Maputo

★ Official language: Portuguese
★ Population: 21,669,278
★ Currency: Meticais
★ Area: 308,642 sq miles (799,380 sq km)

Amazing Animal Gentle dugongs have made their home in Mozambique's Bazaruto Archipelago.

Taking a tilt at stilts Makua tribesmen get a leg up by dancing around their villages on stilts, wearing masks and bright outfits.

OLÁ (oh lah)

Mozambique is a heady mix of Portuguese, African, Indian, and Arabic cultures. It is becoming more modern, but it hangs on to old ways of doing things. Many people still live in traditional villages, in round mud houses. Each village has a fence of sharp sticks around it to keep out hungry lions. Off the coast lie two island chains, with coral reefs full of bright fish and creatures such as dugongs. In the rugged Chimanimani Mountains scary log bridges still cross rushing streams.

Face facts Makonde people create carvings and masks. The masks are often used in ritual dances.

How's the Dhow?

People still use *dhows* (simple sailboats) when they want to carry items along the coast or in waterways through the mangroves.

Copping an Eiffel Maputo train station was designed by Gustave Eiffel, the man who designed the Eiffel Tower in Paris, France (see page 48).

Funky Food Mozambique is famous for its giant LM (Lourenco Marques) prawns. They are caught off the country's coast.

Village life Traditional Malawi villages are constructed from materials such as wood, mud, and thatch, just as they have been for hundreds of years.

MALAWI
★ Lilongwe

★ Official languages: English, Chichewa
★ Population: 14,268,711
★ Currency: Malawian kwachas
★ Area: 45,747 sq miles (118,484 sq km)

Secret Behind the Mask

The Chewa people are known for their strange-looking masks and their secret societies that are in contact with the spirits of ancestors. There are two large clans, the Phiri and the Banda.

MONI (mown ee)

The Great Rift Valley tears through Malawi, slowly ripping it apart. The country is often called the "Warm Heart of Africa" because its people are very friendly and there's lots of sunshine. Lake Malawi dominates the country. It is huge and full of fish. People live on islands in the lake and have unique cultures. The rock art at Chongoni gives an insight into how people lived thousands of years ago. The country's national parks teem with wildlife such as hippos and crocodiles.

Hello to *bao* This might look simple, but *bao* is a very difficult game to play. The game is named after the baobab tree that grows on the shores of Lake Malawi.

Cathedral in the lake St. Peter's Cathedral sits on Likoma Island, in the middle of Lake Malawi.

World's Fishiest Lake

More types of fish live in Lake Malawi than any other lake on Earth. At least 850 species have made their home here.

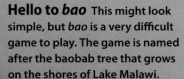

Lake Malawi has more than 300 species of the colorful cichlid fish. They grow to about 12in (30cm) long and have only two nostrils, not the usual four.

ZAMBIA
★ Lusaka

★ **Official language:**
English
★ **Population:** 11,862,740
★ **Currency:** Zambian
kwachas
★ **Area:** 290,587 sq miles
(752,618 sq km)

What's for tea? This eagle likes to go fishing for its dinner. It is called the African fish eagle and has large, sharp talons.

Cop this Zambia has huge deposits of copper. The Copperbelt Province is the mineral-rich area around Kitwe.

BWANJI (bwan ji)

Zambia is a great place for going on safari and spotting wildlife. You might see giraffes, elephants, baboons, antelopes, hippos, crocodiles, leopards, cheetahs, and lions—and about 750 different kinds of birds! Zambia sits mainly on a high plateau, with some hills and mountains. Up to 85 different languages are spoken here. Victoria Falls, or *Mosi-o-Tunya* (Smoke that Thunders), is one of the world's biggest waterfalls.

Crazy Facts

Zambians love riddles and proverbs. Here are some popular sayings:

- A woman without teeth shall be left to the lions.
- An old poacher makes the best gamekeeper.
- Do not look at a visitor's face but at his stomach.
- He who paddles two canoes, sinks.
- If you are ugly, learn how to dance.

Basket case
The Tonga people of Zambia are skilled weavers and make very beautiful baskets.

Fierce faces
Wild Zambian masks are made of bark and mud and have fierce faces painted on them, often in red, black, and white.

Plain Flight

Every year, villages in the Barotse Floodplain get flooded. In the *Kuomboka* ceremony (which means "get out of the water"), the Lozi king leads his people to higher ground!

All together now A walking safari is a great way to see the animals. Just don't let the armed ranger out of your sight or you might end up as lunch!

What's in a Name?

Zambia entered the 1964 Summer Olympics under its old name, Northern Rhodesia. It declared its independence on the day of the closing ceremony, when it changed its name. Zambia was the first country to start the Olympics with one name, and leave it with another.

Time off These Angolan boys have a fun time playing on the beach, but about 30% of Angolan children aged 5 to 14 years have to work.

ANGOLA
★Luanda

★ Official language: Portuguese
★ Population: 12,799,293
★ Currency: Kwanzas
★ Area: 481,354 sq miles (1,246,700 sq km)

Rule of thumb
The thumb piano is a simple musical instrument made from wood and small metal tongues. You play it with your thumb, of course.

OLÁ (oh lah)

Angola is rich in oil, gold, copper, and diamonds, but unfortunately the country has seen years of war, with many people blown up by landmines. At one stage there were more landmines in Angola than children! It also has beautiful beaches. A huge statue of Jesus, named Cristo Rei, which looks like the statue Christ the Redeemer in Rio de Janeiro, Brazil (see page 35), stares from a hill across the city of Lubango. A favorite Angolan dish is *cabidela*, which is chicken's blood with rice.

Amazing Animal

Large, cute, blobby West African manatees swim around off Angola's coast. They have flippers for front legs, a paddlelike tail, and nibble daintily on sea grass.

Diamonds lose their sparkle
Angola has many beautiful diamonds, but some diamonds are sold to buy deadly weapons and fund wars. These diamonds are called "blood diamonds."

Hideous History

Up to 1.5 million people were killed in the 27-year Angolan Civil War, which ended in 2002.

Angola has nearly a dozen international chess masters!

PERIGO MINAS !!

DANGER MINES !!

Life on another planet Angola's Miradouro da Lua (Valley of the Moon) looks like it came from outer space!

Very Able Sable

The giant sable antelope is Angola's national animal. It nearly died out in Angola's civil war. The adult male's horns can grow up to 5ft (1.5m) long. The horns appear on the logos of the country's national airline and the national soccer team.

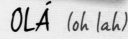

NAMIBIA
★ Windhoek

- ★ Official language: English
- ★ Population: 2,108,665
- ★ Currency: Namibian dollars
- ★ Area: 318,261 sq miles (824,292 sq km)

ONGIINI (on jeen ee)

Namibia has two deserts: the Kalahari Desert and the Namib Desert. The Namib has the world's largest sand dunes and is considered to be the world's oldest desert. It is the only one inhabited by elephants, oryxes, rhinos, giraffes, and lions. The moisture in the fog that rolls in from the sea every morning is just enough to keep these hardy animals alive. Namibia has a long coastline, savanna, forests, woodlands, mountains, and canyons. It is rich in diamonds, wilderness, and wildlife.

Huts on the move The Himba people live in cone-shaped houses made with branches covered in mud and poo! They move often to graze their animals, so they must be able to build new homes quickly and easily.

Crazy Fact

The Namibian Ultra Marathon is a 78-mile (126-km) running race through the Namib Desert. Runners have to carry their own food and water during the 24-hour race. The temperature can reach 113°F (45°C) during the day, and drop to 32°F (0°C) at night.

Visitor from space The Hoba meteorite is the world's largest intact meteorite. It weighs about 67 tons (60 tonnes). This big chunk of iron fell to Earth 80,000 years ago.

All aquiver The San people hollow out the branches of quiver trees to make quivers (holders) for their arrows.

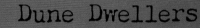

Dune Dwellers

An oryx is a type of antelope that lives in the dry parts of Africa. It doesn't mind spending its days on the dunes.

Dressed to excess
Although it can get extremely hot in Namibia, Herero women wear old-fashioned European hats and huge, heavy dresses with petticoats. They were influenced by the fashions of early German missionaries who settled here.

Amazing Animal

An aardvark is a mammal that lives in the ground and eats ants and termites. In Dutch, its name means "earth pig." It has a long tubelike snout and is a fast digger.

Take a peak The Spitzkoppe is known as the "Matterhorn of Africa." Its amazing granite peaks rise 5,577ft (1,700m) over the Namib Desert.

Trumpeting their size You'll find the world's largest elephant herds in the Chobe National Park.

BOTSWANA
★Gaborone

★ Official language: English
★ Population: 1,990,876
★ Currency: Pulas
★ Area: 224,607 sq miles (581,730 sq km)

The ancient Greeks thought that a giraffe was a cross between a camel and a leopard, and called it a "camelopard." Giraffes are the world's tallest mammals.

DUMELA (doo mell ah)

Most of Botswana is flat, and much of it is covered by the Kalahari Desert. The hunter-gatherer "Kalahari bushmen" live in the desert. They call themselves the San people. At the edge of the Kalahari is the Okavango River, which has a huge delta. Botswana is a great safari spot and is rich in diamonds. People in the south of the country like to munch on mopane worms, which are a good source of protein! Traditional homes are decorated with *lekgapho*, a beautiful type of art.

Weaving their magic
Women in the villages of Etsha and Gumare weave traditional bowls and baskets from palm leaves.

Pole position The Okavango Delta is the world's largest inland delta, with huge floodplains. People cross it using *mokoros* (traditional canoes).

What makes them click? The San people of the Kalahari Desert make a distinct "clicking" noise when they speak.

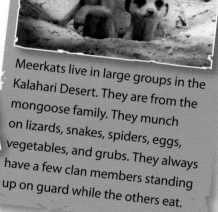

Amazing Animal

Meerkats live in large groups in the Kalahari Desert. They are from the mongoose family. They munch on lizards, snakes, spiders, eggs, vegetables, and grubs. They always have a few clan members standing up on guard while the others eat.

Zebras Crossing

Every year 25,000 zebras travel 150 miles (240km) from the watery Okavango Delta to Makgadikgadi Pans National Park. They travel all that way just so they can lick up special salts, which contain life-giving minerals.

ZIMBABWE
★ Harare

★ Official language: English
★ Population: 11,392,629
★ Currency: Zimbabwean dollars
★ Area: 150,872 sq miles (390,757 sq km)

Shona people often wear traditional clothing, and many still live in villages. They have created amazing stone sculptures and totems.

MHORO (mor oh)

Zimbabwe, which was once called Rhodesia, is a beautiful country with incredible wildlife and many national parks, but it has suffered a very troubled history and terrible financial problems. Zimbabwe is rich in natural resources. Dramatic Victoria Falls, located on the Zambezi River, straddles the border between Zimbabwe and Zambia. Its combined width and height produces the world's largest sheet of falling water.

Hair-raising ride The Zambezi Swing at Batoka Gorge is not for the fainthearted. If you're game, you can slide across a wire 328ft (100m) above the Zambezi River!

Feathers of stone
The carved stone Zimbabwe bird is a national emblem of the country.

Breeding them big Zimbabwe's many national parks (such as Mana Pools National Park) are home to big animals such as buffalo, elephants, lions, hippos, and zebras.

Where's everyone gone? The ruined town of Great Zimbabwe was once home to 12,000 people, and contains some of the oldest buildings in sub-Saharan Africa. It was abandoned more than 500 years ago.

In the Shona language, Zimbabwe means "house of stone."

Over the Top

Victoria Falls is 1.1 miles (1.7km) wide and drops 328ft (100m) onto the rocks below. Dr. David Livingstone was believed to be the first white person to see it.

Strike it rich If you've ever dreamed of being a trillionaire, you should visit Zimbabwe. It introduced a 100 trillion dollar note in 2009, which was worth about $300 (£185).

Meals on wheels Keep your windows up when you go on safari, or you might become lunch!

Yum! Boerewors is a type of tasty sausage they like to eat "round" here.

SOUTH AFRICA
★Pretoria

★ Official languages: Zulu, Xhosa, Afrikaans, Pedi, Sepedi, English, plus six others
★ Population: 49,052,489
★ Currency: Rands
★ Area: 470,693 sq miles (1,219,090 sq km)

Invented Here

In 1967 famous heart surgeon Christiaan Barnard performed the world's first human heart transplant in Cape Town.

SAWUBONA (sow bone ah)

South Africa has 12 official languages—more than any other African nation. It is a beautiful country and its national parks are great places to go on safari to spot elephants, rhinos, lions, and leopards, as well as giraffes, zebras, and many other animals. You might eat dried meat called *biltong*—a dish from the days before fridges were invented—or some spiral-shaped sausages. South Africa once had a policy called apartheid, based on racial segregation.

Modern hero Nelson Mandela is a modern South African hero. He spent 28 years in prison because he tried to get equal rights for black people. He won the Nobel Peace Prize in 1993, and was South Africa's first freely elected president, from 1994 to 1999.

World's Biggest

The Cullinan diamond is the world's biggest diamond. It was found in 1905. It weighed 3,106 carats, and nine smaller diamonds were cut from it—the biggest being the Great Star of Africa.

Shark alley Many great white sharks lurk in the coastal waters near a small fishing village called Gansbaai. You can go under water in a cage and swim with them!

Feared warriors Zulu people are the largest ethnic group in South Africa. They were great warriors, and built a powerful kingdom that many people feared.

Spring in its step The springbok is a jumping gazelle and the national animal. The South African rugby team is named after it.

Where Oceans Collide

The most southern point of Africa is Cape Agulhas, in South Africa. It is where the Atlantic Ocean and the Indian Ocean meet.

INDIAN OCEAN ◄ ► ATLANTIC OCEAN

SWAZILAND
★ Mbabane

MOZAMBIQUE
Mhlume •
⚜ **Mbabane**
• Manzini
• Hlathikulu
SOUTH AFRICA

★ Official languages:
  Swati, English
★ Population: 1,123,913
★ Currency: Emalangeni
★ Area: 6,704 sq miles
  (17,364 sq km)

Hunted for Horns
Rare black rhinos can weigh 1.1 tons (1 tonne), but are dying out because people are still killing them for their horns.

SAWUBONA (sow bone ah)

Swaziland is the only African country that still has an absolute monarch. It is a very traditional country and many people still follow old customs. Some even wear traditional robes to work. Swaziland has many nature reserves where you can see all sorts of wildlife. You can even see wildlife on its money—the flower-shaped 20-cent coin has an elephant on it. A Swazi politician was sacked after he stole some of the king's cow poo to make a magic spell!

Buzz in the village You will see round beehive huts in villages. Some men have more than one wife, but each wife has her own hut.

Fine feathers
The violet-crested turaco is Swaziland's national bird. It has a purple crest, red eyes, and a black beak.

Crazy Facts

- There is only one museum in Swaziland.
- National service consists of weeding the king's millet fields for two weeks.
- The King of Swaziland rules jointly with his mother, who is known as the "Great She-Elephant." He is believed to have about 13 wives.

Crafty creations Swazi arts and crafts include beautiful dolls, woven baskets, and mats.

Reed All Right

Every year, thousands of young women from all over the kingdom bring the Queen Mother reeds to fix up holes in the fence around the royal village. The ceremony is called *umhlanga*, or reed dance, and lasts eight days.

What Hat Is That?

A Basotho hat is the country's national emblem. It is cone-shaped, made from straw, and topped by a knot.

Hill full of history
Thaba Bosiu (Mountain at Night) was used by the 19th-century chief Moshoeshoe as a fortress to protect the Basotho people from attack. Today you can climb to the top and meet some of the locals who graze animals there.

Aloe there
The spiral aloe is a rare and beautiful plant from the Maluti Mountains. It is not found anywhere else. The aloe is the country's national flower.

LESOTHO
★ Maseru

★ Official languages: Sesotho, English
★ Population: 2,130,819
★ Currency: Maloti
★ Area: 11,720 sq miles (30,355 sq km)

SOUTH AFRICA

Pitseng
◆ **Maseru**
Mokhotlong
Semonkong

LUMELA (doo mel ah)

Lesotho is a tiny nation contained within the borders of South Africa and is called the "Kingdom in the Sky" because it is so far above sea level. Being so high up, it is colder here than most other parts of Africa—so do as the locals do and wrap a blanket around your shoulders. Many people still follow the old ways, including playing traditional musical instruments such as the *lekolulo*, a kind of flute used by herding boys. You can see many instruments at the Morija Arts and Cultural Festival.

It's a Wrap
It gets cold up here, so big, bright blankets help keep Basotho horsemen warm when they ride the ranges of Lesotho.

Lesothosaurus (lizard from Lesotho) was a small dinosaur found in Lesotho. It stood only about knee high but was a fast runner.

LESOTHO 5s

Cool surprise
Even in Africa you can find snow! Beating a drum helps keep out the cold.

Do you live round here?
A *rondavel* is a traditional house. It is usually round and has stone walls and a thatched roof.

135

MADAGASCAR
★ Antananarivo

★ Official languages: Malagasy, French, English
★ Population: 20,653,556
★ Currency: Malagasy ariary
★ Area: 226,658 sq miles (587,041 sq km)

MANAO AHOANA (man na own er)

Did you ever see the animated *Madagascar* movies? Well, this is where those movies were set. Madagascar, hundreds of miles off the coast of Africa, is the world's fourth-largest island—almost as big as Spain and Denmark put together, or slightly bigger than France. It's a special place because most of its plants and animals are found nowhere else on the planet. That's because it separated from Africa millions of years ago and its animals evolved differently.

Freaky finger The lemur has a bushy tail and a long claw on its second finger for grooming and scavenging. It taps that finger on trees to find grubs, then scoops out the grubs with it.

Biggest bird! The elephant bird was the largest bird ever. It grew 9.8ft (3m) tall and weighed 882lb (400kg). It couldn't fly and was killed off in the 1600s. It laid an egg 12in (30cm) long.

Catching on Madagascans go fishing in *pirogues*, which are traditional fishing boats with sails.

Scary Stuff

Every seven years, families carry out a special ceremony called the "Turning of the Bones." They remove the remains of dead relatives from the family tomb, wrap them in new silk, then put them back in the tomb again. They have a big party to honor their relatives.

World's Largest and Smallest

Madagascar is the home of the world's largest as well as smallest chameleons! Almost half of the world's chameleon species live here. Their big bulging eyes look in all directions and their skin has the magical ability to change color.

Big Fat Trunks

Madagascar has seven species of baobab trees. Their trunk can soak up 31,700 gallons (120,000 litres) of water during the wet season, so they can survive the dry season. The fruit is called "monkey bread."

Tall story The *aloalo* are tall carved pole sculptures placed on the tombs of important people. They tell the story of the person's life.

SEYCHELLES
★ Victoria

Scary Stuff

Shark Bank is an amazing dive spot full of whitetip reef sharks. Gray stingrays and eagle rays also flap around.

Rare plants The jellyfish tree is found on only one island, Mahé. It gets its name because the flower looks like jellyfish tentacles. There are believed to be only eight of these trees in the world!

★ Official languages: English, French, Creole
★ Population: 87,476
★ Currency: Seychelles rupees
★ Area: 176 sq miles (455 sq km)

Praslin / La Digue
Silhouette
Victoria
Mahé
SEE ENLARGEMENT
Amirantes Group
Alphonse Group
Coétivy
Cosmolédo Group
Providence Atoll
Farquhar Atoll
INDIAN OCEAN

World's Largest

Aldabra Atoll is the world's largest raised coral atoll. It is home to the world's largest known number of giant tortoises.

They're hooked Fishing helps feed much of the local and tourist populations.

BONZOUR (bon zoor)

The Seychelles has the smallest population of any country in Africa. This group of 115 islands in the Indian Ocean is famous for its white sandy beaches. Nobody lived here until the French arrived in 1770; there are some islands people still don't live on! People in the Seychelles have come from many parts of the world, including Africa, the Middle East, China, and India. Some of the islands have steep, jungle-covered hills, and half of all the country's land is set aside as nature reserves.

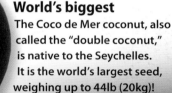

World's biggest
The Coco de Mer coconut, also called the "double coconut," is native to the Seychelles. It is the world's largest seed, weighing up to 44lb (20kg)!

Bare peak Towering over a national park, Morne Seychellois is the country's highest peak at 2,969ft (905m).

Pink Beach

Anse Source d'Argent Beach has beautiful pinky-colored sand and great, big, dark granite boulders.

COMOROS & MAYOTTE
★ Moroni and Mamoudzou

- ★ Official languages: Arabic, French
- ★ Population: 976,203
- ★ Currency: Comoran francs
- ★ Area: 1,007 sq miles (2,609 sq km)

Dhow's that? A *dhow* is a large boat with triangular sails.

SALAMA (sahl ahm ah)

Comoros is one of the world's smallest countries. Its name comes from an Arabic word meaning "moon." A local folk story says the largest island was created when a jewel was dropped into the sea and became a volcano, Mt. Karthala. Mayotte is part of the Comoros Islands region but its people voted to remain under French rule. About 180,000 people live on Mayotte's small islands, making it very densely populated.

Heaven Scent

Comoros is the world's greatest producer of the strange ylang ylang (lang lang) plant. The yellow flowers have a precious oil that is used in perfumes. Other plants grown on plantations on the islands include jasmine, orange, cloves, nutmeg, and vanilla.

World's Largest

Mt. Karthala, an active volcano, is the country's highest point. It's on Ngazidja, Comoros' largest island. It blew up in 2005, destroying villages.

Looking good
For celebrations and weddings women from the island of Ngazidja decorate their body with traditional designs.

Living fossil The coelacanth is an ancient fish. It was thought to have died out 65 million years ago, but it still lives in the seas around Comoros.

Beautiful mosque The central mosque in Moroni, the capital of Comoros, is a spectacular building that looks out over the city's peaceful harbor.

MAURITIUS
★Port Louis

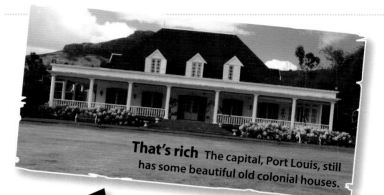

That's rich The capital, Port Louis, still has some beautiful old colonial houses.

★ Official languages: English, French
★ Population: 1,284,264
★ Currency: Mauritian rupees
★ Area: 788 sq miles (2,040 sq km)

What's in a Name?

Dead as a Dodo

The name "dodo" comes from a Portuguese word meaning "simpleton." This funny-looking bird was about 3ft (1m) tall and weighed 44lb (20kg). It was discovered in 1598, but sadly became extinct by 1681.

BONJOUR (bon joor)

Mauritius is a volcanic island nation, with white sandy beaches and steep hills covered in rain forest. Mauritians are descended from African, Indian, Chinese, and French settlers and have a rich Creole culture. The people live together peacefully—perhaps that's why the country doesn't have a proper army! In the sea there is an underwater walk. When people go on the walk they have to wear a big helmet so they can breathe.

Slave to the dance *Sega* is the national dance. It came from the African slaves who once lived here. Women wear big, bright skirts and sway their hips while shuffling their feet. Men play goatskin drums.

Crazy Fact

The Mauritian orange one penny and blue two penny stamps are among the world's rarest stamps. So if you find one, don't lose it—they're worth heaps of money! You can see them in a Port Louis museum.

Floating giants You can almost walk across the giant water lilies at Pamplemousses Botanical Gardens.

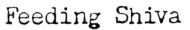

Feeding Shiva

During *Maha Shivaratri*, the most important Hindu festival, celebrated over three days, most of the island's Hindus go to the holy lake of Grand Bassin, to offer food to the Lord Shiva.

GEORGIA
★ Tbilisi

★ Official language: Georgian
★ Population: 4,615,807
★ Currency: Laris
★ Area: 26,911 sq miles (69,700 sq km)

What's in a Name?
Caucasians come from the Caucasus mountain range that divides Europe from Asia. "Caucasian" is also the term for "European with white skin." In 1800 a German scientist decided the Georgians were the "Most Beautiful Race on Earth." Lots of other races might disagree with that!

GAMARDJOBA (gam ah joh vah)

Welcome to Georgia, where possibly the world's most beautiful people live (or is that *your* country?). One not-so-beautiful person who came from here was Joseph Stalin. This land has dark forests, where a brown bear, leopard, or wolf might leap out of a very deep cave to surprise you. You can enjoy a great feast here and be entertained by a real party king, but you might want to leave early…the day after the feast Georgians like to drink *khashi,* a soup made of cow's entrails and garlic.

World's Deepest

Going Down?

Voronya Cave is the world's deepest cave and it keeps getting deeper! The first explorers measured it at 5,610ft (1,710m) in 2001. In 2004 it measured 6,562ft (2,000m). But in 2005 another team found a new tunnel and measured it as 7,021ft (2,140m).

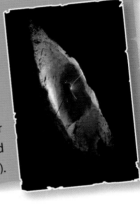

Life on film
The medieval village of Shatili is hidden in a 4,593-ft (1,400-m) deep gorge. Its fortresses and stone houses are used as film settings for Georgian movies. A few families still live here.

King of the party
Georgians enjoy a good *supra* (feast), sometimes drinking from an animal horn. The king of the table is called the *Tamada.* He makes the jokes—and everyone has to laugh at them!

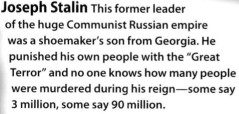

Joseph Stalin This former leader of the huge Communist Russian empire was a shoemaker's son from Georgia. He punished his own people with the "Great Terror" and no one knows how many people were murdered during his reign—some say 3 million, some say 90 million.

Scary Stuff

Some very large, scary carnivores still live in Georgia's deep, dark forests. If you go into the woods you might meet a brown bear, Persian leopard, wolf, or lynx.

AZERBAIJAN
★ Baku

Legendary jump
The Maiden Tower is part of Baku's city walls. Legend says it was given its name because the unwed daughter of the Khan of Baku threw herself from the top into the Caspian Sea below.

★ Official language: Azeri
★ Population: 8,238,672
★ Currency: Azerbaijani manats
★ Area: 33,436 sq miles (86,600 sq km)

SALAM (sal ahm)

This is a very ancient land: so ancient that Neanderthal man used to hang out here. Azerbaijan is the largest of what are called the "Southern Caucasus States" (with Armenia and Georgia). Baku, the capital, sits on the banks of the Caspian Sea and was once a supplier of oil to the world. Earth's heat belches forth from mud volcanoes, and trees are heavy with fairy-tale pomegranates. Chess, backgammon, and wrestling are all favorite pastimes here.

Funky Food

Pomegranates

You might prefer tomato sauce or lemon with your fish, but a favorite dish in Azerbaijan is fish with pomegranate sauce. In October a Pomegranate Festival is held in Goychay, with parades and huge tables full of food made from the town's pomegranate harvest.

Volcanoes of Mud
Qobustan mud volcanoes belch, bubble, burp, and fart out Earth's gases 24 hours a day. Better out than in, they say!

Epic Event

Azykh Cave is where Neanderthal man lived. We know this because archaeologists found a jawbone in the 1960s. The bone is more than 300,000 years old. There is still a bit of woolly mammoth clamped in the mouth—only kidding!

World's First

We might think oil wells are modern, but one was dug in this country in 1594—a stone at the bottom of the well has the date carved on it. In 1900 Baku supplied half the world's oil. Thousands of years ago the people here called oil "fire water," and "eternal fires" burned on the surface of Earth.

Wrestle! Azerbaijan hasn't won many Olympic medals but it does have some for wrestling. These days the wrestlers are enormous, wear lycra leotards, and wrestle in a ring. In ancient times they were slim and did a traditional dance in embroidered trousers to warm up before fighting!

ARMENIA
★ Yerevan

★ Official language: Armenian
★ Population: 2,967,004
★ Currency: Drams
★ Area: 11,484 sq miles (29,743 sq km)

BAREV (bah rev)

Welcome to Armenia. This country spreads across the highlands around Mt. Ararat, where Noah's Ark is said to have floated to dry land after the biblical flood. The Armenians were busy people early in their history—archaeologists have found the world's first leather shoe, skirt, and wine press here. Armenia was tragically caught between the Ottoman and Russian empires in World War I, then became part of the Soviet Union until 1991, when it gained its independence again.

Funky Food

Armenia is famous for its apricots, which are supposed to taste better here than anywhere else in the world. The scientific name for apricot is *Prunus armeniaca* (Armenian plum).

Big, Fat Mountain

Mt. Ararat isn't the highest mountain on Earth but it's one of the largest in overall size. This snow-capped volcano is where biblical Noah's Ark may have come to rest. It's also the national symbol of Armenia…even though it's across the border in next-door Turkey!

World's first wine-lovers? The world's oldest winery was found in Armenia. A wine press and jars for grapes from 6,000 years ago were found in a cave. There is also a shallow basin where ancient Armenians trod grapes.

Oodles "To eat" in Armenian is *oodel*…so in this land you could *oodel* noodles. (Except they eat flat bread, not noodles, in Armenia. They eat noodles, called *laghman*, in nearby Kyrgyzstan.)

Hideous History

Remember…

An eternal flame burns in honor of the victims of the Armenian Genocide, which took place during World War I. On April 24, 1915, Turkish troops (part of the Ottoman Empire) killed 250 Armenian leaders and teachers. Then the soldiers killed more than 1 million Armenians in the Syrian desert.

Big-headed builders?

Zvartnots Cathedral was built in AD 642 by Nerses the Builder (not Bob the Builder) and was called the "Most Beautiful Building in the World." Parts of it collapsed in an earthquake in AD 930 and it was never rebuilt.

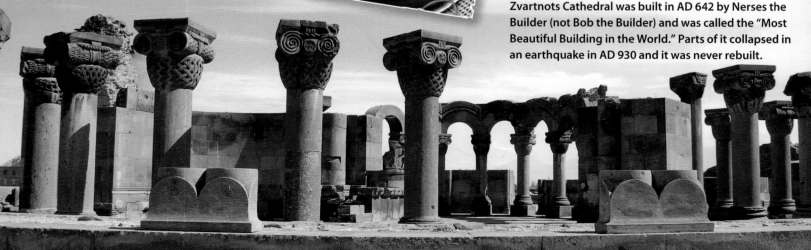

Whirling like a dervish
Dervishes are religious beggars, but they are only allowed to beg for others, not for themselves. They chant poetry, dance to incessant music, and whirl around to reach a state of ecstasy. Sounds like a party!

TURKEY
★Ankara

★ Official languages: Turkish, Kurdish
★ Population: 76,805,524
★ Currency: Turkish liras
★ Area: 302,535 sq miles (783,562 sq km)

Amazing Animal

Flopsie Mopsie

The luscious, long-haired angora from Ankara was the first rabbit to be kept as a pet. The French royals started a craze for these in the 18th century.

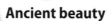

Ancient beauty
The Hagia Sophia has been a church, mosque, and now a museum. For 1,000 years it was the biggest cathedral in the world.

MERHABA (mer ha ba)

Turkey has played a major role in the history of humanity. If you wanted to live in a town 9,000 years ago, Turkey was the place for you...it had the only town in the world, Catal Huyuk. Plus, two of the Wonders of the Ancient World—the Temple of Artemis at Ephesus and the Mausoleum at Halicarnassus—were in Turkey. You can now find a bizarre underground rock city here. Its largest city, Istanbul, is on two different continents and has been the capital of four different world-conquering empires.

Don't trust the horse!
The Trojan Horse was wheeled up to the gates of Troy, in Turkey, by the canny Greeks, who had hidden soldiers inside it.

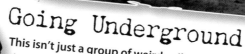

Going Underground

This isn't just a group of weird spiky rocks...there's also an ancient underground city below. Cappadocia was carved out of soft volcanic rock 2,500 years ago because there was no wood nearby for building. Once, more than 20,000 people lived here, with houses, stables, tombs, and schools all underground.

Funky Food

Turkish Delight

In *The Lion, The Witch, and The Wardrobe* the White Witch tempts Edmund with Turkish Delight. This pink rosewater sweetie was made in the Ottoman Empire from the 15th century.

CYPRUS
★ Nicosia

★ Official languages:
  Greek, Turkish
★ Population: 796,740
★ Currency: Euros
★ Area: 3,572 sq miles
  (9,251 sq km)

YIASOU (yah soo)

Cyprus is an "ophiolite," which means it rose up out of the sea. If you missed this on the news that's because it happened 20 million years ago. This is perhaps where the legend of Aphrodite, Goddess of Love, being born from the waves first started. The much-loved English king Richard the Lionheart married here in 1191 (the only time an English royal wedding has taken place overseas) and this country is where 13 suddenly became an unlucky number.

What's in a Name?

"Copper" comes from the name "Cyprus." Thousands of years ago copper was lying on the ground here, ready to be picked up and made into tools. In the Copper Age, 3000–2500 BC, tiny Cyprus sold its copper around the world.

Tomb of the kings Like the Egyptian pyramids, these underground rock tombs were carved out (in 4000 BC) to bury the posh people and leaders of Cyprus. No kings were actually buried here, but "Tomb of the Posh People" doesn't sound quite as cool, does it?

Grape jelly
The favourite sweet thing in Cyprus is *soutzoukos*, a jelly made from almonds and grape juice. The mixture is rolled into long strings and left to dry.

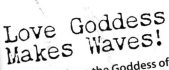

Love Goddess Makes Waves!

Cyprus is where the Goddess of Love was born. According to legend, Aphrodite (or Venus to the ancient Romans) appeared out of the water near Paphos. She grew from foam in the sea and floated to shore on a scallop shell. That must have been a very big shell!

Hide and seek The Cyprus coast has plenty of hiding places in the sea caves in its limestone cliffs. Pirate treasure, anyone?

Not-So-Epic Event

Ever wondered why Friday the 13th is unlucky? It's the day, in October 1307, when many of the Knights Templar were murdered. These rich Christian soldiers had bought Cyprus to use as their base. Unlucky them!

Flatbreads Instead of rice, mashed potatoes, or fries, Syrians eat bread with almost every meal. And, if the bread is big and flat, what better place to carry it than in a big flat basket on your head?

SYRIA
★Damascus

★ Official language: Arabic
★ Population: 20,178,485
★ Currency: Syrian pounds
★ Area: 71,498 sq miles (185,180 sq km)

Bring me water!
In the 12th century clever Syrian farmers built these water wheels to lift water from the Orontes River, drop it into canals, and send it along to water the crops in their fields.

Anyone for Raw Lamb?

The Arab answer to steak tartare (see page 161), raw lamb is mixed with bulgur wheat and as much red pepper as the human mouth can bear (perhaps to shock everyone's taste buds into not noticing that the lamb is raw).

MARHABA (mar ha ba)

Syria is a paradise for archaeologists—the spectacular dead city of Palmyra lay hidden in the sand here for many years. But Syria is also a "paradise on Earth." Legend says that the Prophet Muhammad, on a journey from Mecca (see page 150), gazed down from the mountains on Damascus but refused to enter the city because he wanted to "enter Paradise only once—when he died." How flattering!

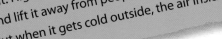

Palmyra's Dead Zone

Something happened here in the 16th century, something big...but no one knows what it was. Once a huge, rich population of people lived in this collection of 700 Byzantine towns, but for some spooky reason they all left home in the 16th century and never came back.

Shopping city A *souk* is the Arab version of a shopping center but more exciting. A maze of little streets is covered and filled with shops that sell everything from clothes to spices.

If you don't mind living in something that looks like a tea cosy, these are the best homes in the desert. These beehive houses have thick mud walls to trap cool air inside and keep the sun out. High domed ceilings collect hot air and lift it away from people sleeping on the floor. But when it gets cold outside, the air inside stays warm.

LEBANON
★ Beirut

★ Official language: Arabic
★ Population: 4,017,095
★ Currency: Lebanese pounds
★ Area: 4,015 sq miles (10,400 sq km)

The Green Line

Lebanon fought a terrible civil war from 1975 to 1990. Christians in East Beirut were separated from Muslims in West Beirut by a no-go zone. Because no one went there, grass grew between the buildings and it was given the name the "Green Line."

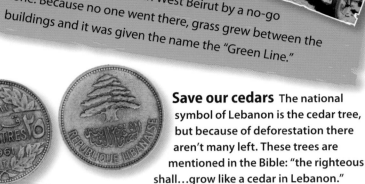

Save our cedars The national symbol of Lebanon is the cedar tree, but because of deforestation there aren't many left. These trees are mentioned in the Bible: "the righteous shall…grow like a cedar in Lebanon."

MARHABA (mar ha ba)

Today Lebanon is well known for its delicious food and long civil war, but this was once a place of Roman temples and spreading cedar trees. Lebanon is named for the beautiful snow-covered mountains of the land, and Lebanese ancestors were named for their talent for dyeing things purple! Keanu Reeves, star of *The Matrix* movies, was born here, and the world's largest ever bank robbery happened in Lebanon in 1976—the burglars got away with $40.8 million (£25 million)!

More Roman than Rome? The ancient Roman temples to the gods in Baalbek were said to be even bigger and more impressive than those in Rome. The stone glows orange at sunset.

The year AD 551 was a bad one for Beirut. It was destroyed by an earthquake, a tsunami, and then a fire.

Lebanese food is popular all over the world. Some Lebanese dishes you might have eaten are: tabbouleh, hummus, baba ghanoush, fattoush, stuffed vine leaves, falafel, kibbe, kofta, and baklava.

Lebanon is the only Middle Eastern country that doesn't have a desert.

What's in a Name?

The name Lebanon comes from the Arabic word *lubnan*, meaning "white," for the snow on the mountains.

Purple Phoenicians The ancient Leb were called Phoenicians, from the Greek *phoinikes* for "purple." They collected rare snails and made purple dye from them.

Work together Traditionally Jewish families lived together on large farms called *kibbutzim*, where everything was shared. Now *kibbutzim* are more like factories, making goods from jewelry and Wellington boots to toilet seats!

Crazy Fact

Albert Einstein was invited to become president of Israel in 1952. He turned down the offer.

ISRAEL
★ Jerusalem

★ Official language: Hebrew
★ Population: 7,233,701
★ Currency: New Israeli shekels
★ Area: 8,522 sq miles (22,072 sq km)

SHALOM (shall om)

This country was only created in 1948, but this biblical land is the world's oldest historical travel destination—everyone has wanted to come here, from Moses to Mark Twain. Today young Jews from around the world travel to Israel to work on *kibbutzim* and pray at the Wailing Wall, where King Solomon's Temple once stood. If you like prickly pears, you'll love it here. You can snorkle with amazing fish, but don't eat any seafood that doesn't have scales and fins!

Wailing Wall
The western wall of the Temple of Jerusalem was the only part left when it was destroyed by the Romans in AD 70. The world's Jews come to pray at this sacred place, while those who can't come send prayers which are poked into the cracks in the wall.

Funky Food

Kosher Food
Some Jewish people follow strict kosher laws for what they can eat. Animals must have "cloven feet" and "chew the cud" (eat grass). So cows can be eaten but never pigs; beef burgers are allowed, but not bacon sandwiches. Seafood must have fins and scales, so fish is eaten but not shellfish such as prawns or oysters. Even the glue on stamps is kosher.

Diving on the Great Barrier Reef? No, this is not Australia, but the amazing coral reefs of Eilat in Israel.

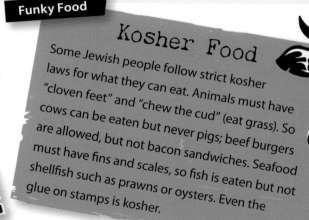

Prickly pears? Jewish people born in Israel are given the nickname "sabras." A sabra is a type of cactus also known as a prickly pear. The name is because Jewish Israelis are seen as being prickly on the outside but soft and squishy on the inside!

The Dead Sea Scrolls When the Romans destroyed the Jewish cities of Jericho, Jerusalem, and Qumran on the Dead Sea, village priests hid sacred parchment scrolls. Some of these scrolls were hidden in caves on sheer cliffs and found by archaeologists in 1947.

PALESTINE
★No official capital

★Official language: Arabic
★Population: 4,013,126
★Currency: New Israeli shekels
★Area: 2,849 sq miles (7,378 sq km)

World's lowest place The shore of the Dead Sea in Palestine is the lowest land on Earth. The Dead Sea is "dead" because the water is so thick with salt that no fish can live there and you can float on the water without any effort. In fact, you can loll around on top of the water reading a book.

MARHABA (mar ha ba)

If you've read the Bible, you'll recognize the names of many places in Palestine. This is the biblical land of Canaan, of Bethlehem where Jesus was born, and the Sea of Galilee, where He turned water into wine and walked on the water. But it's also a holy land for Jews and Muslims as well as Christians. Since Israel was created in 1948, the Palestinians and Israelis have been fighting over much of this land and it is now split into two parts: the West Bank and the Gaza Strip.

Funky Food

Kanafeh is a sweet pastry made of thin wheat shreds and warm goat's cheese soaked in sugary syrup. It might sound like an odd sweet–savory combination but the Palestinians love it.

PALESTINE'S TOP 5 Biblical Places

1. Nazareth
2. Bethlehem
3. Canaan (the old name of Palestine)
4. Sea of Galilee
5. The Wilderness (mountains of eastern Palestine)

Political scarf? Palestinian men wear a *keffiyeh* around their head to protect them from the sun. This square of white cloth has patterns woven on it in black, orange, or red. The colors have come to indicate the politics of the wearer.

Don't Look Down!

Wadi Qelt is a deep river gorge that runs through the wilderness between Jerusalem and Jericho. St. George's Monastery is built into its steep cliffs—to reach it visitors must walk across a narrow pedestrian bridge over the gorge.

JORDAN
★Amman

★ Official language: Arabic
★ Population: 6,342,948
★ Currency: Jordanian dinars
★ Area: 34,495 sq miles (89,342 sq km)

TOP 5 MOVIES
Filmed in Jordan

1. Indiana Jones and the Last Crusade (1989)
2. Red Planet (2000)
3. Mortal Kombat: Annihilation (1997)
4. Son of the Pink Panther (1993)
5. Lawrence of Arabia (1962)

Crazy Fact

Jordanians believe that praising children brings bad luck and should be avoided.

City of mosaics

Madaba looks like an ordinary town but hidden under almost every house is a Byzantine mosaic. Most have been uncovered but who knows what could be in the basement!

MARHABA (mar ha ba)

The land of real-life daredevil Lawrence of Arabia and film setting for fictional daredevil Indiana Jones is also home to the "Rose-red City" that is "half as old as time." Petra disappeared off the map for 1,000 years until a Swiss explorer disguised himself as a Muslim trader and sneaked into this legendary lost city. Be careful what you admire in a Jordanian home—the people of this land are so generous, they'll offer you any of their possessions that you like.

7 ONE OF THE NEW WONDERS OF THE WORLD

Rosy Stone

Petra is one of the world's most amazing abandoned cities. It was carved into rock 2,000 years ago and called the "Rose-red City" because of the color of the stone. In AD 700 Petra was abandoned after a huge earthquake and wasn't found again by a European until 1812.

Lawrence of Arabia During World War I, Colonel T. E. Lawrence of the British Army hid himself and his Arabian troops in Wadi Rum, in the strange rock pillars. He died in a motorbike accident in England, leading to the invention of crash helmets.

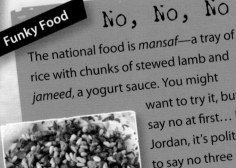

Funky Food

NO, NO, NO

The national food is *mansaf*—a tray of rice with chunks of stewed lamb and *jameed*, a yogurt sauce. You might want to try it, but say no at first… In Jordan, it's polite to say no three times before you accept a meal.

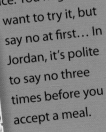

SAUDI ARABIA
★Riyadh

- ★ Official language: Arabic
- ★ Population: 28,686,633
- ★ Currency: Saudi riyals
- ★ Area: 830,000 sq miles (2,149,690 sq km)

Oil Rich

Saudi Arabia has the world's largest supply of oil and is the world's largest exporter of oil. This makes it an extremely rich country.

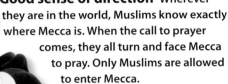

Good sense of direction Wherever they are in the world, Muslims know exactly where Mecca is. When the call to prayer comes, they all turn and face Mecca to pray. Only Muslims are allowed to enter Mecca.

MARHABAN (mar ha ban)

Several times a day Muslims all over the world turn in the direction of Saudi Arabia to pray. Mecca, where Muhammad was born, is the spiritual center of Islam and a place every Muslim must visit once in their life. This country has not a single lake or river—instead it has the "Empty Quarter," the world's biggest desert. In this land of oil and sand you can feast on sheep's eyes, then clean your teeth with *miswak*, the root of the arak tree.

Staying covered Many Muslim women wear a long, black cloak called an *abaya* with a veil or eye-mask to keep their face and hair hidden from strangers.

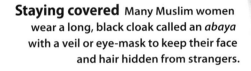

Walking Together

Mecca is the center of the Muslim world; Muhammad was born here in AD 570. The center of Mecca is a cube-shaped building called the Kaaba. Every Muslim in the world must journey to Mecca and walk around the Kaaba seven times to perform the Hajj. Around 3 million Muslims can do this at the same time!

World's biggest desert Rub' al-Khali desert, or "Empty Quarter," in southern Saudi Arabia is the biggest sand desert in the world (bigger than the Sahara). It is more than 250,000 sq miles (650,000 sq km), as large as France, but hasn't a single village.

Sauce with That?

Yes, you really can eat sheep's eyeballs in Saudi Arabia. The whole sheep is roasted for a banquet and the eyeballs are considered the most yummy special part. So yummy and special that they're often offered to guests!

King Fahd's Fountain This is the tallest fountain of water in the world. Water sprays 1,024ft (312m) into the air above the Red Sea and can reach a speed of 233mph (375km/h). The fountain was opened in 1985 and uses salt water from the sea instead of tap water.

Plain sailing The traditional Arab sailing boat is called a *dhow*. Dhows were used to carry heavy goods around the coast instead of over land. Large *dhows* had a crew of 30 people and traded dates, fish, and mangrove timber between Africa and the Persian Gulf.

Dates

YEMEN
★San'a

- ★ Official language: Arabic
- ★ Population: 23,822,783
- ★ Currency: Yemeni rials
- ★ Area: 203,850 sq miles (527,968 sq km)

MARHABAN (mar ha ban)

Yemen is a land of date palms and sand, but also sailing boats with billowing sails—the traditional Arabian *dhows* were copied by the Portuguese to make their grand *caravels*. The deep river valleys in the desert here are called *wadis* and houses were often built in them as they contained the only water for miles around. A thousand years ago this was the New York City of the desert—although the skyscrapers made of mud bricks look very different to today's high-rise buildings.

World's First Skyscrapers

These 500 tall narrow houses were built 1,000 years ago of mud bricks in Wadi Hadramaut. They were built close together to act as a fortress and keep enemies out. The ground floors have no windows (animals were kept there) but higher up were colored windows.

Hubbly bubbly
In the Arab world people smoke as part of their culture. They don't smoke cigarettes… they smoke a *narghile* or *sheesha*, aka hubbly bubbly. Some *narghiles* have several hoses so that friends can smoke together.

Amazing Animal

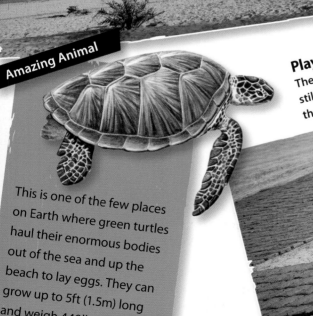

This is one of the few places on Earth where green turtles haul their enormous bodies out of the sea and up the beach to lay eggs. They can grow up to 5ft (1.5m) long and weigh 440lb (200kg).

Playing with mud
The traditional mud brickmakers are still busy in Yemen today, but now the houses are large, with garages!

Crazy Fact

Qat's that?
Yemenis often have cheeks bulging with a green leaf, *qat*, which they chew to relax. The government is now worrying about the amount of time spent on *qat*-chewing instead of work…

OMAN
★ Muscat

- ★ Official language: Arabic
- ★ Population: 3,418,085
- ★ Currency: Omani rials
- ★ Area: 119,499 sq miles (309,500 sq km)

MARHABAN (mar ha ban)

This country once sat on the seabed and its gravel desert still holds the fossilized treasures of that time. Bedouins move across the baking sands and, on the shore of the Gulf of Oman, forts perch to watch out for foreign invaders. If you're looking for an unusual gift, frankincense is harvested here and you might be able to photograph a mythical unicorn. Camels and falcons are favorite animals, but make sure your falcon has its passport before you set off to the airport.

Favorite fort Fort al Jalali sits on a high rock guarding the entrance to the Gulf of Oman. In medieval times many European nations were keen to capture it. In 1507 the Portuguese were successful and kept it for a century.

Amazing Animal

Birdie Passports

In ancient times Bedouins trained falcons to hunt for food. Now falconry is a popular sport. Good hunting falcons are so valuable that they are given passports to prevent them being smuggled out of Oman.

Always on the move Bedouins are often the only people living in Arabian deserts. These nomadic people don't build homes but move around continually.

Crazy Fact

Under the Sea?

Millions of years ago Oman was at the bottom of the sea. Because of this, there are millions of fossilized seashells lying in the huge gravel desert that covers much of this land.

Happy birthday! Looking for the perfect gift for a baby? Try frankincense. This scented resin from the *Boswellia* tree is used in perfume and incense. It was traditionally used to anoint newborn babies. Think of baby Jesus and the Three Wise Men.

Squint a Bit!

The Arabian oryx is the animal that is supposed to have started the myth of the unicorn. Spotted from the side, in hazy desert light, the oryx looks as if it has only one horn. Really!

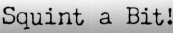

UNITED ARAB EMIRATES
★ Abu Dhabi

(see page 81)

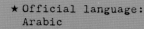

TOP 5
World Records of Burj Khalifa:

1. Building with most stories (160)
2. Highest and fastest elevator (40mph 64km/h)
3. Highest mosque (on the 158th floor)
4. Highest nightclub (on the 144th floor)
5. Highest swimming pool (on the 76th floor)

★ Official language: Arabic
★ Population: 4,798,491
★ Currency: Emirati dirhams
★ Area: 32,278 sq miles (83,600 sq km)

World's tallest building

Burj Khalifa is about as tall as two of New York's Empire State Building on top of each other. It is the tallest man-made structure ever built at 2,717ft (828m). It cost $1.5 billion and breaks many world records.

MARHABAN (mar ha ban)

The United Arab Emirates (UAE) is a rival to the Russian Federation (see page 81) in the world record stakes. In 1991 there was only one skyscraper here; today Dubai's Burj Khalifa is the world's tallest tower and Capital Gate leans farther than the Leaning Tower of Pisa (see page 57) —on purpose! Dubai is one of the seven emirates that make up the UAE. The average rainfall here is just 5in (13cm) a year, so all these futuristic buildings and indoor ski slopes are built on desert.

(see page 57)

Crazy Fact

Desert Snow

Just because you live in the desert, it doesn't mean you have to miss out on winter sports. One Dubai shopping center, Mall of the Emirates, has its own indoor ski slope!

The world's largest horse racing track is in Dubai.

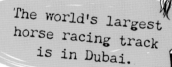

Man-made Islands

As well as tall towers, the people of Dubai like to create islands—the Palm Islands are in the shape of a palm tree. The World Islands are still being made—private buyers can purchase an island in the shape of any country they want to own. So, if you had enough money, you could buy the USA!

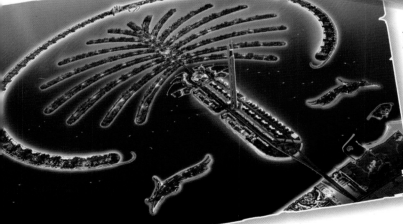

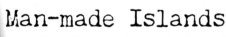

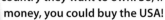

World's Longest

Dubai made the world's longest gold chain in 1999. The chain was 2.6 miles (4.2km) long and made of 22-carat gold. After it was measured, it was cut into necklace- and bracelet-sized bits; 9,600 people bought a piece.

Ahoy, me hearties! Until the early 20th century this part of the Persian Gulf coast was called the Pirate Coast. It was an important trade route, which made it a good place for pirates to hang around and rob people!

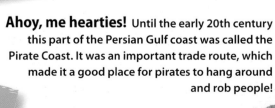

QATAR
★ Doha

Persian Gulf
Al-Khuwair
• Dukhan
Doha ✦
Mesaieed •
SAUDI ARABIA

* Official language: Arabic
* Population: 833,285
* Currency: Qatari riyals
* Area: 4,473 sq miles (11,586 sq km)

Adapted to Deserts

Bedouins, nomadic Arabs, describe camels as a "gift from Allah" because they're so perfect for the desert. Their long eyelashes keep out dust, their nostrils close in a sandstorm, and their broad feet don't sink in the sand. And their urine, which is thick and syrupy, can be collected and used for washing with. Only if you're really desperate!

دولة قطر
State of Qatar

MARHABAN (mar ha ban)

Welcome to the world's richest people. Qatar's capital, Doha, was once a pearl-fishing village, but today it looks more like the film set of a science-fiction movie. In this hot desert country, camels are king—they're perfectly made for the desert (although you might not like to use them for everything the Bedouins do). Al Jazeera, the Arabic news station, broadcasts from here. The locals holiday beside an inland sea and you'll get a good cup of coffee wherever you go.

Amazing Animal

Faster!

Camels don't run quite as fast as horses but they can race. Often they don't have human jockeys, but robot riders who are put on their back to whip them. The camel owners drive their cars alongside the race track, blowing their horns to make the animals go faster.

Nice little cup of coffee Arabian coffee is spiced with cardamom pods and served in tiny thimble-shaped cups. In many homes a vacuum flask of coffee is made in the morning and kept ready in case visitors come calling.

Let's go inland...to the beach The Khor al Adaid is a little inlet of the Persian Gulf that's become separated from the rest of the water. English speakers in Qatar call this the "Inland Sea."

The sticky tree Qatar's capital is called Doha, which means "the big tree" or "the sticky tree" in Arabic. Where this amazing futuristic city now sits was once a little pearling village... with a very big sticky tree.

Hideous History

Zubara Fort

This fort looks ancient, but don't be fooled. It was built in 1938 and was a police station, with prisoners held in the tops of the towers that could be reached only by ladder. The 3-ft- (1-m-) thick walls have strange twisted holes in them—they let in light but enemies can't fire through them into the fort.

Is This Paradise?

Bahrain is thought to be the site of the biblical Garden of Eden where Adam and Eve ate the forbidden fruit.

BAHRAIN
★ Manama

★ Official language: Arabic
★ Population: 727,785
★ Currency: Bahraini dinars
★ Area: 286 sq miles (741 sq km)

Al-Budayyi ● **Manama** ⚬
Al-Zallaq ● ● Awali
● Askar

Persian Gulf

Crazy Fact

Grand Prix

In 2004 Bahrain built an international racing car track and held the first ever Formula One Grand Prix in the Middle East. As Bahrain is a Muslim country, the winner does not spray alcoholic champagne around the podium when they win, but a nonalcoholic, fizzy rosewater drink called *waard* is used to celebrate victory instead.

MARHABAN (mar ha ban)

Welcome to the smallest Arab nation. This archipelago of 33 islands is 92% desert; only a tiny 3% of its land can be used to grow food. Food isn't important anyway, because Bahrain is known for its water...its salty seawater and the sweet spring water which encourages pearls to grow in the oysters. This might be the setting of the Garden of Eden where Eve ate the apple, but remember your manners and don't eat in public during Ramadan in this Muslim land.

Hold your breath

The pearls from Bahrain's oysters are thought to be the world's best and helped make this country rich. Pearls were more valuable than diamonds 200 years ago, and 30,000 pearl-divers held their breath to dive for them here.

What's in a Name?

Bahrain means "two seas": the sweet-water springs that bubble up off the shore and the salty sea around them. The sea around Bahrain is so shallow that the Bahrainis sometimes fill in the gaps between sandbanks to get more land.

Slow builders Bahrain Fort is built on a 36-ft (12-m) mound of earth that humans worked on for thousands of years, from 2300 BC to the 18th century. The fort on top was once called the Portuguese Fort. (Those Portuguese got everywhere!)

Respectful Ramadan

During the month of Ramadan, Muslims are not allowed to eat or drink even water during daylight hours. In Bahrain no one eats or drinks in public during Ramadan out of respect for the Muslim fasters.

KUWAIT
★Kuwait City

★ Official language: Arabic
★ Population: 2,691,158
★ Currency: Kuwaiti dinars
★ Area: 6,880 sq miles (17,818 sq km)

Woven stories The Bedouins are well known for their skill in weaving wool into stunning patterns. They are always on the move and don't write down their history in books. Instead, they weave patterns that tell stories about the desert.

Funky Food

The Kuwaiti favorite food is *machboos* and it's made for sharing. A huge plate of rice is topped off with layers of mutton, chicken, or fish. At noon on Friday, after prayers, the main family meal of the week is served and guests are often invited to come over to share.

MARHABAN (mar ha ban)

This country is built on oil—and not much water. Kuwait is relatively small, but most of that is desert on top of oil. This country earns 95% of its money from selling oil to the rest of the world and its citizens are the sixth richest on the planet. The men here wear long white *dishdashas* to protect them from the fierce desert sun and the women cover their faces with *yashmaks*. Any strange-shaped buildings seen here might turn out to be water tanks.

Look up! Kuwait has an annual kite-flying festival. On February 15, 2005 the world's largest kite was flown here—a huge Kuwaiti-flag kite, 82ft (25m) long and 131ft (40m) wide—bigger than a tennis court!

Epic Event

In 1990 diplomatic relations between Iraq and neighboring Kuwait deteriorated and Iraq invaded Kuwait, gaining control of its oilfields. Iraq occupied the country for seven months until the USA led troops into Kuwait to free it.

Big Buckets?

Kuwait Towers might look like just another groovy landmark for a capital city but they are actually very important and useful. These bulging buildings are water storage towers in this desert land of little rain.

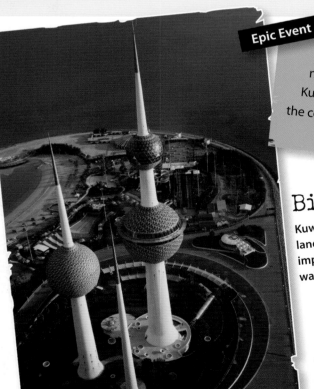

Striped funnels These water towers are so oddly shaped that they're called the "Mushroom Towers." Can't imagine why...

Baghdad was once the largest city in the world, with 1.2 million inhabitants. It was built on the Tigris River between AD 900 and 1200.

IRAQ
★ Baghdad

★ Official language: Arabic
★ Population: 28,945,657
★ Currency: Iraqi dinars
★ Area: 169,235 sq miles (438,317 sq km)

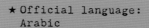

Hanging Gardens The gardens of Babylon were one of the Seven Wonders of the Ancient World. They didn't hang in the air, but King Nebuchadnezzar built them on a high rooftop for his wife, who was homesick for her mountainous homeland.

MARHABAN (mar ha ban)

Some wonderful things have happened in Iraq. About 7,000 years ago the first writing was created in this land, then called Mesopotamia and nicknamed the "Cradle of Civilization." The Sumerians lived here and invented carts with wheels on them, the first writing (called 'cuneiform'), and school (isn't that wonderful?). The Hanging Gardens of Babylon were one of the Seven Wonders of the Ancient World, but not many people find the screaming spiders of Iraq's deserts very wonderful.

Yippee, School!

This land is known as the "Birthplace of Writing." Pictures and marks were scratched on soft clay and the first school books were these clay tablets, made to be memorised by lucky children.

Striding lions One hundred and twenty of these painted life-size lions lined Babylon's Processional Way.

Screaming Spiders!

The camel spider can't kill you with its bite, but it might scare you to death. This spider likes to scream at you! It can run very quickly, as fast as a human, screaming at the same time. And, if that's not scary enough, it can also leap 3ft (1m) into the air. It loves shadows...so watch out for dark corners.

Terrified of Nanna?

Ziggurat means "house whose foundations cause terror" and the Great Ziggurat of Ur certainly looks terrifying. It was built in about 2100 BC as the control center of Ur and a shrine to the city's saint and moon god, Nanna.

TOP 5 Bible Stories:

1. Noah's Ark was built here
2. The Tower of Babel was built here
3. Abraham was born here
4. Daniel was thrown into the lions' den in this country
5. The Three Wise Men set out from here

IRAN
★ Tehran

★ Official languages: Persian, Azari, Kurdish
★ Population: 66,429,284
★ Currency: Iranian rials
★ Area: 636,372 sq miles (1,648,195 sq km)

The caracal is a fierce wild cat found here, although it hides so well that it's hardly ever seen. Its name means "black ears" in Persian.

Older than your grandma Persepolis is a ruin of pillars and sculptures in the desert. This 2,500-year-old city was once the capital of ancient Persia.

SALAAM (sah lahm)

Human history was made in this country 12,000 years ago. It was the Persian people of Iran, in the Zagros Mountains, who learned to grow crops and look after animals rather than just run around killing them. The invention of farming meant people started to stay in one place and build towns and cities. The city of Persepolis here is one of the world's great ruins, with huge decorated pillars, walls, and doorways soaring spookily upward out of the desert sands.

Crazy Fact

Everyone thinks of Iran as a hot sandy country and not somewhere for winter sports, but there are ski slopes in the mountains around Tehran. An Iranian boy went to study in France and learned to ski there. He came home in 1938, showed local carpenters how to make skis, and the sport became popular.

Backgammon Chess was invented in India and the emperor sent a chess set to the Persian king, as an example of how "wisdom and logic" shape life. The Persian king devised backgammon and sent it back to prove that "logic and luck" shape life.

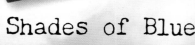

Precious gems Persian turquoises have been mined for more than 5,000 years. This is Iran's national gemstone.

Shades of Blue

The Masjed-e Emam is covered in millions of tiny blue tiles that change color depending on where the sun is in the sky.

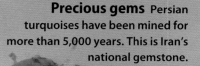

Ghostly Goats

In Nokhur village the gravestones are made from the horns of mountain goats. The locals think the horns will protect the tombs. (Perhaps from all the goat ghosts trotting around this cemetery looking for their horns?)

TURKMENISTAN
★Ashgabat

★ Official language: Turkmen
★ Population: 4,884,887
★ Currency: Turkmen manat
★ Area: 188,456 sq miles (488,100 sq km)

Take Care How You Do Your Hair

The old men of this country wear shaggy sheepskin hats (no, that's not his hair!) and grow long beards. They are respected for their wisdom and called *aksakals* (white beards). If a man wants to marry here, it's easy to pick out a bride: women with two braids are single, while those with one braid are already married.

SALAM ALEYKUM (sah lahm a lay coom)

Most of this country is covered by the Karakum Desert—a vast expanse of black sand, dinosaur footprints, and burning gas craters. One of these craters is 197ft (60m) across and thousands of spiders occasionally run together into its fire in a sort of mass suicide. Ashgabat, the capital, was destroyed on October 6, 1948, during an earthquake that measured 9 on the Richter scale and killed two thirds of the city's people. It's been rebuilt with marble palaces and golden statues.

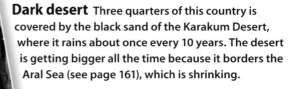

Dark desert Three quarters of this country is covered by the black sand of the Karakum Desert, where it rains about once every 10 years. The desert is getting bigger all the time because it borders the Aral Sea (see page 161), which is shrinking.

(see page 161)

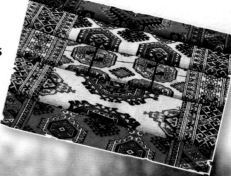

Carpet-makers
Shops all over the world sell the famous carpets of Turkmenistan. You might even have one in your house.

Golden Horse

The golden Akhal-Teke horse is the national emblem. It's famous for its speed and fitness on long marches (the Turkmens were traditionally nomads so this horse hardly ever got a rest). It's also famous for its shiny metallic-looking coat that can look like gold in the sunlight.

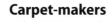

UZBEKISTAN
★ Tashkent

★ Official language: Uzbek
★ Population: 27,606,007
★ Currency: Uzbekistani soums
★ Area: 172,742 sq miles (447,400 sq km)

Marco Polo

Of all the travelers who journeyed along the Silk Road, Marco Polo is the most famous. He set off with his family in 1271 from Venice to China, through Uzbekistan. Before that, no one had traveled along the entire road. He went on foot, horseback, and camel, and the journey took his family more than three years.

SALOM (sal om)

Unless you live in this part of the world you might not even have heard of Uzbekistan, but in the 14th century this country was the center of the world. The reason was the Silk Road; it wasn't really a road, more a route to be followed between Europe and China. The Silk Road passed right through Uzbekistan, making some of this country's cities the most important on Earth at that time. If you wanted to go shopping, or you had something to sell, this was the place to come.

Bread luck *Lipioshka* (bread) is never placed upside down and it must never be put on the ground, even if it's in a bag.

Slave trade Ichan Kala looks like the world's most perfect sandcastle but inside these 30-ft (10-m) high walls there was a slave market until 1873.

The Silk Road

A thousand years ago merchants from Europe discovered the way to the Far East. They started to carry jewels, gold, and silver along a 4,000-mile (6,500-km) path to trade them for Chinese silks, spices, and carpets from the East. To protect themselves from robbers, merchants traveled in groups called "caravans."

Silk Road Shopping List

Don't forget to buy: silk tunics, umbrellas, paper, and medicine from China; pomegranates and carrots from Rome; honey and slaves from northern Europe. Oh, and a couple of peacocks, please. See you in three years!

Road to school Six hundred years ago, cities that were on the Silk Road became hugely important. Great Islamic schools were often built in places such as Samarkand.

KAZAKHSTAN
★Astana

★ Official languages: Kazakh, Russian
★ Population: 15,399,437
★ Currency: Tenge
★ Area: 1,052,090 sq miles (2,724,900 sq km)

Get on your horse
This is thought to be the land where humans first sat on a horse, thousands of years ago, and then didn't get off for a very long time. *Stan* means "land," and *kazakh* means "wanderer."

Funky Food
Steak Tartare
Raw beef with an egg yolk on top...This delicious concoction was named for the Tartars, a nomadic tribe who ate raw meat while riding because they didn't have time to get off and cook. They kept the meat under their saddles to make it tender.

SALEM (sal em)
The people of this land were traditionally nomadic, wandering the great flat *steppes* of their country on horseback—and getting dinner ready while they galloped! Once they finally dismounted from their horses, they discovered the apple trees of their largest city and the beluga sturgeon swimming in their local Caspian Sea. Caviar that is sold for about $4,545 per lb (£6,000 per kg) in the rest of the world can be bought here for $114 (£152).

The Endless Steppe
This isn't just a huge field: it's a *steppe*. These enormous plains of grasslands with no trees are often very cold. This climate zone is not quite dry enough to be called desert.

What's in a Name?
Almaty means "full of apples" and that's what Kazakhstan's biggest city is famous for. Apples grew on snowy hillsides here for thousands of years before they became popular around the world. Some are enormous. (But remember: never eat anything bigger than your head—even an apple!)

Hideous History
Shrinking Sea
The Aral Sea used to be the fourth-largest inland sea in the world, but it has shrunk to a tenth its original size. The huge Soviet Union piped away much of its water for irrigating crops.

Expensive eggs
The beluga sturgeon lives in the Caspian Sea here. Its eggs are sold as beluga caviar, one of the world's most expensive foods.

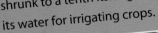

1973   1987   1999   2001   2004   2007   2009

Deadly desert Where the Aral Sea once lapped, boats are left aground. The dust from here carries pesticides that have been found in the blood of penguins in Antarctica, the glaciers of Greenland, the forests of Norway, and the fields of Russia.

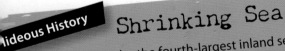

KYRGYZSTAN
★ Bishkek

- ★ Official languages: Kyrgyz, Russian
- ★ Population: 5,431,747
- ★ Currency: Soms
- ★ Area: 77,202 sq miles (199,951 sq km)

Epic Event ## Black Death

Issyk Kul means "Hot Lake," and although this lake is surrounded by snowy mountains, it never freezes. It's thought the Black Death (bubonic plague) started here. Some doctors treating plague victims wore primitive masks shaped like a bird beak.

SALAMATSYZBY (sal a mat zi bee)

This high, glacial, mountainous country is called the "Switzerland of Asia" and was a land of (very cold?) nomads. *Kyrgyz* is from the Turkish word for "forty" —there were 40 nomadic clans in this land who came together as one Kyrgyz people. *Yurta* are the traditional tent homes here (do they have central heating?) and the men wear high hats of felt or sheepskin. Scientists now think that Kyrgyzstan's Hot Lake might have been a bubonic plague hot spot.

Ice skating, anyone?
The Inylchek Glacier is 37 miles (60km) long, which makes it one of the largest glaciers in the world that is *not* in the Arctic or Antarctic.

Get your walnuts here Kyrgyzstan is home to some of the largest natural walnut forests in the world.

Has Someone Got the Tent Poles?

Yurta are the traditional tents used by the nomads of the *steppes* who need to move their homes around. Modern *yurta* can have solar panels and satellite dishes— living in a tent doesn't mean you have to miss an episode of The Simpsons!

On the flag The sun on the flag of Kyrgyzstan has 40 rays coming from it to show the 40 tribes of this land. In the middle of the sun is a bird's eye view of the crown of a *yurt*.

Peaks galore Kyrgyzstan shares the Tien Shan mountain range with China. The mountains take up only a small part of enormous China, but cover 75% of Kyrgyzstan.

Kingdom of the kids Nearly half the population of this land are under the age of 14. That makes Tajikistan one of the "youngest" countries in the world.

TAJIKISTAN
★ Dushanbe

★ Official language: Tajik
★ Population: 7,349,145
★ Currency: Tajikistani somoni
★ Area: 55,251 sq miles (143,100 sq km)

Amazing Animal

Call That a Horn?

Marco Polo sheep were named for the merchant who saw them in the Pamirs. They are bigger than other sheep and have very long spiral horns.

SALAM ALEYKUM (sah lahm a lay coom)

Until 1991, when the huge Soviet Union broke apart into independent countries, this land was closed to the outside world. When they controlled Tajikistan, the Soviets (Russians) sent researchers into the Pamirs to try to find the "giant snowman" that supposedly roamed there, terrifying travelers who had to spend many days in the wilderness crossing these high mountains. If you want someone to play with, this "young country" is a good place to visit.

Epic Event
Hidden until 1991

This was a very secretive land that allowed in no "foreign devils." In 1891 an English explorer sneaked in but was found by the Russians, who closed the country to the outside world for 100 years…just like Sleeping Beauty.

Funky Food

Samsa are a favorite snack here. These filled pastries are like Indian *samosas*.

Wizard's gate The only bit left of the huge Hissar Fortress is this monumental gate. The walls are 3ft (1m) thick. Legend says that the fortress was owned by an evil wizard.

Roof or Legs?

Are the Pamirs the "Roof of the World" or the "Legs of the Sun"? They have been given both nicknames (although the Chinese call them the "Onion Mountains"). It takes 12 days to cross the Pamirs on horseback.

A monster called the "giant snowman" is rumored to live in the Pamirs.

AFGHANISTAN
★Kabul

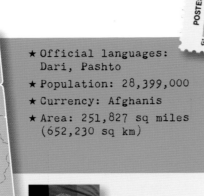

- ★ Official languages: Dari, Pashto
- ★ Population: 28,399,000
- ★ Currency: Afghanis
- ★ Area: 251,827 sq miles (652,230 sq km)

World's weirdest sport?
Buzkashi means "grab the goat." The aim is to pick up a headless, disemboweled goat while galloping on a horse, then throw the goat across a goal line. Sort of like polo...only with a headless animal instead of a ball.

Camel's choice
Mazar-e Sharif is built on a spot chosen by a camel. The animal was carrying the body of a murdered man whose family followed it through the desert for weeks. Where the camel died, they buried their relative and built the Shrine of Hazrat.

SELAM (she lam)

This country might have the strangest national sport in the world, and it once had the most amazing giant Buddhas, too. The beautiful (but not very clever) Afghan hound was brought to Europe from here in the 1800s by returning soldiers (it makes up in beauty what it lacks in brains). Afghan coats were popular with hippies in the 1970s, but don't worry, they weren't made from Afghan hounds. The famous Khyber Pass, 33 miles (53km) long, links Afghanistan and Pakistan.

Hideous History

The Hunt for bin Laden
In 2001, after the September 11 attacks on America by al-Qaeda, US and UK forces invaded Afghanistan and defeated its Taliban government. The forces were trying to find Osama bin Laden, but he managed to escape from them through a huge maze of mountain caves at Tora Bora. He was found and killed in 2011.

Naan (like "gran") This flat bread is served at every meal.

Amazing Animal

Daft Dogs?

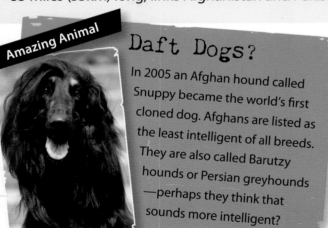

In 2005 an Afghan hound called Snuppy became the world's first cloned dog. Afghans are listed as the least intelligent of all breeds. They are also called Barutzy hounds or Persian greyhounds —perhaps they think that sounds more intelligent?

The Buddhas of Bamiyan
Travelers on the Silk Road were amazed by the two Buddhas of Bamiyan. The largest was 180ft (55m) tall. They were carved into the sandstone cliffs in the 6th century and decorated with gold and jewels. In 2001 the Taliban government of Afghanistan blew them up with dynamite; now these Buddha-shaped holes hold the ruins.

Deadly poppies Poppies are the most popular crop in Afghanistan. But these poppies aren't for putting in a vase—they are opium poppies. They can be used to manufacture medicines but also to make illegal drugs such as heroin.

Turquoise jam? The Minaret of Jam is a 200-ft (65-m) high tower, built with mud bricks in the 12th century. It might be the last remains of Turquoise Mountain, the lost Afghan capital of the Middle Ages.

Funky Food

The national drink of Pakistan is sugarcane juice (not a big favorite of dentists). This drink, called *roh*, is sold on roadsides. Drink it quick, or it turns black.

PAKISTAN
★ Islamabad

★ Official language: Urdu
★ Population: 176,242,949
★ Currency: Pakistani rupees
★ Area: 307,374 sq miles (796,095 sq km)

SALAAM (sal arm)

In 1947 India was partitioned, making Pakistan a separate country. The second-highest mountain on Earth, K2, is part of the Karakoram Range here, and the meadows of Lalazar have been called the world's "Most Beautiful Place" more often than anywhere else. While the Indians invented numbers, it was in Pakistan that the all-important number 0 was created—imagine trying to do math without it. Here's a bit of math—80% of all soccer balls are made in this country.

Life in the Fast Lane

The Karakoram Highway (aka KKH) is a bit like the USA's Route 66—one of the world's most famous roads. This thin strip of tarmac runs 750 miles (1,200km) from Islamabad to China. It follows the ancient Silk Road, but is packed with minibuses and trucks, not camel caravans.

Invented Here

Game of Kings, King of Games

Polo was invented in Pakistan and this game of "hockey on horseback" is played fiercely here. The name "polo" means "ball" in the local language. Competitions are held every year high in the Hindu Kush and the rules are tougher than anywhere else in the world. Actually there are no rules other than to stay on your horse (and try not to get hit by your opponent's mallet).

Turn left at the end of the road

Is this where town planning started? Mohenjo Daro was built 4,000 years ago and is the first example of a city with streets in a grid pattern.

Reward for a good life?

The city of Uch is famous for two reasons: it was founded by Alexander the Great (see page 68) and it is home to many spectacular Muslim tombs built for *sufis* who devoted their life to God.

Snake eaters?

In Persian, *mar* is "snake" and *khor* is "eat." But, like other goats, the markhor eats plants, not snakes.

INDIA
★ New Delhi

★ Official languages:
  Hindi, English, Bengali,
  plus 13 others
★ Population:
  1,166,079,217
★ Currency: Indian rupees
★ Area: 1,269,219 sq miles
  (3,287,263 sq km)

NAMASTE (nah mah stay)

This land is famous for its people—and there are many of them. India's population is only just behind China's, but all these people are crowded into a much smaller area. That hasn't stopped the Indians inventing more useful objects than any other race and building one of the New Seven Wonders of the World at Agra. An Indian man holds the record for the longest combined length (20ft 4in/6.2m) of fingernails on one hand, but he certainly can't pick his nose!

Amazing Animal
Sacred Cows

Hindus believe that cows are holy animals so they don't eat them, and eight out of every ten Indians are Hindu. According to Hindu teaching, 330 million gods and goddesses live in the body of a cow.

Holy bath time
Every year millions of Hindus make a pilgrimage to the holy city of Varanasi in north India to worship in one of the temples there. Then they walk into the Ganges River to wash away their sins.

Hollywood or Bollywood?
More than 800 films a year are made in India—double the number that are made in Hollywood. The film industry is nicknamed Bollywood and is famous for making action movies with singing and dancing.

Invented Here

- Pajamas
- Numbers 1–9 (these were called Hindu numerals but when the Arabic nations adopted them they became Arabic numerals)
- Bangles
- Dentists (and their dentist drills!)
- Buttons
- Hospitals
- Ovens
- Plastic surgery (but as a type of punishment!)
- Shampoo
- Swimming pools

The Taj Mahal

A lot of people have called this the most beautiful building in the world. The Mogul emperor Shah Jahan would be pleased to hear that! He built the Taj Mahal in memory of his favorite wife. It took 20,000 workers 21 years to build and was completed in 1653.

India has 16 major languages and hundreds more lesser ones.

CHERRAPUNJEE
THE RAINIEST PLACE ON PLANET EARTH
A LAND OF BREATHTAKING BEAUTY AND EXOTIC PEOPLE.
CHERRAPUNJEE IS LOCALLY KNOWN AS SOHRA.
AVERAGE ANNUAL RAINFALL (1973-2006) 11931.7 mm.
JAN, FEB, NOV, DEC, RECEIVE NO OR NOMINAL RAINFALL.
CHERRAPUNJEE HOLIDAY RESORT
WWW.CHERRAPUNJEE.COM
PH.03637-244218, 244219, 244220 (M) 94361-15925, 98630-79856
ELEVATION-1364 m ABOVE MSL.

World's Wettest

Cherrapunjee is the wettest place on Earth—during monsoon, of course!

7 ONE OF THE NEW WONDERS OF THE WORLD

Charming snakes!
How on earth does this work? The charmer pipes music and the deadly cobra sways up out of a basket without going bonkers and biting him? It's done by hypnotism.

Enough! One banyan tree on its own can look like an entire forest. Every branch of the tree grows roots down into the ground, which then send up more tree trunks. One tree in Sri Lanka has 350 large trunks and over 3,000 smaller ones.

Tea for Two, or a Million?

Tea has been grown here for 150 years and now more than 1 million Sri Lankans work in the tea industry.

SRI LANKA
★Colombo

★ Official languages: Sinhalese, Tamil
★ Population: 21,324,791
★ Currency: Sri Lankan rupees
★ Area: 25,332 sq miles (65,610 sq km)

A'YUBOWAN (au bo wan)

If you have Buddha's tooth, legend says you can become ruler of this land. Luckily, the tooth is kept safe in a temple in Kandy. This country was called Ceylon until 1972, and if you like tea, you might find your tea bags come from here. Sri Lanka grows the world's largest fruit and trees that can sprout hundreds of trunks. Speaking of trunks, the Pinnawela Elephant Orphanage has the largest captive herd of elephants in the world. And a lot of them still drink milk from a bottle!

The elephant orphanage
All these orphaned baby elephants are bathed twice a day in the river and fed bottles of milk by volunteers until they are three years old.

Scary Stuff

Stepping off the End of the World

World's End is a 2,854ft (870m) sheer cliff. It's often in cloud, so take care where you step.

World's Largest

The world's biggest fruit that grows on a tree, one single jackfruit can weigh as much as 125 apples (55lb/25kg). It has spiny skin, an egg-shaped seed, and sour pulp.

Lion's rock Inside this rock fortress there is ancient graffiti. On the walls are drawings of beautiful women—the graffiti says 500 women, but many have been cleaned off in case they "distract meditating monks."

MALDIVES
★ Male'

★ Official language: Divehi
★ Population: 396,334
★ Currency: Rufiyaa
★ Area: 115 sq miles (298 sq km)

Island skyscrapers Male' Atoll is the second most densely populated island in the world, after Ap Lei Chau in Hong Kong (see page 185). The people live in brightly colored, tall, thin skyscrapers—so that more people can fit on each bit of land—and a sea wall is built around the city to stop it being washed away.

SALAAMU ALAIKUM (sala mu a li kum)

It might look as if a little wave could just wash away this low, flat group of islands, but they've been written about in history since the 5th century BC. There are about 1,200 coral islands here, and 200 have people living on them. Not surprisingly, the Maldivians are worried about global warming—as sea levels rise, they have less island to live on! If a big wave does come washing up the beach, you could pick up some ancient money, but watch out for sharks!

Crazy Fact

Money Shells

Two hundred years ago cowrie shells were used as ornaments and jewelery and eventually as money. The Maldives had many cowrie shells lying on its beaches, so was nicknamed the "Money Islands." Imagine money just lying around on the beach!

Tiger shark

TOP 5
Sharks with Odd Names

1. Snaggle-tooth sharks
2. Big-nose sharks
3. Slit-eye sharks
4. Zebra sharks
5. Tiger sharks (scary man-eaters)

World's Flattest

This is the flattest, lowest country in the world. The highest spot in the whole country is just 7ft 7in (2.3m)—probably about as high as your bedroom ceiling. The islands are made of coral—the coral's limestone remains clump together to make reefs. The Maldives are ancient coral reefs that grew around prehistoric volcanoes. The volcanoes sank into the ocean, leaving these coral islands behind.

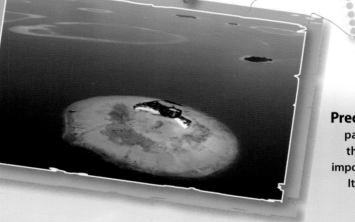

Precious palm The coconut palm is the national tree of the Maldives and the most important plant in the country. It's grown on all the islands and its timber is used in houses and boats. The leaves are used for roofs.

That's Abominable!

Enormous footprints like those of a bare-foot man or huge ape have been found in the snow here. Many people have been terrified by a huge hairy monster lurking in the gloom of the mountainside. Stories of the Yeti, or Abominable Snowman, have been told for hundreds of years and many expeditions have set out to find it. Even Sir Edmund Hillary led one.

NEPAL
★ Kathmandu

★ Official language: Nepali
★ Population: 28,563,377
★ Currency: Nepalese rupees
★ Area: 56,827 sq miles (147,181 sq km)

NAMASTE (nuh muh stay)

Although the main religion here is Hinduism, this is the famous birthplace of Buddha. Nepal is best known for Mt. Everest, the highest point on Earth, but eight of the world's ten highest peaks are here in the Himalayas. Himalaya means "home of snow" and these mountains grow a tiny bit higher each year, pushed upward by Earth's crust. If you're lucky, a Sherpa will help you up the mountain, but beware—somewhere in the icy darkness, something abominable could be lurking.

Someone's looking at you! Bodhnath Stupa was built in the 5th century. This huge shrine is decorated with the all-seeing eyes of Buddha.

Birthplace of Buddha
Lumbini, Nepal, is where Siddhartha Gautama, the Lord Buddha, was born in 623 BC. The village later fell into ruins and was redisovered in 1895 by a German archaeologist.

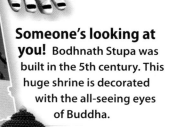

Super-Sherpa! Since people started climbing Everest, they've used Sherpas as mountain guides and to help carry their luggage. Sherpas are the local people—their bodies are used to thin air and they can carry heavy loads, including the climbers themselves! They call Everest *Chomolungma*, or "Mother of the World."

South Base Camp
Each climbing season, up to 1000 people live in a huge city of tents partway up Everest to acclimatize to the altitude. At higher altitudes, the air becomes thinner and breathing becomes even more difficult.

Mt. Everest

Mt. Everest is the highest point on Earth at 29,035ft (8,850m). The first people to reach the summit were Edmund Hillary and Sherpa Tenzing Norgay, in 1953. Nepal is also home to Annapurna, the world's 10th highest peak, thought to be the world's most dangerous mountain to climb—by 2011 only 153 people had reached its summit, and 58 had died.

TIBET
★ Lhasa

★ Official languages: Tibetan, Mandarin Chinese
★ Population: 2,840,000
★ Currency: Renminbi
★ Area: 474,288 sq miles (1,228,400 sq km)

Fed to the birds
When a Tibetan family requests a sky burial, the body is taken to a mountaintop, cut into pieces by a monk (and sometimes even pounded to a pulp), and then vultures are called to feast on the body.

Hideous History
In 1950 the Chinese army marched into Tibet and took over the country. Many people were killed and monasteries were destroyed. In 1959 the Tibetans rebelled, but the Chinese soldiers stopped them. The Dalai Lama was forced to leave his country and escape across the Himalaya mountains to exile in India.

TASHI DELEK (ta she duh lek)

To the north of the Himalayas lies Tibet, the "Land of Snows" and spiritual home of the Dalai Lama. This is a place of yaks, fluttering prayer flags, and funeral rites that might give you nightmares. Tibet has been battling China for 1,500 years. Foreign tourists have only been allowed to enter Tibet since the 1980s, and although you can climb Mt. Everest from here, you need the government's permission. Wenzhuan in Tibet is the world's highest city at 16,467ft (5,019m).

Prayer flags These colorful squares of thin cotton have Buddhist symbols and prayers printed on them. As the wind blows the flags and frays their edges, prayers are released to the heavens.

Amazing Animal

There is a myth that yak's milk is pink—but it's white, just like cow's milk, and can be churned into butter. The Tibetans like to drink yak butter tea, or *sud-ja*, with salt and globs of butter floating in it. Some Tibetans drink up to 40 cups a day.

Searching for the Dalai Lama
The first Dalai Lama was born in a cowshed in Tibet in 1391. When the Dalai Lama dies, Tibetans believe he is reincarnated into a baby born soon afterward.

Earthquake-proof

Potala Palace has foundations made of copper so that it can withstand earthquakes. It was built in AD 637 by the Tibetan king as a present for his bride, and then became the Dalai Lama's home until 1959. Its sloping walls are more than 15ft (5m) thick at the base.

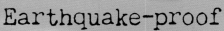

Rumbling Thunder

This country is nicknamed "Land of the Thunder Dragon" because of the noise of the terrible thunderstorms during monsoon season. The dragon on the flag is called Druk, and so is the national airline.

BHUTAN
★ Thimphu

★ Official language: Dzongkha
★ Population: 691,131
★ Currency: Ngultrum
★ Area: 14,824 sq miles (38,394 sq km)

Aim, shoot! Archery is the national sport and neighbouring villages often hold competitions against each other.

Pink Elephant?

No, this is a blue sheep. Its horns grow up and back, like a back-to-front moustache. Unfortunately, it is the favourite snack of the snow leapard.

TASHI DELEK (ta she duh lek)

Welcome to the "Land of the Thunder Dragon," where many homes have no television, phone, or Internet, but the people are very happy. It's illegal to sell cigarettes here because they're bad for your *karma* as well as your health; Bhutan hopes to soon become the world's first smoke-free nation. Foreign tourists have been allowed to enter here since 1974. Bhutan claims the world's highest unclimbed peak, Gangkar Puensum—the government can't afford rescue parties so no one is allowed to climb it.

Radish copycat Chorten Kora is a copy of Bodhnath Stupa (see page 169) that was made in 1740 by Lama Loday. Loday went to Nepal and carved a model of Bodhnath into a radish so he could remember how to rebuild it in Bhutan. It's not an exact copy because the radish shrank during his journey home and became shriveled and twisted!

Asia's happiest country

This country isn't rich or important, but in a 2006 survey the people of Bhutan were found to be happiest of all Asian people. Buddhists value happiness above wealth.

No Crane or Bulldozer?

Tiger's Nest Monastery was built on a cliff edge in 1692, near a cave where the second Buddha meditated. He is said to have been carried to the cave on the back of a tiger.

BANGLADESH
★ Dhaka

Rangpur
INDIA
Sylhet
Dhaka
INDIA
Khulna
Chittagong
UNION OF MYANMAR
Bay of Bengal

★ Official language: Bengali
★ Population: 156,050,883
★ Currency: Taka
★ Area: 55,598 sq miles (143,998 sq km)

Star apple If you cut this favorite fruit in half, you'll find a perfect star shape in its center.

Spice it up Spices are added to food here for their flavor and color, but also to heal and give energy.

Epic Event

Bangladesh's 1998 monsoon floods were the worst in human history. Two thirds of this country flooded, 1,000 people died, and 30 million were left homeless.

SUNCHHEN (soon chen)

Bangladesh is home to the man-eating Bengal tiger, so anyone paddling in the mangrove swamps here should watch our for stripes hiding behind a tree! The tigers have many potential snacks in this country, which is one of the most crowded in the world. Everything here is busy: the markets are full of brightly colored spices and fruit and the streets of Dhaka are packed with more than half a million rickshaws, but when the monsoon rains come it's time to take cover.

Spot the stripes The Sundarbans (the name means "beautiful forest" in Bengali) is the largest mangrove forest in the world. Move carefully here: it's the home of many Bengal tigers.

Bengal tiger
A tiger's markings are like fingerprints—no two have the same stripes.

Join the Crowd

Bangladesh is one of the most crowded countries in the world with more than 1,000 people per 0.4 sq mile (1 sq km) of land.

Sitar

The sitar looks a bit like a guitar, only longer! It is played in Bangladesh and India but suddenly became popular around the world in the 1960s, when the Beatles and Rolling Stones "discovered" it and used it in the songs "Norwegian Wood" and "Paint It, Black."

How's that possible? *Kyaiktiyo*

(Golden Rock) is a huge boulder that hovers on the edge of a cliff, looking as if it's about to crash down at any second. Legend says it is balanced on a strand of Buddha's hair. The rock is covered in pieces of gold leaf that are stuck on by the Buddhists who come to see it.

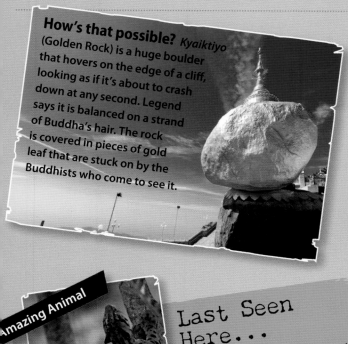

UNION OF MYANMAR
★ Nay Pyi Taw

* ★ Official language: Burmese
* ★ Population: 48,137,741
* ★ Currency: Kyats
* ★ Area: 261,228 sq miles (676,578 sq km)

Amazing Animal

Last Seen Here...

The clouded leopard is extinct in much of the rest of the world but can still be found living in the wild here.

MINGALARBAR *(min gala bar)*

In the Union of Myanmar (Burma) you'll find ruby mines, clouded leopards, a huge rock balancing on a hair, and an ancient deserted capital city. Here are tribal women whose necks look as if they've been stretched (although it's their collarbones that have been pushed down) and Buddhist monks with a troop of well-trained pets. If you've ever wondered why these monks all wear spice-colored robes, it's because that's what they used to have to dye their cloth with.

Long-necked ladies

The Padaung women are famous for the stacks of brass rings around their necks—they believe these will protect them from tiger attacks. Rings are added each year so that their necks look longer and longer.

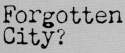

Red as a pigeon's blood

Rubies are mined in north Myanmar. The most valuable is called the "pigeon-blood red ruby."

Forgotten City?

A thousand years ago Bagan was the capital of Myanmar and had over 13,000 temples. The Irrawaddy River has washed away one third of this ancient city, and thieves and earthquakes have destroyed many buildings. There are now only around 2,200 temples left.

Crazy Fact

The monks at Nga Phe Kyaung Monastery have taught their cats to jump through hoops. (They must have a lot of patience and spare time…)

THAILAND
★ Bangkok

★ Official language: Thai
★ Population: 65,905,410
★ Currency: Baht
★ Area: 198,117 sq miles
  (513,120 sq km)

Bangkok's Thai name is the longest place name in the world (see Wales, page 43). This city is called *Krung Thep Mahanakhon Amon Rattanakosin Mahinthara Yuthaya Mahadilok Phop Noppharat Ratchathani Burirom Udomratchaniwet Mahasathan Amon Phiman Awatan Sathit Sakkathattiya Witsanukam Prasit.* Thais don't call their city Bangkok (that's just for foreigners); they call it *Krung Thep* (City of Angels).

SAWAT DI (sa wat dee)

Welcome to Thailand, known as the "Land of Smiles" because the people here are so friendly. You can watch a game of elephant polo or nip through the busy Bangkok streets in a crazy *tuk tuk*. This is a country of golden Buddhas and temples, and a capital city that really does have the longest name in the world. Spicy noodles are cooked up in Thai street stalls, and when you hear someone asking for a plate of "cow pat," don't be alarmed—they just want fried rice.

Buddha rules! There is a strict set of rules for making statues of Buddha. Buddha is shown flat-footed, with long ear lobes, thin fingers, and toes that are all the same length.

In Thailand it's illegal to leave the house with no underwear on.

Supersize polo In this country polo is played on elephants, using a ball the size of a soccer ball.

Floating Market

When you go shopping here, don't get seasick. Bangkok's floating market consists of long thin boats piled with goods, parked together on the river. Buyers hop between shops, taking care not to fall in.

Tuk Tuk!

These crazy-looking vehicles will take you anywhere you want to go. This Thai version of a taxi dashes through the traffic, weaving between larger vehicles. The name comes from the noise the engine makes!

Fill your basket During the full moon the That Muang Sing Festival is celebrated. Thousands of plastic shopping baskets are hung out with offerings to the gods.

LAOS
★ Vientiane

★ Official language: Lao
★ Population: 6,834,942
★ Currency: Kips
★ Area: 91,429 sq miles (236,800 sq km)

nky Food

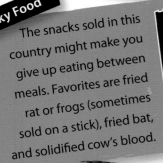

The snacks sold in this country might make you give up eating between meals. Favorites are fried rat or frogs (sometimes sold on a stick), fried bat, and solidified cow's blood.

SABAIDEE (sa bai dee)

The word "Laos" sounds like "cow," not "mouse." Many towns in this country have a night-time curfew, which means the government tells you what time you have to be home—and it tells your parents, too! If you're wondering why everyone's hanging out their plastic supermarket basket, look up and you may find that it's a full moon. The national dish doesn't need a knife and fork, just a lettuce leaf, but the snacks sold in this country might surprise you.

Buddha and the pumpkin This bizarre sculpture park looks ancient, but Buddha Park was built in 1958. It has more than 200 Hindu and Buddhist statues, including gods, animals, people, and...a giant pumpkin. The park has three levels, representing Heaven, Earth, and Hell. The gateway is a huge demon's head.

Finger food A favorite food in Laos is *larb*. This meat salad, often made with chicken or beef, is flavored with fish sauce and lime juice. Using their fingers, Laotians wrap up the *larb* in a crisp lettuce leaf, then eat it.

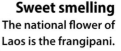

Amazing Animal

That's a Whopper!

The world's largest freshwater fish lives in the Mekong River. Mekong catfish can grow 10ft (3m) long. The largest one ever caught weighed 646 lb (293kg).

Sweet smelling The national flower of Laos is the frangipani.

World's Grooviest Hat?

These circular, embroidered, and beaded hats are Laotian traditional dress for girls. The boys wear caps that are smaller but also very colorful.

VIETNAM
★ Hanoi

★ Official language: Vietnamese
★ Population: 86,967,524
★ Currency: Dong
★ Area: 127,881 sq miles (331,210 sq km)

Bring a towel Water puppet shows have been performed here for 1,000 years. The puppeteers have to stand in waist-deep water behind a screen, using the surface of the water as the stage. The front row of the audience often gets very wet.

XIN CHAO (sin djow)

The Vietnamese don't have to worry about forgetting a friend's birthday—everyone turns one year older on the same day here! *Tet* is like Christmas, New Year, and a birthday rolled into one huge celebration. This land is home to the pot-bellied pig, the overcrowded motorbike, and some very wobbly-looking boats. There's a rumor that the Vietnamese eat dogs—they do, but only in special doggy restaurants. And snake wine can be drunk to wash the meal down.

Crazy Fact

Would *you* dare paddle out to sea in a little wicker basket? Basket boats are made of woven bamboo with a coating of tar to keep them waterproof. They can even surf over waves.

Saddle up! Buffalo are used like horses in Vietnam. They pull carts and plows and work in the fields, but children also ride them home from school.

Amazing Animal

Big Bellies

The Vietnamese pot-bellied pig has a huge belly that can sometimes drag on the ground. It can be kept as a pet and trained to open the fridge on its own (it's got to keep that belly nice and fat).

Happy New Year! Celebrate with these sticky rice and banana leaf parcels called *banh chung*.

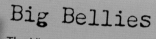

Musical kites The Vietnamese take kite-flying very seriously. Some kites here even play a tune as they fly—they have bamboo flutes tied to them. The faster the kite flies, the louder the flutes play.

Bike Overload

How many people can fit on one motorbike? The Vietnamese are famous for using the motorbike as a family car. Often mom, dad, and several children squeeze onto the same bike.

CAMBODIA
★ Phnom Penh

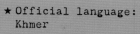

Irrawaddy dolphins live in the Mekong River. They can survive in both fresh and saltwater, but river pollution is causing them to die.

Cruel rule The Khmer Rouge controlled Cambodia from 1975 to 1979. During this time they killed nearly 2 million people.

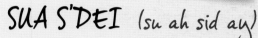
★ Official language: Khmer
★ Population: 14,494,293
★ Currency: Riels
★ Area: 69,898 sq miles (181,035 sq km)

THAILAND LAOS
Battambang
Stung Treng
Kompong Chhnang
★ Kratie
Phnom Penh
VIETNAM
Gulf of Thailand
South China Sea

SUA S'DEI (su ah sid ay)

Cambodia is still recovering from the horror of its Khmer Rouge government in the 1970s. The men of this country wear bright-colored sarongs to make up for the years when only black or dark blue clothing was allowed. A *wat* is a Buddhist temple or monastery, and near Cambodia's ancient capital, Angkor, is the largest religious monument in the world, Angkor Wat. One creepy-crawly street snack that's sold here—with eight legs!—is called the "Caviar of Cambodia."

Epic Event

The Cow Gets to Choose!

For centuries, Cambodian farmers have chosen what to grow based on the Royal Plowing Ceremony. Seven cows are led to seven golden trays containing rice, corn, seeds, beans, grass, water, and wine. Depending on what they scoff down, the farmer plants his crop.

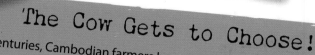

Stilt villages
Houses are sometimes built on 20-ft (6-m) high stilts. In the wet season the water laps at the front door and everyone travels by boat.

Wat's This?

Angkor Wat is a temple complex built for a Khmer king in the 12th century. Construction in the area lasted for 300 years. The palaces and houses were made of wood and rotted away long ago, but more than 100 stone temples still stand in a little patch of jungle that's been cleared. There are many more still covered with vines. Nearby Angkor Thom was the setting for *Lara Croft: Tomb Raider*.

Funky Food

Fried Spiders

If you suffer from arachnophobia, you might not like this snack. These aren't tiny little spiders, they're great big tarantulas that are fried whole—legs, fangs, and all. Crisp on the outside and gooey inside!

MALAYSIA
★ Kuala Lumpur

★ Official language: Bahasa Malaysia
★ Population: 25,715,819
★ Currency: Ringgits
★ Area: 127,355 sq miles (329,847 sq km)

Tallest Twins

Kuala Lumpur's Petronas Twin Towers were the world's tallest buildings from 1998 to 2004, and they are still the tallest twin towers. In 2010 Burj Khalifa in the United Arab Emirates (see page 153) took the honor of the tallest building.

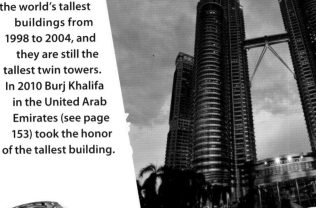

Malay lacewing butterfly

HELO (hell oh)

Malaysia can seem like two separate countries. The mainland peninsula of western Malaysia is a land of tall towers and modern cities. On the island of Borneo, orange-haired orangutans still survive in the mountain forest. Not so long ago the tribal people lived in longhouses and shot their enemies with poisoned darts—then cut their heads off, shrunk them over a fire, and put them on sticks as a warning to other enemies!

Poison pipes

The Penan tribe used blowpipes for hunting. The hollow pipe could be up to 6ft (2m) long and the darts were sometimes dipped in poison.

Amazing Animal

Borneo is famous for its wild orangutans. The Malaysian noticed the similarity between humans and orangutans and named them because of it: the word *orang* means "man," while *utan* means "forest." These great apes use tools and make cozy beds at night from branches and leaves.

World's Smelliest

Hold Your Nose

Rafflesia is the largest flower in the world and is found in the rain forest here. It can grow to 3ft (1m) wide and weigh up to 22 lb (10kg) but has no stem or leaves. The flower is famous for another, more horrible, reason—its nickname is "corpse flower" or "meat flower" because it smells like rotting flesh. This foul smell attracts plenty of flies to it.

No fighting with your neighbors

Traditionally in Borneo, a whole village of up to 200 families could live together in one building called a "longhouse."

Point with your thumb, never your finger.

Funky Food

This large, heavy fruit has spines and drops from the tree when ripe, so don't sit under a durian tree! Its smell is strong, even before it's cut open. Most people here love it, but others (especially tourists) find durian's smell so disgusting that it is banned in some hotels and on public transportation.

BRUNEI
★ Bandar Seri Begawan

★ Official language: Malay
★ Population: 388,190
★ Currency: Bruneian dollars
★ Area: 2,226 sq miles (5,765 sq km)

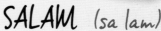

SALAM (sa lam)

Brunei is famous for its super-rich ruler, pristine rain forest, and villages on stilts. The Sultan of Brunei could drive a different car to work every day and it would still take him more than four years to get through the contents of his garage. This tiny country on the island of Borneo is completely surrounded by Malaysia, but centuries ago, before the Dutch arrived, it owned a huge rich empire. The capital of Brunei has such a long name that the locals just use its initials: BSB.

No competition This mosque was built in 1958 by Brunei's 28th sultan, Omar Ali Saifuddien. Its tallest minaret is 144ft (44m) high and no building is allowed to be taller. A nearby bank had to have its top floor removed for being too high.

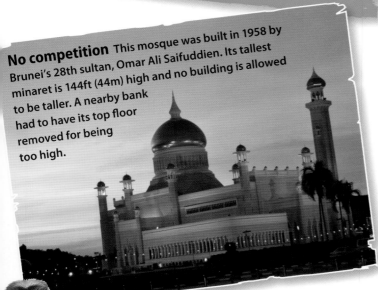

Are you looking at my nose? Proboscis monkeys, with their large noses, live in the swampy rain forest here. They live in colonies of about 20 members, with one male for approximately 12 females, plus juveniles.

Which Bathroom to Use?

The Sultan of Brunei is a very rich man. He owns the world's largest lived-in palace (in fact, it is the world's largest private home), which has 1,788 rooms, including 257 bathrooms. The banqueting hall can fit 4,000 people for dinner, so let's hope he has many friends.

Taxi! Many of the people of Brunei live in stilt villages over the water. They travel to and from their homes in water taxis.

Crazy Fact

What do you give the man who has everything? A new car, of course. The Sultan of Brunei collects cars: he reportedly owns 983 Mercedes-Benzes, 230 Rolls-Royces, and 325 Ferraris.

SINGAPORE
★ Singapore

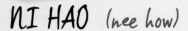

★ Official languages:
  Mandarin Chinese,
  Malay, Tamil, English
★ Population: 4,657,542
★ Currency: Singapore
  dollars
★ Area: 269 sq miles
  (697 sq km)

Sit back and relax If you're feeling really lazy, get a nice gentleman to pedal you around. Rickshaws were invented around 1868.

NI HAO (nee how)

Singapura means "Lion City," which is odd because lions never lived here! Tigers did though, at least until the 1920s, when local legend says the last one was shot under the pool table at the city's famous Raffles Hotel. Many things here are named after Sir Stamford Raffles, the British founder of Singapore. This city-state (the whole country is one city, like Vatican City, see page 59) is famous for its shopping, clean streets, and a dish of noodles you won't find here.

Singapore noodles?
In many Chinese restaurants around the world, you can eat a spicy noodle dish with curry powder called "Singapore noodles." But not in Singapore!

Crazy Fact

Feeling Like a Merlion?
Singapore's Merlion mascot has a lion's head on a fish's body. This isn't an ancient symbol—it was invented by Singapore's tourist board in 1964. Some young Singaporeans now say "I'm going to do a Merlion," when they're feeling sick—because of the water gushing out of the Merlion's mouth.

Where's the nutmeg tree? Singapore was once a little fishing village and, just 80 years ago, its famous shopping street, Orchard Road, really was the path that led to the fields of nutmeg, pepper, and fruit trees.

TOP 5
Things You Won't Find in Singapore
1. Chewing gum (illegal)
2. Graffiti (illegal)
3. Spitting in public (illegal)
4. Litter (illegal)
5. Traffic jams (so rare they make headline news)

No Nails Needed
The Thian Hock Keng Temple was built in the 1840s by Chinese immigrants. They dedicated it to the goddess of the sea for letting them arrive safely in Singapore. The whole building was made without using any nails...and it doesn't look as if it's going to fall down any time soon!

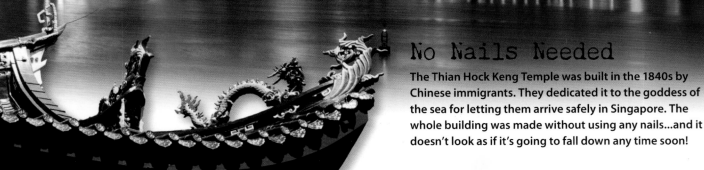

Funky Food
Mangosteens

England's Queen Victoria loved this fruit. She even offered a reward to anyone who could carry some back to England for her so quickly that they didn't turn bad on the way.

Cup of cat's poo, anyone?

Kopie luwak is the rarest, most expensive coffee in the world. But it's made from the poo of a cat called the *luwak*. The *luwak* eats ripe coffee beans but can't digest them. So, out they come again!

Set your worries free

A sky lantern is made of bamboo and rice paper with a little candle inside. The candle flame heats the air in the lantern and it floats up. It's good luck to release sky lanterns—they symbolize all your problems and worries floating away.

INDONESIA
★ Jakarta

- ★ Official language: Bahasa Indonesia
- ★ Population: 240,271,522
- ★ Currency: Indonesian rupiah
- ★ Area: 735,358 sq miles (1,904,569 sq km)

SELAMAT SIANG (se la mat see ahng)

This is the world's biggest "archipelago nation"—many islands making one country. Indonesia has 17,000 islands, with people living on 6,000 of them. This land also has 129 active volcanoes and in 1815 the eruption of Mt. Tambora was the biggest in modern history—its ash caused a volcanic winter so bad that in 1816 Europe had a "year without a summer." In 1912 the longest snake ever seen (33ft/10m) was shot here, but the Komodo dragon still roams free.

Shadowy stuff These leather shadow puppets are moved by a puppeteer (*dalang*), who sits behind a screen. Most of the audience watch the show but some sit with the *dalang* to watch his skill.

Amazing Animal
Danger Dragon!

Giant Komodo dragons can grow 9ft (3m) long and weigh 150lb (70kg) although, sadly, they don't breathe fire! This is the world's largest living lizard, and it's a meat-eater, so watch out! The Komodo is top dog on its island, but even at the Los Angeles Zoo, one attacked a VIP guest who was on a private tour.

Balinese Dance

The island of Bali is part of Indonesia. Here dancing is taken very seriously and even five-year-old girls can represent their village in the *legong* dance.

EAST TIMOR
★ Dili

★ Official languages: Tetun, Portuguese, Indonesian, English
★ Population: 1,131,612
★ Currency: US dollars
★ Area: 5,792 sq miles (15,000 sq km)

What's in a Name?

According to local legend, this land was once a great crocodile. Centuries ago sea merchants, looking for somewhere to land their boats, spotted it in the mist and gave it the name "Land of the Sleeping Crocodile."

OLA (oh la)

This "Land of the Sleeping Crocodile" is made of limestone and rose up out of the sea 4 million years ago. It's still rising a tiny 0.1in (3mm) every year. From the 16th century until 1975, this land was (yet another!) Portuguese colony, but when the Portuguese left, the Indonesians moved in. Tiny East Timor has only been independent since 2002. The people here have a tradition of carving and coffee-growing, and if you see someone who looks like a vampire, don't panic!

Sacred house These little stilt houses are scattered around the countryside. They are called *uma lulik* and were built to hold the village's heirlooms.

Scary Stuff

Blood-red Teeth

No, she isn't another Count Dracula—she's just an East Timorese lady chewing betel nut (*pinang*). The nut makes a blood-red stain over the teeth and gums, which sometimes runs down the chin. It "relaxes" the chewer (but maybe not the people watching).

Peaceful Peak

Mt. Ramelau is East Timor's highest mountain at 9,724ft (2,964m). A 9-ft (3-m) statue of the Virgin Mary stands on the peak of the mountain. She came all the way from Italy and was put up here in 1997.

Time to celebrate
After being ruled over by the Portuguese and Indonesians, the East Timorese celebrated their independence in 2002.

Hideous History

Between 1975, when the Portuguese left and the Indonesian army arrived, and 1979, East Timor lost one third of its people to starvation, disease, and war. The Indonesians stayed here until 1999, and when they did finally leave, they destroyed most of the country as they went.

MAY PEACE PREVAIL ON EARTH

ASIA

PHILIPPINES
★Manila

The Chocolate Hills

More than 1,775 hills look like perfect mounds of chocolate across the countryside (they're really limestone covered in grass, which turns brown in the dry season). Legend says they were piles of poo made by a greedy giant who had to lose weight to win the love of a beautiful woman.

Ginger root

★ Official languages: Filipino
★ Population: 97,976,603
★ Currency: Philippine pesos
★ Area: 115,831 sq miles (300,000 sq km)

Batanes Islands · Philippine Sea · South China Sea · Manila · Legazpi · Puerto Princesa · Cebu · Zamboanga · Davao · MALAYSIA

Tinkling The national dance imitates long-legged *tikling* birds dodging bamboo traps set by rice farmers. The dancers weave their feet between bamboo poles.

KAMUSTA (com moo sta)

This is a tricky place for bad spellers: the Philippines is the country, but its people are the Filipinos. This land is made up of 7,107 islands, and in the waters off Gato Island thousands of sea snakes writhe and breed. Beware the Aswang, a legendary monster who's half-vampire, half-witch and steals children from their beds, leaving twigs in their place. Here you can dance like a bird or text with the best, and you'll always know when this country's at war—it flies its flag upside down!

The Philippines is nicknamed the "Text Capital of the World." About 400 million text messages are sent every day here. Lots of Filipinos don't even use their phones for making calls, just for sending text messages!

Beep, Beep, Jeep!

These colorful "jeepneys" are used as buses in the Philippines. They are rebuilt American military jeeps that were left here after World War II.

Balut eggs are a popular snack sold from carts on the side of the road, just like hot dogs in the USA... only not quite. You'll certainly be surprised when you crack open this egg! The egg is boiled just before it's due to hatch. So you get to eat the egg and the baby chick at the same time.

Tiny tarsier At 3.3in (8.5cm), the tarsier is one of the smallest primates.

183

TAIWAN
★ Taipei

Everyone together In the very early morning here, huge groups of people do their *t'ai chi* exercises together in city parks.

East China Sea

Taipei

Changhua · Hualien

Makung

Kaohsiung

South China Sea

★ Official language: Mandarin Chinese
★ Population: 22,974,347
★ Currency: New Taiwan dollars
★ Area: 13,892 sq miles (35,980 sq km)

Not-So-Epic Event

The "French Spiderman"

Taipei 101 was the world's tallest building until Burj Khalifa opened (see page 153). Alain Robert is famous for climbing the world's highest buildings, usually without ropes. He scaled Taipei 101 in December 2004, just before its grand opening. The 1,667-ft (508-m) climb was legal, but heavy rain meant it took him four hours instead of two.

A long, long, long way to go...

NI HAO (knee how)

Taiwan, with its mountains and hot springs, is also called *Ilha Formosa*, meaning "Beautiful Island." It was christened in 1544 by the Portuguese sailors who were the first Europeans to see it. This island lies off the southeast coast of China and is potato-shaped, so the locals call themselves the rather less-beautiful-sounding "Children of the Sweet Potato." In Taiwan red is the color of good luck, white is the color of death, and the number 4 is very unlucky.

TAIWAN'S TOP 5
Amazing Animals

1. Black bears
2. Pangolins (these look prehistoric!)
3. Flying foxes
4. Flying frogs
5. Salamanders

Funky Food

Bubble Tea (*boba*) is made with milk and tapioca pearls and was invented in Taiwan in the 1980s.

Put on a happy face There are plenty of palm readers in the world, but here you can have the lines on your face read.

Look Up!

In this land some of the most amazing artwork is up on the roof. Colorful carved dragons and lions are often featured.

Same hat, different name This conical straw hat is worn in many lands. The "rice hat," "sedge hat," or "paddy hat" is even shown on road signs.

HONG KONG
★No official capital

Dragon boat racing In Chinese mythology dragons are the rulers of rivers, lakes, and seas.

★ Official languages: Cantonese, English
★ Population: 7,055,071
★ Currency: Hong Kong dollars
★ Area: 426 sq miles (1,104 sq km)

CHINA

New Territories

Kowloon

Hong Kong Island

South China Sea

LEI HAO (lay how)

The streets of Hong Kong are some of the most tightly packed in the world. This was a British colony from the 1840s until 1997, when it was handed back to China. The Queen of England's crown was removed from Hong Kong's stamps, but English is still taught in schools. Here you can eat shredded jellyfish, celebrate with mooncakes, watch dragons race, or buy a new goldfish. Hong Kong possibly has the world's best-dressed dead people.

nky Food

Mooncakes are filled with sesame seeds, lotus seed paste, or salted duck egg and eaten to celebrate the Moon Festival.

Look smart after death
In Hong Kong's funerary stores, paper clothes are sold for dead people. Some have matching watches.

Bang!
Firecrackers were invented by the Chinese to flash, bang, and pop at special occasions.

Amazing Animal

Take your pick At the goldfish market you can buy any fish you want.

Dim sum These little snacks are served with Chinese tea, often for breakfast.

Full Up?

Hong Kong is one of the most densely populated areas of the world. Ap Lei Chau is the world's most densely populated island, with 60,000 people squeezed into every 0.4 sq mile (1 sq km).

CHINA
★Beijing

★ Official language:
  Mandarin Chinese
★ Population:
  1,338,612,968
★ Currency: Renminbi
★ Area: 3,705,407 sq miles
  (9,596,961 sq km)

NI HAO (knee how)

China has the largest population (1.3 billion) of any country—one out of every five people on the planet lives here. But, if you want to be alone, head for the "Pole of Inaccessibility" in China's Dzoosotoyn Elisen Desert—it's farther from the sea (1,645 miles/2,648km) than anywhere else on Earth. Women's feet were once bound for beauty here, the Great Wall was built, and siblings are rare. Chinese tradition says not to save someone's life in case you interfere with their fate.

All alone Are you sick of your pesky little brother or annoying sister? Chinese children don't have to worry about sibling rivalry because the government allows married couples living in cities to have only one child.

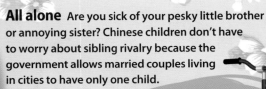
In 1987 there were more than 500 million bicycles here.

Amazing Animal Cuddly Giant?

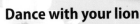

The world's only giant pandas live in the bamboo forests here. There are fewer than 1,600 in the wild, but it's difficult for zoologists to help them increase their numbers because the females can only mate for three days each year.

Terracotta Warriors The Chinese emperor Qin Shi Huang had more than 6,000 life-size clay soldiers made and buried with him to guard his body. It took 700,000 workers 38 years to build his tomb.

Dance with your lion
The lion dance is often performed at Chinese New Year.

7 ONE OF THE NEW WONDER OF THE WORLD

Greatest thing? The Great Wall of China is the longest structure ever built on Earth. It is 2,150 miles (3,460km) long and was built along the border of Inner Mongolia in 210 BC to keep out invaders from the north. It took many Chinese dynasties to complete it.

Harbin Ice Festival
Ice sculptures are carved from the frozen Songhua River. The festival lasts for one month and then the sculptures are allowed to melt away.

Funky Food How Old?

To make "thousand-year-old eggs," fresh duck, chicken, or quail eggs are buried in a mixture of clay, ash, lime, salt, and rice for weeks or even months. The eggs turn black and give off a strong smell of sulfur (like bad eggs) and ammonia (like urine). These are a delicacy in China.

Eagle eyes The nomads here still train eagles to hunt for them. They keep their eagle for seven years, then set it free again.

MONGOLIA
★ Ulaanbaatar

★ Official language: Mongolian
★ Population: 3,041,142
★ Currency: Tögrög
★ Area: 603,909 sq miles (1,564,116 sq km)

Egg hunt Fossilized dinosaur bones and nests of eggs can be found lying around on the surface of the Gobi desert. They were first discovered in the 1920s by American explorer Roy Chapman Andrews, whose adventures are thought to have inspired the Indiana Jones movies.

SAIN UU (say noo)

Mongolia was once called "Outer Mongolia," making it sound very remote! This country is most famous for the fierce leader of its nomadic peoples: Genghis Khan. He was born in Outer Mongolia, although the Chinese, Koreans, and Japanese all try to claim him as their own. In the Gobi desert you might find a nest of fossilized dinosaur eggs, a two-humped camel, or a gerbil—yes, this is where those cute pets hang out when they're not runnning on a wheel in a hutch.

Amazing Animal

Snowy Cats

One quarter of all the world's rare snow leopards live in Mongolia. A snow leopard can leap 50ft (15m) and jump 20ft (6m) straight up—but, bizarrely, it cannot purr or roar.

Hero or Horror?

The nomadic Mongols were led by Genghis Khan. Europeans think of him as a bloodthirsty tyrant but Asian nations see him as a hero. This 131-ft (40-m) statue of Genghis Khan, located near Mongolia's capital, sits on the world's biggest statue of a horse.

World's Coldest

Ulaanbaatar is the world's coldest capital city. This was once a truly nomadic city—it used to move three times a year! Ulaanbaatar means "red hero."

Wacky race The Mongol Car Rally starts in London and ends in Ulaanbaatar. The 10,000-mile (16,000-km) race has cars, taxis, fire engines, and ice-cream vans!

There are 13 horses for every person in this country.

Extreme bactrian The two-humped camel can survive temperatures from −58°F (−50°C) to more than 122°F (50°C).

NORTH KOREA
★ Pyongyang

CHINA
Chongjin
• Kanggye
• Sinuiju
Sea of Japan
✪ Pyongyang
Kaesong
SOUTH KOREA

★ Official language: Korean
★ Population: 22,665,345
★ Currency: North Korean won
★ Area: 46,540 sq miles (120,538 sq km)

Epic Event

In 1950 North Korea invaded South Korea and the Korean War started. The USA and other nations came into battle to help South Korea, while China fought with North Korea. The two countries still aren't friendly neighbors. Soldiers guard the concrete wall that marks the boundary between North and South Korea.

AHN NYEONG (on nyoung)

Welcome to the "Hermit Kingdom," the world's most secretive country. The land of Korea was split into two countries (North and South) after World War II. The two halves went to war in 1950 and are still great enemies. North Korea is known for its military strength and its mass games, when hundreds of thousands of dancers and gymnasts perform together. It's also famous for its everlasting leader, who still rules the country, even though he's dead!

Military might
The Korean People's Army is part of the government here. North Korea is the most "militarized" country in the world...which means it has a lot of soldiers and weapons.

Stamp of celebration
The founding of this country in 1948 is often celebrated by its government.

Quite a personality
The leader of North Korea since 1945 is Kim Il-sung. Even though he died in 1994, he is still president! He was given the title "Eternal President" although his son, Kim Jong-il, now runs the country. North Koreans are often told that Kim Il-sung "created the world" and his son "controls the weather."

Crazy Fact

Tower of Years
The Juche Tower was built in 1982 to commemorate Kim Il-sung's 70th birthday. The tall spire contains 25,550 blocks (70 x 365)—one for each day of his life up until then.

Mass Games

To celebrate special occasions, large groups perform dances or gymnastics together to show teamwork and "strength in unity." Around 100,000 people often take part. Imagine how much practice that takes!

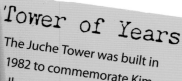

Switch off now! South Koreans love technology, which makes Seoul a lively city. But that's not always good for everyone. A 28-year-old man from Seoul died while playing video games. He had been playing for 50 hours.

SOUTH KOREA
★Seoul

★ Official language: Korean
★ Population: 48,508,972
★ Currency: South Korean won
★ Area: 38,502 sq miles (99,720 sq km)

Korean Ginseng

Ginseng is believed to bring health, energy, and wisdom and South Korea's ginseng is supposed to be the best in the world. You can buy it raw, peeled, shaved, sliced, honeyed, wind-dried, skewered, steamed, or bottled as wine.

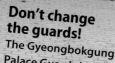

AHN NYEONG (on nyoung)

South Korea's fast-moving, buzzing capital, Seoul, is one of the world's biggest cities. These people love technology—but it's not always good for their health! In the countryside are snow-covered mountains, old men made of stone, rice paddies, and fishing villages (where any octopus with good sense stays well hidden). And, if you can't see over your garden wall, the women of South Korea have come up with a good idea to get you airborne.

Don't change the guards! The Gyeongbokgung Palace Guards have protected the palace gates since 1469.

Crazy Fact

Into the Sky

Neolttwigi is a game for Korean girls that sounds like fun. A girl stands on either end of a seesaw and one jumps so that the other flies up into the air. It's said that Korean women invented *neolttwigi* so they could see over the high walls around their homes—back in the days women were only allowed out of their living compounds at night.

Sticky stuff Octopus is often cooked before being served but *sannakji*, live octopus, is also eaten here. The octopus is quickly cut into pieces, seasoned, and served squirming on the plate. It sometimes sticks to the roof of your mouth...

Stone Grandfathers

Stone *dol hareubang* are believed to protect villages from evil. They're carved with bulging eyes, large stumpy noses, and slight smiles, and have their hands resting on plump bellies. Is that like your grandfather?

JAPAN
★ Tokyo

★ Official language: Japanese
★ Population: 127,078,679
★ Currency: Yen
★ Area: 145,914 sq miles (377,915 sq km)

KONNICHIWA (kon nee chee wah)

Tokyo is the world's most populated city and the people here are used to not having much space. Some hotel rooms are just beds in little capsules, and if you take the train at rush hour, be prepared to be squashed in like a sardine. Japan has many volcanoes—the most famous is snow-capped Mt. Fuji, which last erupted in 1707. A favorite food here is sushi, but if you find puffer fish on the menu, make sure there's a good chef in the kitchen.

Amazing Animal

Japanese macaques live farther north than any other primates apart from humans. These are clever monkeys—in the freezing Japanese winter, they bathe in hot springs. And for fun, they throw snowballs at each other!

Perfect paper The traditional art of folding paper to make models is called *origami*—from *kami,* the Japanese word for "paper." These figures of birds, animals, and people can have hundreds of intricate folds.

Squeeze In

Tokyo is home to around 13 million people. So many workers cram into the city's trains that special guards called "pushers" pack them in and get the doors shut.

Ancient flower arrangers? Samurai warriors were Japan's fighting knights. They were trained in fencing, wrestling, archery, and acrobatics and wore huge horned helmets— more to scare their enemies than protect themselves. However terrifying they looked, they also took lessons in painting, poetry, and flower-arranging!

Scary Stuff

Puffer fish

Chefs have to be careful with this Japanese food or diners might end up in the cemetery. The deadly puffer fish, or *fugu*, is the ultimate delicacy in Japan, even though its skin and insides are more poisonous than cyanide. Only expert chefs are allowed to prepare puffer fish.

The bigger, the better! Sumo wrestlers are known for their skill and strength... and their big bottoms!

Comic business Manga cartoons aren't just for children—science, history, romance, and business books are published in this style.

PALAU
★ Melekeok

What a dive! Palau has some of the richest varieties of sea life in the world, making it a brilliant place to dive or snorkel.

★ Official languages: English, Palauan
★ Population: 21,093
★ Currency: US dollars
★ Area: 191 sq miles (494 sq km)

ALII (ah lee)

Palau is like an adventure playground. This small nation has more than 500 islands—but only nine of them have people living on them. There's lots to explore, both on land and in the big blue sea. The islands are thick with trees that hide secret waterfalls, beautiful birds, and walking trails. Under the water you'll find a magical world of caves, shipwrecks, coral gardens, and even giant clams. Some of these colorful clams are even heavier than two big, fat men!

Telling stories Before they had pens and paper, people from Palau recorded their myths and legends on wooden storyboards.

Scary Stuff

Rumbles in the Jungle

Palau is a peaceful place today, but terrible battles were fought here in World War II and many people died. If you're stomping through the jungle, be careful where you walk—you might encounter an old bomb or sea mine and go KABOOM! Better take a good map, too, because the jungle is so thick it's easy to get lost. And look out for those jungle swamps—they might be full of grinning crocodiles...snap!

Shark Friends

Palau created the world's first shark sanctuary in 2009, protecting about 232,000 sq miles (600,000 sq km) of ocean from shark fishing.

Squishy If you've ever had a bath in custard, you'll know what it feels like to swim in Jellyfish Lake, which is home to millions of soft, blubbery, pale pink jellyfish. Luckily they don't have stingers.

Not-So-Epic Event

Let's Face Up

No one knows where the ancient stone monoliths and faces on the large island of Babeldaob came from.

PAPUA NEW GUINEA
★ Port Moresby

* ★ Official language: English
* ★ Population: 6,250,000
* ★ Currency: Kinas
* ★ Area: 178,704 sq miles (462,840 sq km)

Party time In July tribes from all over the country enjoy a three-day mask festival. Papua New Guinea is the place for a face.

GUDE (goo day)

There are more ways to say "hello" in Papua New Guinea than in any other place on the whole planet. Can you believe about 850 different languages are spoken here, and that there are more than 700 tribes of people? This is a land of steep mountains, hot jungles, and colorful birds and coral reefs. It is also a face-painting paradise—if you colored your cheeks red, your lips yellow, and put blue dots over your face, you would fit right in.

World's Largest | Widest Wingspan

The Queen Alexandra's birdwing butterfly flutters only in Papua New Guinea. It is the largest butterfly in the world. Its wingspan is a whopping 12in (30cm). One of the world's biggest moths can be found in Papua New Guinea, too. It isn't called Giant Hercules for nothing—its wingspan is also a massive 12in (30cm).

30cm (12in)

Lost World?

Papua New Guinea is one of Earth's least-explored places. Biologists believe many plant and animal species there are yet to be discovered.

Lofty living Have you ever stood on stilts? Well, houses in Papua New Guinea do. This helps the air flow underneath the houses, keeping them cool.

PAPUA NEW GUINEA'S TOP 4 Weirdest Critters

1. Bizarre spike-nosed tree frog
2. Huge tame woolly rat
3. Yellow-eyed, gargoyle-like gecko
4. Tiny forest wallaby (the smallest in the kangaroo family)

Spike-nosed tree frog

Hideous History

Feed Me the Facts

Cannibalism is the practice of eating human flesh. It was only banned in Papua New Guinea as recently as the 1950s!

AUSTRALIA
★Canberra

AUSTRALIA'S TOP 10
Deadliest Creatures

1. Box jellyfish
2. Irukandji jellyfish
3. Saltwater crocodile
4. Blue-ringed octopus
5. Stonefish
6. Red-back spider
7. Brown snake
8. Tiger snake
9. Great white shark
10. Funnel-web spider

Red-back spider
This deadly little spider loves lurking in nooks and crannies. In the old days, some even hid under backyard toilet seats—eek!

★ Official language: English
★ Population: 21,007,310
★ Currency: Australian dollars
★ Area: 2,967,909 sq miles (7,686,850 sq km)

G'DAY (gid day)

Welcome to the "Land Down Under." It gets this name because the whole country sits south of the equator. Some people call Aussie-land the world's smallest continent; others say it is the world's largest island. It's certainly big and flat, with a huge desert in the middle. If you went walkabout here, you would see the world's largest rock, the largest group of coral reefs, and the largest cattle station. You would also get a big dose of sun and fun if you went surfing at its 7,000 beaches!

Great white shark This mighty predator can grow up to 20ft (6m) long, weigh 4,400lb (2,000kg) and swim 43mph (70km/h).

Scary Stuff

One-way Ticket

Long ago Australia had different kinds of birds—jailbirds! In 1787 the UK started to send prisoners from its overcrowded jails to Australia. Back then, stealing got you a one-way ticket on a convict ship. Most prisoners were jailed for 7 or 14 years.

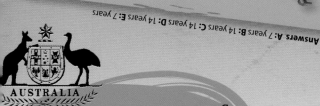

Guess the time to the stealing crime:

A. 1 loaf of bread
B. 1 silver spoon
C. 4 geese and 11 ducks
D. 1 pair of shoes, 1 hat, and 2 handkerchiefs
E. 1 bucket

Answers A: 7 years B: 14 years C: 14 years D: 14 years E: 7 years

Miles of tiles
Sydney Opera House:
• 1,000 rooms
• 20,000 light fittings
• 1 organ with 10,000 pipes
• 1,057,000 glossy, white roof tiles (all self-cleaning!)

AUSTRALIA

The Australian coat of arms has a kangaroo and an emu on it. These animals are famous for something else, too. Neither of them can walk backward!

NEXT 10 KM

Uluru (oo loo roo)
aka Ayers Rock

NEW ZEALAND
★ Wellington

★ Official languages: English, Maori, Sign Language
★ Population: 4,315,800
★ Currency: New Zealand dollars
★ Area: 103,738 sq miles (268,680 sq km)

Old geysers Near Rotorua (ro to roo ah), the inside of Earth is trying to burst out. At Whakarewarewa (fuk ar ray wa ray wa) Thermal Valley, mud boils and water spurts out of the ground, high into the air.

KIA ORA (kee ora)

A country with two main islands, New Zealand is known as the "Shaky Isles" because it has an average 365 earthquakes a year—one a day! The local Maori (mow ree) people call the country Aotearoa, which means 'Land of the Long White Cloud'. Maori came from eastern Polynesia, in the Pacific Ocean. New Zealand has a famous rugby team, the All Blacks, and a basketball team called the Tall Blacks.

Scary Stuff

Many Maori have face and body tattoos, called *tā moko*, which are like a passport showing their family ties. In the old days these tattoos were made using chisels (OUCH!), but now needles are often used (also ouch!).

Little green men

A tiki is a Maori charm carved out of a rock called *pounamu*, or greenstone. It is worn on necklaces.

Leap of Faith

Who'd be crazy enough to jump off a bridge tied to a rubber band? That's what Alan Hackett did in Auckland in 1986—the world's first modern bungee jump. Now thousands of people do it all around the world. People in Vanuatu have been "land diving" for centuries (see page 195).

There are 12 sheep for every person in New Zealand!

Amazing Animals

There are five species of kiwi in New Zealand: the great spotted kiwi, the little spotted kiwi, the rowi, the tokoeka, and the North Island brown kiwi. None of these birds can fly!

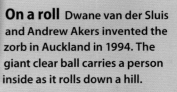

On a roll Dwane van der Sluis and Andrew Akers invented the zorb in Auckland in 1994. The giant clear ball carries a person inside as it rolls down a hill.

VANUATU
★ Port Vila

Land diving While many boys play sports on Saturdays, boys on Pentecost Island jump off 98-ft (30-m) wooden towers with only a vine attached to their leg! Villagers dance and stomp feet while the boys leap. It's a bit like bungee jumping (see page 194) and helps celebrate the yam harvest.

★ Official languages: Bislama, English, French
★ Population: 212,000
★ Currency: Vatus
★ Area: 4,710 sq miles (12,200 sq km)

ALO (al oh)

Vanuatu is made up of 83 islands, with thick forests, white and black sandy beaches, and thousands of sea creatures. It lies on the Pacific Ring of Fire, so it has plenty of volcanoes. More than 100 local languages are spoken here. Many people still live in thatched hut villages and grow food in tiny gardens, deep in the jungle. Some tribes still wear grass skirts and believe in black magic. Pigs are highly valued, and are traded and given as gifts. Their tusks are made into bracelets.

Sky high You can climb up to the rim of Mt. Yasur volcano and peer into its fiery insides.

deous History

Resident birdie The only kind of swallow on Vanuatu, Pacific swallows build their cuplike mud nests under cliff ledges and overhangs.

Cannibal Kitchen

People here used to be cannibals—the last known person was eaten in 1969! They would dig a hole, put in hot stones, then put the chopped-up person on top. They'd add vegetables for a healthy meal, then cover it up with banana leaves, and cook for a few hours. The chief ate the person's head. Crunchy!

Island magic Ambrym Island is famous for its wood carvings, but it's also the home of black magic and sorcery, and a mysterious *rom* dance in which participants wear masks 3ft (1m) high.

Nemo Found!

Remember the cute little clownfish from the 2003 movie *Finding Nemo*? If you go snorkeling in Vanuatu, you might just find him hiding in the colorful coral.

SOLOMON ISLANDS
★Honiara

★ Official language: English
★ Population: 581,318
★ Currency: Solomon Islands dollars
★ Area: 10,985 sq miles (28,450 sq km)

In the 1800s, sailors from "blackbirding" ships stole people from the islands and made them work on big sugar plantations in Queensland, Australia, and Fiji.

Money bites Solomon Islanders used dogs' teeth for money until the 20th century.

HALO (al oh)

The Solomon Islands are a group of nearly 1,000 islands, in which about 70 languages are spoken. Many of these islands are small and remote. On some islands, shells and red feathers are still used as money. Fishing is an important part of life, and the rich sea life brings in visitors who enjoy activities such as snorkeling, scuba diving, big game fishing, surfing, and kayaking. Others like relaxing on its lovely beaches. Soccer, rugby, and beach soccer are popular sports among the locals.

War scars Among the coral reefs around the Solomon Islands, divers can explore hundreds of sunken planes and ships—submerged wrecks left behind from World War II.

Say What?

You'll hear about 70 native languages in the Solomon Islands, with pijin being the day-to-day one.

Here are five pijin sayings:

Aftanun ol'ta! Good afternoon everyone!

Wanem nao datwan? What is that one?

No wariwari. Hem oraet nomoa. No worries. It is all right (no more).

Diswan hem bagarap. This (thing) is broken.

On air Some remote islands don't get TV signals, so radio is the best way to catch up on news.

Smoky pokey Many of the Solomon Islands were formed by old volcanoes. Some volcanoes in the area poke straight out of the sea, like this one.

Head start Solomon Islanders were once feared as cannibals (human flesh-eaters) and head-hunters. Ancient head-hunters entombed the skulls of their victims on Kundu Hite (Skull Island).

Every Person Counts

Epic Event

Nauru's favorite public holiday is Angam Day (October 26), which celebrates the time when the island's population reached 1,500—the minimum number of people it needs to survive.

★ Official language: Nauruan
★ Population: 13,770
★ Currency: Australian dollars
★ Area: 8 sq miles (21 sq km)

Phosphate Stockpile

Parliament House

Government House

PACIFIC OCEAN

Lost riches Nauru is an island built on bird poo. This poo, or phosphate, was used in fertilizers and was mined between the early 1900s and the late 1980s. Now it's all gone and nothing much grows on the island.

EKAMAWIR OMO (e kam a weer o mo)

Tiny Nauru has a land size of just 8 sq miles (21 sq km), making it the world's smallest island nation. It sits just south of the equator, and its name is believed to mean "I go to the beach." It is so small it doesn't have a capital city. The island's flag has a white star with 12 points—one for each of its 12 original tribes. Many big fish, such as barracuda, marlin, and tuna, live in the clear blue sea around Nauru. Pandanus trees, coconuts, pineapples, and bananas grow on the island.

Money laundering All that bird poo made Nauru very rich for a while, but it lost much of its money through some bad investments. To make more cash, it became a place where criminals could hide their illegal profits.

About 40% of Nauru's population has type 2 diabetes (a blood sugar disease)—more than any other nation.

Hideous History

Between 1878 and 1888, 12 native tribes fought the Nauruan Tribal War. By the end of the war, one third of the population (about 500 people) had died.

Dressing up On special occasions people like to wear more traditional outfits, such as these grass skirts, made from pandanus palm leaves.

Taking terns Islanders catch birds called noddy terns with lassos as they fly in from feeding at sea. The noddy is then killed, plucked, cleaned, cooked, and eaten. Yum!

Weighty Wonders

Nauruans are excellent weightlifters. They have won medals for the sport in every Commonwealth Games since 1990.

FEDERATED STATES OF MICRONESIA
★Palikir

★ Official languages: English, State Languages
★ Population: 107,665
★ Currency: US dollars
★ Area: 271 sq miles (702 sq km)

HELLO (hal oh)

Spread over 1 million sq miles (2.6 million sq km), the Federated States of Micronesia is a group of 607 islands in the western Pacific Ocean. If you go visiting, don't be scared if you see people with red teeth—they like to munch on betel nuts, which makes their mouths red! They also eat lots of seafood, breadfruit, and yams. The pirate Bully Hayes was shipwrecked on the island of Kosrae in 1874 and may have buried his treasure there. No one has found it yet!

Cold hard cash People on the island of Yap earn big money—some of it up to 13ft (4m) across! The money disks are made of stone and have a hole in the middle. Luckily all the islanders know who owns each piece, so they don't have to carry it around.

Crazy Fact

What Are You Wearing?
Micronesians tried to ban wearing baseball caps, ties, and T-shirts on the islands. They wanted to keep their old ways alive.

Epic Event

Ghost Fleet
In World War II, Americans bombed Japanese forces in Chuuk Lagoon, sending 60 ships and 275 airplanes to the bottom. They are still there today.

What's Down There?
• Human remains • Fighter planes • Tanks • Bombs
• Bulldozers • Motorcycles

History mystery Nan Madol is a ruined city off the island of Pohnpei. It has small man-made islands linked by canals, and is called the "Venice of the Pacific," after Venice, Italy (see page 57), which is famous for its canals.

Coming clean Every day hundreds of giant manta rays glide into M'il Channel and Manta Ray Bay, where wrasse fish clean them of pesky little parasites.

People on the island of Pohnpei consider dog a delicacy, and sometimes eat it.

Flower power Many of the Marshall Islands' atolls are dotted with beautiful flowers such as flame of the forest, hibiscus, and different colored plumeria.

MARSHALL ISLANDS
★Delap-Uliga-Darrit

★ Official languages: English, Marshallese
★ Population: 63,174
★ Currency: US dollars
★ Area: 70 sq miles (181 sq km)

PACIFIC OCEAN

Bikini Atoll

Kwajalein Atoll

Delap-Uliga-Darrit ○
Majuro Atoll

EXPLODING SWIMWEAR

The bikini was named after Bikini Atoll in the Marshall Islands. The two-piece bathing suit first went on sale in France in 1946, just days after the first atomic test on Bikini Atoll. It was an instant hit.

IOKWE (ee awk way)

The Marshall Islands are named after British sea captain John William Marshall, who sailed by in 1788. Its 29 atolls (coral-ringed lagoons) and five remote islands are divided into two "sunrise" and "sunset" chains. They are part of Micronesia, and are just north of the equator. Local people call the islands *jolet jen Anij*—"gifts from God"—because of the nice climate and rich marine life. Its many World War II wrecks are also popular with scuba divers.

Stick it to them
Until the 1950s Marshall Islanders traveled by canoe between islands using "stick charts," which acted like modern-day maps, showing islands and ocean currents.

Hideous History

What a Blast

The US set off 67 atom bombs in the Marshall Islands between 1946 and 1958. In 1956 the Atomic Energy Commission said the Marshall Islands were "the most contaminated place in the world."

Get Cracking

You wouldn't want to get nipped by a coconut crab. Their massive claws are strong enough to crack open coconut shells! The crabs, which can weigh more than 9lb (4kg), have a leg span of 3ft (1m).

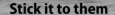

TUVALU
★ Funafuti

Nanumea Atoll

Vaitupu

Nukufetau Atoll
Funafuti Atoll ○ **Funafuti**

SOUTH

PACIFIC

OCEAN

Niulakita

★ Official language:
Tuvaluan
★ Population: 12,177
★ Currency: Tuvaluan
dollars
★ Area: 10 sq miles
(26 sq km)

TALOFA (tah lo fah)

Tuvalu is a group of nine very small islands. Its name means "eight standing together," since one island isn't inhabited. It is the world's least populated nation, except for Vatican City (see page 59). The islands of Tuvalu are only just above sea level, and local people are scared rising sea levels will soon swallow their little islands up and they'll have nowhere to live. They love singing, dancing, and feasting on coconuts, taro, pandanus, bananas, breadfruit, and seafood.

Flatty and Skinny

In most islands of Tuvalu, people believe that the eel and a flat fish called the flounder created Tuvalu. The flounder's flat body became the flat islands; the eel's thin, round body became the coconut trees growing on the islands.

Lovely leaves This girl is wearing a traditional outfit that has been woven by hand, from hand-dyed pandanus leaf strips. Other Tuvalu handcrafts are also popular throughout the Pacific.

Fun time Tuvaluans sure know how to celebrate. Villagers often gather together at a central meeting house (*maneapa*) for days of feasting, dancing, music, and games.

See turtles Green turtles breed in Tuvalu, and hawksbill and leatherback turtles are sometimes seen.

Stamps of approval Tuvalu makes money by selling beautiful coins and stamps, which are popular with collectors.

Sinking Feeling

Tuvalu's highest spot is only 15ft (4.5m) above sea level. It could be one of the first nations to disappear under the waves, thanks to rising sea levels caused by climate change.

Crazy Fact

Web Barons

Tiny Tuvalu sold its little internet suffix—.tv— to a company in California for a huge amount of money: as much as several million dollars a year!

FIJI
★ Suva

Hideous History

In the old days, Fijians killed their enemies and rivals and ate their flesh. One man, Ratu Udre Udre, is said to have eaten 872 people, leaving a big pile of stones for every one he ate. Fijians also fed people to pesky missionaries, who didn't realize what they had eaten!

★ Official languages: English, Fijian
★ Population: 861,000
★ Currency: Fijian dollars
★ Area: 7,066 sq miles (18,300 sq km)

BULA (boo lah)

Fiji was once nicknamed the "Cannibal Isles." In 1789 Captain William Bligh sailed for his life through the islands after a mutiny on HMS *Bounty* (see page 202), with hungry locals in hot pursuit. Fiji is a chain of more than 332 islands and 500 islets and is a popular place for vacations. Fijian men were once feared warriors, but today they relax by sipping *kava*, a muddy brew made from a plant root. Many Indian and Chinese people now also live here. Fijians play a mean game of rugby.

Sea gardens The clear waters off the islands of Fiji are great spots for snorkeling. They are filled with bright coral gardens and zillions of darting fish.

Scary Stuff

That's Hot!

In an ancient ritual on Beqa Island, the Sawau people stroll over a pit of hot stones. Fijian Indians also firewalk to purify themselves—they stick forks into their cheeks, hands, ears, nose, or tongue, then walk over red-hot coals!

Don't fall off Brave (or crazy) surfers from all around the world come to Cloudbreak— a huge offshore wave near Tavarua Island, which smashes onto a razor-sharp coral reef.

Dances with spears The *meke* is a song and dance to loud drumming and stick beating, telling of legends, love, and history. The men wear full warrior costume and do scary spear dances.

Join the Club

A warrior's wooden club was his best friend. After each kill, it was decorated with a human tooth, and gained extra deadly powers.

TONGA
★ Nuku'alofa

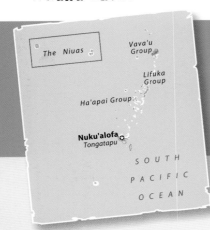

* ★ Official languages: English, Tongan
* ★ Population: 119,009
* ★ Currency: Pa'angas
* ★ Area: 277 sq miles (718 sq km)

No Sail

The mutiny on the HMS *Bounty* occurred off Tonga in 1789, after the ship's crew decided they didn't want to sail anymore. They thought it would be much nicer to laze about in tropical Tahiti (see page 205).

Whoosh!

The Mapu'a 'a Vaca blowholes are geyser-like blowholes that stretch out for about 3 miles (5km) and squirt fountains of seawater high up into the air.

MALO E LELEI (mah low eh leh leh ee)

Known as the "Friendly Islands," Tonga is a kingdom of 176 South Pacific islands. It is ruled by a king, who lives in a royal palace. People here used to wear richly decorated *tapa* cloths, made out of tree bark, and love singing and feasting. Tonga and its neighbor Samoa (see page 203) are only 557 miles (896km) apart by sea, but they have a time difference of 24 hours—if it's Friday in Tonga it will be Saturday in Samoa because they are separated by the International Date Line.

World's Heaviest

In the 1970s Tonga's king, Taufa'ahau Tupou IV, was the heaviest monarch in the world, weighing over 440lb (200kg). When he visited Germany, they made special chairs that would not snap when he sat on them!

Leaping giants Humpback whales come to breed in the warm waters of Ha'apai and Vava'u between June and November.

Eat up Tongan feasts are prepared in an *umu* (underground oven). On the menu you might find taro and sweet potatoes, roasted suckling pig, chicken, corned beef, fish, and shellfish.

Crazy Fact

No Jo

King Taufa'ahau Tupou IV had some stra money-making ideas, helped by his "co jester," Jesse Bogdonoff. The king o wanted to turn Tonga into a nuclear wa dump, and to burn smelly old car tires generate energy. He also kept a Boeing 7 plane in New Zealand that couldn't even f

That's nutty No Pacific paradise is complete without coconuts. Today Tongans are even producing energy from coconuts.

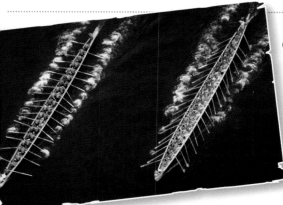

Oar-some Samoans used to get around in longboats, called *fautasi*. Today they have big longboat races, with up to 40 paddlers in each boat!

SAMOA
★Apia

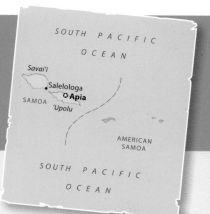

★ Official languages: Samoan, English
★ Population: 186,100
★ Currency: Talas
★ Area: 1,133 sq miles (2,934 sq km)

Flow-on Effect

When Mt. Matavanu erupted last century, lava flowed across the island of Savai'i, burying villages in its path. The lava was more than 328ft (100m) deep in some places.

Ic Event

TALOFA (tah loh fah)

Samoa used to be called Western or German Samoa, so it wouldn't get mixed up with American Samoa, a group of islands to the east. It has nice beaches, waterfalls, and forests. Samoans are very relaxed and friendly and have strong family bonds. A favorite food is *oka* – raw fish, marinated in lime juice and coconut milk. Robert Louis Stevenson, who wrote *Treasure Island* and *The Strange Case of Dr Jekyll and Mr Hyde*, lived in Samoa. His grand old house is now a museum.

Worms rising In October or November, palolo reefworms rise from the coral to mate, and that's when Samoans wade into the lagoons to catch them. The worms look like spaghetti and taste like caviar. Yum!

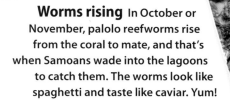

Gimme shelter
You wouldn't have your own room if you lived in a Samoan *fale*. This traditional house has no walls, but you can let down a curtain or two whenever you want a bit of privacy.

Scary Stuff

'To the Point
Samoan tattoos, usually from the waist to the knees, are very elaborate—and getting them done really hurts. It can take up to three months for a tattoo to be completed.

Sit, Slap, Dance
Samoans have many traditional dances. Some involve lots of leaping! There is also a noisy "slap" dance, where people slap themselves—like they're swatting mosquitoes. The *sasa* is a group dance performed sitting down, to beating drums.

KIRIBATI
★ Tarawa

★ Official languages: English, Gilbertese
★ Population: 112,850
★ Currency: Australian dollars
★ Area: 313 sq miles (811 sq km)

Going, Going...Gone!

Two small Kiribati islands, Tebua Tarawa and Abanuea, disappeared underwater in 1999. Luckily no one was living there at the time. More islands will be swallowed by the sea if sea levels keep rising, because the ice in Earth's polar caps is melting.

Flying high The frigatebird is so important to the people of Kiribati that they have it on their flag, and do a special dance that imitates how the bird walks and flies. The bird helps guide home fishermen lost at sea.

MAURI (mor ee)

Kiribati (kee ree buss) is a tiny nation of about 313 sq miles (811 sq km). It sits on the equator and is made up of 33 small coral islands. To get from one island to another, it's best to hop in a very speedy boat, because they're sprinkled over 1.37 million sq miles (3.55 million sq km) of the Pacific Ocean! One island is called Christmas Island, because explorer Captain Cook happened to sail past on Christmas Eve in 1777. Kiribati has plenty of fish and coconut, breadfruit, pandanus, and pawpaw trees.

Our daily bread Who says bread doesn't grow on trees? Breadfruit trees are a good source of food on many Pacific islands.

Oarsome races

The men of Kiribati love their canoes almost as much as they love life. They often test their strength and skill by taking part in canoe races.

War Wrecks

Terrible battles were fought around the islands of Kiribati in World War II. On Tarawa and Butaritari Atoll you can still see big rusted defense guns and solid concrete bunkers. At low tide you can see rusted tanks, shipwrecks, and plane wrecks on the shores.

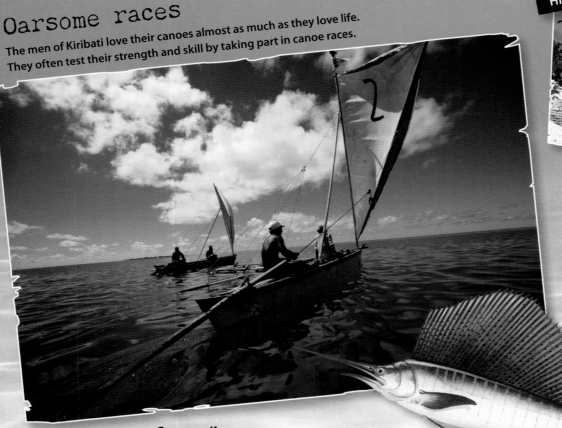

Scary sailors Sailfish use the soaring sail on their back to make themselves look big and scary. They thrash their pointy nose around as a dangerous weapon. The color of their skin can change instantly to confuse their prey.

TAHITI & FRENCH POLYNESIA

★Pape'ete

Pacific Paradise

French Polynesia is famous for its sleepy lagoons, with white sandy beaches, swaying palm trees, and warm aqua-colored waters.

★ Official language: French
★ Population: 245,405
★ Currency: Comptoirs Français du Pacifique francs
★ Area: 1,351 sq miles (3,500 sq km)

IA ORANA (yo rah nah)

The 117 islands of French Polynesia cover an area of the Pacific Ocean as big as the whole of Western Europe. The largest is Tahiti, a volcanic island which has very steep, rugged mountains covered in lush jungle. This region is part of the Pacific Ring of Fire, and has been nicknamed the "Shark Capital of the Pacific." When you go there, they'll put a *lei*—a necklace made of fresh flowers—around your neck, and a flower behind your ear. They also make beautiful necklaces from shells.

Shake those hips The *'ote'a* is a famous fast swaying dance from Tahiti and is also performed by Cook Islanders. It is usually danced by a group of boys and girls, all dressed in Tahitian "grass skirts"—which are not made from grass at all, but tree bark fibers.

Black magic Beautiful natural black pearls are the major export of French Polynesia. They earn the country millions every year.

Electrifying Electra dolphins, also known as pygmy orcas or melon-headed whales, gather in the hundreds at the island of Nuku Hiva. It's quite a sight.

Mutiny!

The 1789 HMS *Bounty* mutiny occurred after the ship's crew spent six splendid months in Tahiti. Some sailed back to Tahiti; others went south to Pitcairn Island, where their descendents still live.

A big impression Famous French painter Paul Gauguin moved to Tahiti in the late 1890s and painted beautiful impressions of life in paradise. He died in 1903.

WORLD MAP

In the alphabetical list below, each country's page number appears in bold, followed by the country's coordinates (the letter and number combination) corresponding to the map's grid. The map is color-coded to match the regions within the book.

ARCTIC OCEAN

SVALBARD

ARCTIC OCEAN

Laptev Sea

East Siberian Sea

Chukchi Sea

Barents Sea

ARCTIC CIRCLE

Bering Strait

Norwegian Sea

RUSSIAN FEDERATION

SWEDEN FINLAND

NORWAY

Sea of Okhotsk

Bering Sea

SCOTLAND
North Sea
DENMARK
ESTONIA
LATVIA
LITHUANIA

IRELAND
ENGLAND
WALES
GERMANY
NETH.
POLAND
BELARUS

Baltic Sea

BELGIUM
LUX.
FRANCE
SWITZ.
CZECH REPUBLIC
SLOVAKIA
AUSTRIA
LIECHT.
SLOVENIA
HUNGARY
UKRAINE

KAZAKHSTAN

MONGOLIA

Sea of Japan (East Sea)

PACIFIC OCEAN

MONACO
SAN MARINO
ITALY
VATICAN CITY
ANDORRA
CROATIA
BOSNIA & HERCEGOVINA
ROMANIA
SERBIA
MONTENEGRO

Black Sea

Caspian Sea

Aral Sea

UZBEKISTAN

KYRGYZSTAN

NORTH KOREA

PORTUGAL
SPAIN
BULGARIA
MACEDONIA
ALBANIA
GREECE
GEORGIA
ARMENIA
AZERBAIJAN
TURKMENISTAN
TAJIKISTAN

SOUTH KOREA
JAPAN

GIBRALTAR
MALTA
TUNISIA
CYPRUS
LEBANON
ISRAEL & THE PALESTINIAN TERRITORIES
SYRIA
IRAQ
IRAN
AFGHANISTAN

TURKEY

CHINA

Yellow Sea

East China Sea

TROPIC OF CANCER

MOROCCO

Mediterranean Sea

JORDAN
KUWAIT
PAKISTAN

TIBET

TAIWAN

ALGERIA
LIBYA
EGYPT

Red Sea

SAUDI ARABIA
BAHRAIN
QATAR
UNITED ARAB EMIRATES
OMAN

NEPAL
BHUTAN

HONG KONG
MACAU

NORTHERN MARIANA ISLANDS

MAURITANIA
MALI
NIGER
CHAD
SUDAN
ERITREA
YEMEN

INDIA
BANGLADESH
UNION OF MYANMAR (BURMA)
LAOS

South China Sea

Philippine Sea

SENEGAL
BURKINA FASO
BENIN
NIGERIA
DJIBOUTI

Gulf of Aden

Bay of Bengal
THAILAND
CAMBODIA
VIETNAM

PHILIPPINES

GUAM

MARSHALL ISLANDS

GUINEA
SIERRA LEONE
CÔTE D'IVOIRE
TOGO
GHANA
CENTRAL AFRICAN REPUBLIC
SOUTH SUDAN
ETHIOPIA

SRI LANKA

BRUNEI

PALAU

FEDERATED STATES OF MICRONESIA

LIBERIA
Gulf of Guinea
EQUATORIAL GUINEA
CAMEROON
GABON
UGANDA
KENYA
SOMALIA

MALDIVES

MALAYSIA
SINGAPORE

Celebes Sea

KIRIBATI

SÃO TOMÉ & PRÍNCIPE
REPUBLIC OF CONGO
DEMOCRATIC REPUBLIC OF CONGO (ZAIRE)
RWANDA
BURUNDI
TANZANIA

SEYCHELLES

DIEGO GARCIA - BRITISH INDIAN OCEAN TERRITORY

INDONESIA

NAURU

EQUATOR

ASCENSION

ANGOLA
ZAMBIA
MALAWI
COMOROS
MAYOTTE

INDIAN OCEAN

EAST TIMOR

PAPUA NEW GUINEA

SOLOMON ISLANDS

TUVALU

TOKELAU

ST HELENA

ZIMBABWE
MOZAMBIQUE
Mozambique Channel
MADAGASCAR
MAURITIUS

WALLIS & FUTUNA
SAMOA

SOUTH ATLANTIC OCEAN

NAMIBIA
BOTSWANA
RÉUNION

Coral Sea
VANUATU

FIJI

NIUE

NEW CALEDONIA

TONGA

SWAZILAND

AUSTRALIA

TROPIC OF CAPRICORN

TRISTAN DA CUNHA

LESOTHO
SOUTH AFRICA

Tasman Sea

NEW ZEALAND

SOUTHERN OCEAN

ANTARCTIC CIRCLE

ANTARCTICA

THE NOT-FOR-PARENTS TRAVEL BOOK
Cool Stuff to Know about Every Country in the World

1st Edition
Published August 2011

Conceived by Weldon Owen in partnership with Lonely Planet
Produced by Weldon Owen Pty Ltd
Ground Floor 42–44 Victoria Street, McMahons Point
Sydney NSW 2060, Australia
weldonowenpublishing.com

Copyright © 2011 Weldon Owen Pty Ltd

WELDON OWEN PTY LTD

Managing Director Kay Scarlett
Publisher Corinne Roberts
Creative Director Sue Burk
Senior Vice President, International Sales Stuart Laurence
Sales Manager, North America Ellen Towell
Administration Manager, International Sales Kristine Ravn

Managing Editor Averil Moffat
Senior Editor Barbara McClenahan
Designer Jacqueline Richards
Images Manager Trucie Henderson
Production Director Todd Rechner
Production and Prepress Controller Mike Crowton
Proofreader Bronwyn Sweeney
Editorial Assistant Natalie Ryan

10 9 8 7 6 5 4 3 2 1

Published by
Lonely Planet Publications Pty Ltd ABN 36 005 607 983
90 Maribyrnong St, Footscray, Victoria 3011, Australia

ISBN 978-1-74220-814-5

text & maps © Lonely Planet Publications Pty Ltd 2011
photos © as indicated 2011

Printed in China

CREDITS

Key tcl=top center left, tl=top left, tc=top center, tcr=top center right, tr=top right, cl=center left, c=center, cr=center right, bcl=bottom center left, bl=bottom left, bc=bottom center, bcr=bottom center right, br=bottom right, bg=background

Front Cover Getty Images bcr; iStockphoto.com tl, tcl, bcl; Shutterstock bl, b, c, tr

Back Cover iStockphoto.com bg, c, cl, bc, bcr; Lonely Planet bcl; NHPA, br; Shutterstock cr, tr

Spine Shutterstock b, bc

Alamy 41tc, 43br, tl, 92bl, 93br, 94cl, 96cl, 98br, tr, 99tcl, 101br, 102bc, 103tl, cr, 106c, 107cl, 108tr, cr, 109cl, 112br, 114tr, 115bl, 118cl

Bigstock 113cl, 126c, 129bc, 132bcr, 140c, 141tl, 154bc, 155bg, 159br, 161tl, 169bg, 171bc, 182cr, 183tl, bl, 190tc

Bridgeman Art Library 157bg, tc, 160tr

Corbis 48bl, tcr, 52cr, 83c, 93bcl, 100tcr, tc, 102tr, 104cr, 110tc, 112c, 114bl, 116c, 128bc, 135tl, 136tc, 138br, 141cl, 150tr, 159bcl, 160bg, 169c, bl, 175tc, 176bl, 187tc, 191bc, 193cl, bg, br, 195tl, cr, 198cr, 201cr, bl, 203tl, cr

Getty Images 11bl, 12c, 63bl, 80cr, 111tl, 113bc, 119cl, 123tc, 124bg, 126tr, 129bg, 134bg, 140cr, br, 149tc, 159c, 172c, 182cl, 184tcr, 192bc, 197cr, br, 199cr, 203c, 205cr

iStockphoto.com 6bcr, br, cr, tc, tcr, tr, 7bc, bcl, bg, c, tc, 8cl, tc, 9bg, bl, tl, 10bl, br, cr, tr, 11c, 12b, bg, 13cl, 15bl, c, tl, 16bg, cr, tr, 17br, cr, tl, 18bg, bl, tr, 19bg, c, 20cr, tr, 22bg, bl, cr, tr, 23bc, tl, 24cr, tr, 25bc, bl, br, cl, cr, tl, 26bl, 27b, br, 29bc, tc, 30bg, cr, 31cl, cr, 32bl, c, 33br, c, cr, 34bcr, br, 36tc, 37bl, tl, 38c, tc, 41br, bl, c, 43bl, tc, tcl, 45bc, bcl, tcl, 46cl, tr, 47bg, c, cl, 48bc, bcr, br, cl, tr, 49bl, cr, 50c, cr, tc, tr, 51tl, 52bc, bg, bl, 53bc, bl, c, tc, tl, 54br, tcr, 55bl, cl, cr, tc, 56bl, br, 57bl, br, 58br, 59bc, bl, 60bl, c, cl, 61c, 62bl, br, 63c, tl, 64bc, tc, 65bc, cr, 66bcr, c, tc, 67bl, c, cl, tc, 68tc, 69cl, cr, 71bg, 72bc, tl, 82bc, bg, c, cl, tr, 83br, cl, tc, tl, 84br, tc, 85c, cl, tc, 86bcr, bl, 87cl, cr, 88bg, bg, c, 89bl, c, 90cl, tc, 91bg, bl, cl, tc, tl, 92c, 93bg, bl, tc, 94tc, 95cl, cr, tc, 96bg, c, 97bc, bg, tl, 100c, 101bcl, 102bg, cr, tc, tr, 103bg, 104tr, 105br, tl, 106cr, 107bcl, bg, cr, tc, 108bg, c, tc, 109c, 110cr, 111bg, c, 112bl, 114br, 115bc, bg, cr, tc, 116bc, 117c, cl, cr, 118b, tr, 119bg, bl, 120bg, tr, 121bg, 122c, tc, 123bg, c, cr, 124cl, 125br, 126bc, bg, cr, 127c, cr, tl, 128br, tc, 129bl, cr, 130cl, 131bg, cr, tc, tl, 133tc, 134cr, 135br, cl, 136cl, tr, 139bc, 140bl, br, 141cr, 142cl, tr, 143c, cl, 144bl, 145br, 146c, 147br, 148tcr, 149bg, c, cl, tl, 150cl, 151bl, 152bcr, cl, tc, 153bl, br, tl, 154cl, tc, tr, 155br, tl, 156br, 157bcl, cr, 158bc, bg, bl, 160br, tc, 161cl, cr, 162c, tr, 164bl, c, tc, 166bcr, c, tr, 167bl, c, 168bc, cr, 169cl, 170b, 171bg, br, 172bl, tr, 173bg, tl, 174bg, 175br, 176br, cl, tcr, 177bg, 178tc, 179tl, 180bcr, 181br, tl, 183cl, cr, tc, 184bcr, c, tr, 186bcr, tc, tcr, tr, 187bg, 188c, cl, tr, 189bc, tc, 190bg, tr, 191br, tl, 192bg, bl, br, 193c, cr, tl, 194bl, cl, tc, 196bcr, tr, 198br, tr, 199tl, 200br, cl, tr, 201bg, c, cl, 202br, 203bcl, 204bg, br, 205bl

Library of Congress 63tc

Lonely Planet 9bc., 11br, cl, 15bc, 19tl, 23cr, 30tr, 33tl, 36bl, 37bc, 45tc, 50bc, 51br, 61tc, 62tr, 63cl, 64tr, 71bc, tc, 76cl, 83bl, 84tr, 87br, 89tl, 97cl, 98bl, 99bcl, 104b, 109br, 119tl, 121cl, 126bl, 127c, cl, 132tcr, 133bcl, c, 135bcl, bl, 148bg, 154cr, 157tl, 158c, 159tcl, tl, 160cr, 162tcr, 164br, 167br, 173br, 174bcr, 175bc, tl, 177tcl, 180bl, tr, 182bg, c, 184bg, c, 185cl, 189bl, cl, tl, 192c, cr, tr, 194cr, 196br, tcr, 202bc, cr, 203bc, 204bcr, bl

NASA 96cr, 97br

Nature Picture Library 130bg, 134tc, 137c, 152bg

NHPA/Photoshot 99bc, 110bl, 112bc, 120bl, 137tl, 167tl, 173cl

NOAA 26cr

Photolibrary 6br, 7tl, 16bc, 18tcr, 35br, tc, 38cr, 40cr, tr, 41b, 53cl, 66tcr, 73bcl, 79bl, 82c, 85bl, 88bl, 89tc, 90tr, 100b, 101tcl, 104cl, 109tl, 110tr, 111br, tcl, 121tc, 122bg, 125tl, 127tc, 128bg, cl, cr, 129cl, tl, 133tl, 134c, 135cr, 136bl, 137bcl, 138bl, c, 139c, tc, 140tr, 144cr, 145bl, tl, 151bc, 156c, tr, 157bc, 161bl, 164bc, 165bg, 166bl, 177bcl, 178c, 179bg, cr, 181tc, 187tl, 188br, 190tcr, 191tc, 192c, 195bcl, c, 196bl, 197bl, 198bl, 199bl, 200c, 201bc, 202tr

Photoshot 6cl, 88tc, 94bg, 95c, 96tc, 97bl, 102c, 103br, 105bl, 106tcr, 110c, 114cr, 116cr, 117tl, 121cr, tl, 122cl, cr, 124cr, 131c, 133tcl, 135tcl, 138bc, 139cl, 141bc, 145c, 147bl, tl, 150cr, 152tcr, 153cl, 155tc, 156cr, 161bg, 163cl, tl, 164tr, 165cr, tl, 166c, 170c, 171bl, 172bg, 175bl, 187cr

Picture Desk 70br

Shutterstock 6bc, bg, br, 7bl, br, tcl, 8bl, br, c, tr, 10tc, 11tc, 12bc, tc, tr, 13bl, cr, tl, 14bl, br, cl, tc, 16bl, c, 17bl, c, tl, 18c, cl, 19bc, cl, 20bc, c, tcr, 21bc, bl, c, tl, 22br, cl, 23c, 24bg, br, c, 26bg, br, c, tr, 27c, cl, tc, tl, 28bc, br, cl, 29bcl, c, tcl, 30bc, bl, 31br, 32bc, br, cl, tr, 33bl, 34bl, tcr, tr, 35bc, c, 36bc, tr, 37br, cr, 38b, br, cl, tr, 39bl, cr, tl, 40bc, c, tc, 41c, cl, cr, tl, 42cr, 43bc, bcl, cr, 44bc, bl, cr, tc, 45c, cr, 46br, c, tc, 47bc, bl, br, 49bc, c, tc, tl, 51bc, 52c, tc, 54bc, bcr, c, tc, 55bc, br, tl, 56bg, tr, 57bc, bg, c, cl, cr, 58cl, cr, tr, 59c, cl, 60br, tr, 61bc, c, cl, 62bg, c, tcr, 63br, 64c, c, cr, 65c, c, cl, tc, 66bc, 67c, tl, 68bc, bl, tr, 69bg, cl, tc, tl, 70bc, cl, cr, tcr, tr, 71bl, c, cl, 72bl, cl, cr, 73bc, c, cr, tcl, 74bc, bg, br, cl, tcr, 75bc, bcl, c, tcl, 76cr, tc, tr, 77bl, br, cl, cr, 78bg, cr, tr, 79br, cl, tc, tcl, 80c, cl, tc, 81c, tc, 82cr, 83cr, 84bg, c, cr, 85bc, br, 86bg, c, tcr, tr, 87bc, bg, bl, cr, tc, tcl, tl, 88tcr, 89br, c, cl, 90bg, 91br, 92br, cr, 93c, tcl, 95bg, 97tl, 98bc, bg, cr, 99bg, c, 100bcr, tr, 101bg, c, tc, 102br, 103c, 104c, 105c, cl, 106bg, 107tcl, 108br, 109bl, 110br, br, 111bc, bcl, bl, 112bg, tr, 113bl, c, tl, 114tc, 115cl, tl, 116bl, br, 117bg, 118cr, 119cr, tc, 120br, c, cr, 122br, 123c, tl, 124tc, tr, 125bc, c, cl, tc, 127bg, br, 129c, tc, 130b, br, c, tr, 131cl, 132bl, c, cl, 133bg, br, c, 134cl, 135bc, 136bg, 137bg, cr, tcl, 138c, cr, 141bl, c, cl, tc, 142bg, c, 143bl, br, cr, tc, 144bg, tr, 145bc, 146bg, bl, br, cl, cr, tc, tr, 147c, tc, 148bcr, c, cl, tr, 149bc, bl, br, 150bg, bl, br, tc, 151bg, cl, cr, tc, 152cr, 153cr, 154c, 155bl, 156bl, tc, 157br, tcl, 158bcr, tr, 159bg, 160bl, 161c, 162bcr, bg, bl, 163bg, cl, tc, 165br, tl, 166bg, br, cl, tc, 167bc, bg, 168bg, c, tcr, tr, 169c, tc, 170cr, 171cl, tc, 172bc, br, tc, 173c, cr, 174cl, 175cl, cr, 176bcr, c, tc, 177br, c, tc, 178bg, bl, cr, tr, 179tcl, 180bg, tc, 181bl, 182bc, 183bg, br, 184cl, 185bg, bl, c, cr, tc, tl, 186bc, bg, bl, br, c, 187bc, 188bg, cr, 189cr, 190bcr, bl, br, 191c, 193bc, 194bc, c, 195bc, tcl, 196bg, 197cl, 198c, 199bc, bg, tc, 200tc, 203tcl, 204tc, tcr, 205bg, cl

Superstock 53cr, 164cl

Top Foto 37cl, 56cr, 139tl, 153c, 200cr

USG 19bl

Wikipedia 9br, cl, 10cl, 13c, 14tr, 19br, 20bg, bl, 22c, 23bl, 24bl, 28c, 31bc, bl, 32tc, 35bl, cl, 36bc, 39b, cl, 42tc, tr, 44br, tr, 45tl, 46bl, cl, 50cl, 51bcl, tcl, 52bc, br, 54tr, 56bc, c, 58bc, 59cr, tl, 61cr, 62bc, 67bc, 68br, cr, 69bl, 73tc, 78tc, 79bcl, 84bl, 90cr, 94cr, 99cr, tc, 103bl, cl, 106bcr, 116tr, 120tc, 123cl, 132bg, tc, 136c, 137tc, 138bg, 139cr, 141br, 142cr, 144cl, 145bg, 147cl, 151br, 153tc, 158tcr, 165c, 170tr, 171tl, 174tcr, tr, 179br, 180tcr, 181cl, 183c, 187bl, cl, 191bl, 193bl, 197tl, 205bc

All repeated image motifs courtesy of iStockphoto.com

All country flags courtesy of iStockphoto.com, except 21, 28, 33, 57, 103, 111, 122, 133, 167, 169, 170, 173, 180, 184 and 188 courtesy of Shutterstock

Cartography: Will Pringle/Mapgraphx

All other illustrations and images copyright Weldon Owen Pty Ltd

LONELY PLANET OFFICES

Australia Head Office
Locked Bag 1, Footscray, Victoria 3011
phone 03 8379 8000
fax 03 8379 8111

USA
150 Linden St, Oakland, CA 94607
phone 510 250 6400, toll free 800 275 8555
fax 510 893 8572

UK
2nd fl, 186 City Rd, London EC1V 2NT
phone 020 7106 2100
fax 020 7106 2101
Send us your feedback at
lonelyplanet.com/contact

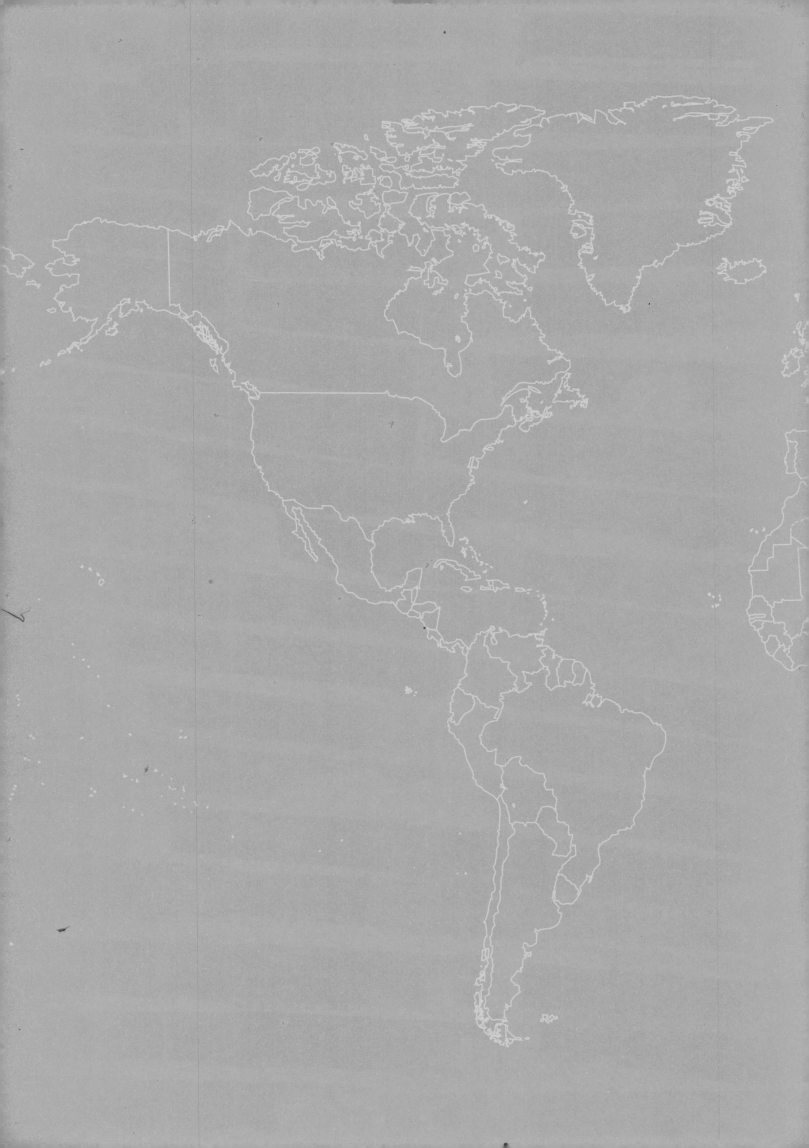